A BOOK OF SCOTLAND

EDITED BY G. F. MAINE

A Book of Scotland

The Molendinar Press

First published by William Collins & Sons Co Ltd 1950

Copyright © William Collins Sons & Co Ltd 1981

This Edition Published by
Richard Drew Publishing Ltd 1981

ISBN 0 904002 67 5

Made & Printed in Great Britain by
William Collins Sons & Co Ltd., Glasgow

FOREWORD

THE first edition of this anthology of Scottish prose and verse (and comments on Scottish life and character by Sassenachs of differing rank and reputation) was compiled by Mr. H. L. Findlay and published in 1933. What I have tried to do is to follow as far as possible the pattern of the book as he conceived it, and to choose from the great wealth of material at the disposal of the anthologist, I hope with feeling and imagination, poems, prose passages and letters that reflect something of the soul of Scotland. I have retained almost everything of Mr. Findlay's choosing and, in addition to much new matter, I have added, as aids to those who are unfamiliar with our historical and literary heritage, a few explanatory notes and indices of authors and the first lines of poems.

Ours is a checkered history. Our roots are deep in the soil; our gnarled branches bear witness of frost and tempest, not, alas !, of soft zephyrs and a ripening sun. Our fruits are not the grape and the pomegranate. But adversity as well as righteousness may exalt a nation and great quarrels bring great emancipations. Thus, out of hardship has grown self-reliance; out of battles for great causes, pride of race and heritage; out of self-discipline, character.

When in 1865 an English historian and man of letters (James Anthony Froude) ventured to address an Edinburgh audience on *The Influence of the Reformation on the Scottish Character* he said, with what wisdom has become increasingly apparent during the present century: "Institutions exist for men, not men for institutions; and the ultimate test of any system of politics, or body of opinions, or form of belief, is the effect produced in the conduct and conditions of the people who live and die under them." And again, "So far as one can look into that commonplace round of things which historians never tell us about, there have rarely been seen in this world a set of people who have thought more about right and wrong, and the judgment about them of the upper powers. Long-headed, thrifty industry; a sound hatred of waste, imprudence, idleness, extravagance; the feet planted firmly upon the earth; a conscientious sense that the worldly virtues are, nevertheless, very necessary virtues; that without these, honesty for one thing is not possible and that without honesty no other excellence, religious or moral, is worth anything at all—this is the stuff of which Scottish life is made, and very good stuff it is." This was a sound appraisement then. Dare we hope it still has the same validity?

There are those who regard anthologies as of the devil, but there are others who, in an age when the tempo of life takes increasing toll of our physical and nervous resources, find them stimulating, even rejuvenating. I hope that Scots at home and beyond the seas will relish this miscellany, and that those of other nationalities who sojourn with us for business or pleasure will find here much that will help them better to understand our nation's life and history.

G. F. MAINE

CONTENTS

CONTENTS

CONTENTS

CONTENTS

PASTORAL

CONTENTS

PEOPLE, GREAT AND SMALL

CONTENTS

HUMOUR AND SENTIMENT

CONTENTS

CUSTOMS, HOSPITALITY

CONTENTS

POEMS, SONGS, BALLANTS

CONTENTS

RELIGIOUS AND MYSTICAL

CONTENTS

INTRODUCTION TO THE 1981 EDITION

Robert Burns, Scotland's national poet, figures largely in this anthology of Scottish history, tales and verse. As a great-great grandson of the poet, I hope that this new edition of A Book of Scotland will reach a wide circle of all those who are interested in Scottish Literature.

IAN BURNS GOWRING
December, 1980

ACKNOWLEDGMENTS

Cordial acknowledgements are here tendered to the following authors, owners of copyrights, publishers and literary agents who have given permission for poems and prose passages to appear in these pages.

EDWIN MUIR and CURTIS BROWN, LTD. for the poem *Robert the Bruce Stricken with Leprosy: to Douglas.*

HUGH MACDIARMID and JARROLDS, LTD. for passage from *Scottish Scene* and the poem *With the Herring Fishers.*

SETON GORDON and MACMILLAN & CO. LTD. for two passages from *Highways and Byways in the Central Highlands.*

PROFESSOR SIR ALEXANDER GRAY for the poem *Scotland.*

LT.-COL. MAURICE MACDONALD for the poems *What the Auld Fowk are Thinkin'* and *Christmas Meditation* by George MacDonald.

MRS. LESLIE MITCHELL and JARROLDS LTD. for passages from *Scottish Scene* and *Sunset Song* by Lewis Grassic Gibbon.

DOUGLAS YOUNG for the poems *For the Old Highlands* and *Last Lauch.*

THOMAS NELSON & SONS, LTD. for passage from *The House With the Green Shutters* by George Douglas.

FABER & FABER, Ltd. for the poem *Alas! Poor Queen* by Marion Angus and passage from *The Lost Glen* by Neil M. Gunn.

LONGMANS GREEN & CO., LTD. and the representatives of the late Andrew Lang for the poems *St. Andrews, Lost Love* and *Endure, My Heart.*

GEORGE CAMPBELL HAY and OLIVER & BOYD, LTD. for the poems *Edinburgh* and *Cuimhne Mach Téid As.*

R. CROMBIE SAUNDERS for the poem *Had I Twa Herts.*

ANDREW DAKERS LTD. for the poems *Daft Sang* and *Recollection of First Love* by William Soutar.

NEVILLE CARDUS for passage from *Autobiography,* herein entitled *A Week-End With Barrie.*

JOHN MURRAY for the poem *Tam I' The Kirk* by Violet Jacob and two passages from *The Psalms In Human Life* by R. E. Protheroe.

MRS. RATCLIFFE BARNETT and JOHN GRANT BOOKSELLERS, LTD. for two passages from *The Road to Rannoch and the Summer Isles* by T. Ratcliffe Barnett.

J. & J. GRAY for *Recipe for Haggis* from *Banquets of the Nations* by Robert H. Christie.

ACKNOWLEDGMENTS

HIS MAJESTY'S STATIONERY OFFICE for passage from *Official Guide to Holyroodhouse* by Sir Herbert Maxwell, Bt.

NOEL F. SHARP for the poem *The Bugles of Dreamland* from *The Hills of Dream*, *The Fairy Chorus* from *The Immortal Hour*, and *The Immortals* and *The Reed Player* from *The Silence of Amor* by Fiona MacLeod.

ISOBEL ADAM and The Editor, *The Bulletin* newspaper, for passage from an article on *Old and New Balmoral*.

CONSTABLE & CO., LTD. for poem *The Whistle* by Charles Murray.

DR. ARTHUR GEDDES for the poem *Ane Playnt of Luve* by Pittendrigh MacGillivray.

MARGARET WINEFRIDE SIMPSON and The Editor, *The Northern Scot* newspaper, for the poem *Young Crusade*.

LEWIS SPENCE and The Editor, *Scotland's S.M.T. Magazine*, for the poem *The Haantit Hoosie*.

MAURICE LINDSAY for the poems *The Exiled Heart* and *Hurlygush*.

DOUGLAS A. KIDD for Latin translation of part of the *Declaration of Arbroath*.

ALEXANDER SCOTT for the poems *Calvinist Sang* and *Poem Before Birth*.

JAMES NISBET & CO., LTD. for two prose passages from *The Story of the Tweed* by Sir Herbert Maxwell, Bt.

SIR REGINALD COUPLAND for passage from *Livingstone's Last Journey*.

HODDER & STOUGHTON LTD. and CURTIS BROWN LTD. for passages from the novel *Auld Licht Idylls* and the play *Mary Rose* by Sir J. M. Barrie.

A. & C. BLACK LTD. for *An American Lady's Farewell to Edinburgh*, from *Penelope's Experiences in Scotland* by Kate Douglas Wiggin.

CASSELL & CO. LTD. for passage from *Malcolm* by George MacDonald.

ALEX. GARDNER LTD. for the poem *Kirkbride* by R. Wanlock Reid.

AGNES MURE MACKENZIE for *Aignish on the Machair*.

MACMILLAN & CO. LTD. for the extract from *The Scenery of Scotland* by Sir A. Geikie.

McGRIGOR, DONALD & CO. and WM. BLACKWOOD & SONS, LTD. for the poem *John o' Lorn* by Neil Munro.

J. P. LOGIE ROBERTSON and WM. BLACKWOOD & SONS, LTD. for *An Ochil Farmer* by J. Logie Robertson.

CHATTO & WINDUS for passage from *Looking Back* by Norman Douglas.

The executrix of IAN MACLAREN (John Watson, D.D.) and HODDER & STOUGHTON, LTD. for *Burnbrae's Prayer* from *Beside the Bonnie Brier Bush*.

WILLIAM HEINEMANN LTD. for the excerpt from *Boswell's London Journal, 1762-1763*, herein entitled *I Come From Scotland*.

PROLOGUE

Breathes there the man, with soul so dead,
Who never to himself hath said,
   This is my own, my native land!
Whose heart hath ne'er within him burn'd,
As home his footsteps he hath turn'd,
   From wandering on a foreign strand!
If such there breathe, go, mark him well;
For him no minstrel raptures swell;
High though his titles, proud his name,
Boundless his wealth as wish can claim:
Despite those titles, power, and pelf,
The wretch, concentred all in self,
Living, shall forfeit fair renown,
And, doubly dying, shall go down
To the vile dust, from whence he sprung,
Unwept, unhonour'd, and unsung.

O Caledonia! stern and wild,
Meet nurse for a poetic child!
Land of brown heath and shaggy wood,
Land of the mountain and the flood,
Land of my sires! what mortal hand
Can e'er untie the filial band,
That knits me to thy rugged strand!

SIR WALTER SCOTT
The Lay of the Last Minstrel

Places

SCOTLAND

Here in the Uplands
The soil is ungrateful;
The fields, red with sorrel,
Are stony and bare.
A few trees, wind-twisted—
Or are they but bushes?—
Stand stubbornly guarding
A home here and there.

Scooped out like a saucer,
The land lies before me;
The waters, once scattered,
Flow orderedly now
Through fields where the ghosts
Of the marsh and the moorland
Still ride the old marches,
Despising the plough.

The marsh and the moorland
Are not to be banished;
The bracken and heather,
The glory of broom,
Usurp all the balks
And the fields' broken fringes,
And claim from the sower
Their portion of room.

This is my country,
The land that begat me.
These windy spaces
Are surely my own.

And those who here toil
In the sweat of their faces
Are flesh of my flesh,
And bone of my bone.

Hard is the day's task—
Scotland, stern Mother—
Wherewith at all times
Thy sons have been faced:
Labour by day,
And scant rest in the gloaming,
With Want an attendant,
Not lightly outpaced.

Yet do thy children
Honour and love thee.
Harsh is thy schooling,
Yet great is the gain:
True hearts and strong limbs,
The beauty of faces,
Kissed by the wind
And caressed by the rain.

SIR ALEXANDER GRAY (1882-1968)

EDINBURGH

Living in Edinburgh there abides, above all things, a sense of its beauty. Hill, crag, castle, rock, blue stretch of sea, the picturesque ridge of the Old Town, the squares and terraces of the New—these things seen once are not to be forgotten. The quick life of to-day sounding around the relics of antiquity, and overshadowed by the august traditions of a Kingdom, makes residence in Edinburgh more impressive than residence in any other British city. I have just come in—surely it never looked

so fair before! What a poem is that Princes Street! The
puppets of the busy, many-coloured hour move about
on its pavements, while across the ravine Time has piled
up the Old Town, ridge on ridge, grey as a rocky coast
washed and worn by the foam of centuries; peaked and
jagged by gable and roof; windowed from basement to
cope; the whole surmounted by St. Giles's airy crown.
The New is there looking at the Old. Two Times are
brought face to face, and are yet separated by a thousand
years. Wonderful on winter nights, when the gully is
filled with darkness, and out of it rises, against the
sombre blue and the frosty stars, that mass and bulwark
of gloom, pierced and quivering with innumerable lights.
There is nothing in Europe to match that, I think.

ALEXANDER SMITH (1830-67)
A Summer in Skye

EDINBURGH
FROM BLACKFORD HILL

Blackford! on whose uncultured breast,
  Among the broom, and thorn, and whin,
A truant-boy, I sought the nest,
Or listed, as I lay at rest,
  While rose, on breezes thin,
The murmur of the city crowd,
And, from his steeple jangling loud,
  Saint Giles's mingling din.
Now, from the summit to the plain,
Waves all the hill with yellow grain;
  And o'er the landscape as I look,
Nought do I see unchanged remain,
  Save the rude cliffs and chiming brook
To me they make a heavy moan,
Of early friendships past and gone.
Still on the spot Lord Marmion stay'd,

27

For fairer scene he ne'er survey'd.
When sated with the martial show
That peopled all the plain below,
The wandering eye could o'er it go,
And mark the distant city glow
  With gloomy splendour red;
For on the smoke-wreaths, huge and slow,
That round her sable turrets flow,
  The morning beams were shed,
  And tinged them with a lustre proud,
  Like that which streaks a thunder-cloud.
Such dusky grandeur clothed the height,
Where the huge Castle holds its state,
  And all the steep slope down,
Whose ridgy back heaves to the sky,
Piled deep and massy, close and high,
  Mine own romantic town!
But northward far, with purer blaze,
On Ochil mountains fell the rays,
And as each heathy top they kiss'd,
It gleam'd a purple amethyst.
Yonder the shores of Fife you saw;
Here Preston-Bay, and Berwick-Law;
  And, broad between them roll'd,
The gallant Frith the eye might note,
Whose islands on its bosom float,
  Like emeralds chased in gold.
Fitz-Eustace' heart felt closely pent;
As if to give his rapture vent,
The spur he to his charger lent,
  And raised his bridle hand,
And, making demi-volte in air,
Cried, "Where's the coward that would not dare
  To fight for such a land!"

SIR WALTER SCOTT (1771-1832)
Marmion

28

THE LEGEND OF
HOLYROOD ABBEY

At this time wes with the king ane man of singulare and devoit life, namit Alkwine, channon eftir the ordour of Sanct Augustine, quhilk wes lang time confessoure, afore, to King David in Ingland, the time that he wes Erle of Huntingtoun and Northumberland. This religious man dissuadit the king, be mony reasonis, to pas to this huntis; and allegit the day wes so solempne, be reverence of the haly croce, that he suld gif him erar, for that day, to contemplation than ony othir exersition. Nochtheles, his dissuasionis litill avalit; for the king wes finalie so provokit, be inoportune solicitatioun of his baronis that he past, nochtwithstanding the solempnite of this day, to his hountis. At last, quhen he wes cumin throw the vail that lyis to the gret eist fra the said castell, quhare now lyis the Cannongait, the staik past throw the wod with sic noyis and din of rachis and bugillis, that all the bestis were rasit fra thair dennis.

Now wes the king cumin to the fute of the crag, and all his noblis severit, heir and thair, fra him at thair game and solace; quhen suddenlie apperit to his sicht the farist hart that evir wes sene afore with levand creatour. The novis and din of this hart rinnand, as apperit, with auful and braid tindis, maid the kingis hors so effrayit, that na renzeis micht hald him; bot ran, perforce, ouir mire and mossis, away with the king. Nochtheles, the hart followit so fast, that he dang baith the king and his hors to the ground. Than the king kest abak his handis betuix the tindis of this hart, to haif savit him fra the strak thairof; and the haly croce slaid, incontinent, in his handis.

The hart fled away with gret violence, and evanist in the same place quhare now springis the Rude Well. The pepil, richt affrayitly, returnit to him out of all partis

29

of the wod, to comfort him efter his trubill, and fell on kneis, devotly adoring the haly croce; for it was not cumin but sum hevinly providence, as weill apperis, for thair is na man can schaw of quhat mater it is of, metal or tre. Sone eftir, the king returnit to his castel; and in the nicht following he was admonist, be ane vision in his sleip, to big ane abbay of channonis regular in the same place quhare he gat the croce. Als sone as he was awalkinnit, he schew his vision to Alkwine, his confessour; and he na thing suspendit his gud mind, bot erar inflammit him with maist fervent devotion thairto.

The king, incontinent, send his traist servandis in France and Flanderis, and brocht richt crafty masonis to big this abbay; syne dedicat it in the honour of this haly croce. The croce remanit continewally in the said abbay, to the time of King David Bruce; quhilk was unhappely tane with it at Durame, quhare it is haldin yit in gret veneration.

BOECE
(*Book* 12, *Ch.* 16)

EDINBURGH CASTLE

There, watching high the least alarms,
    Thy rough, rude fortress gleams afar;
Like some bold veteran, grey in arms,
    And marked with many a seamy scar:
The pond'rous wall and massy bar,
    Grim-rising o'er the rugged rock,
Have oft withstood assailing war,
    And oft repell'd th' invader's shock.

ROBERT BURNS (1759-96)
Address to Edinburgh

RIOT IN ST. GILES'S CHURCH
1637

Charles I being determined to put into execution his favourite scheme, of having all his subjects in Great Britain of the same religion, resolved upon introducing the canons and liturgy among a people to whose principles both were revolting. He vested the power of kirk sessions and presbyteries in bishops; lay elders were dismissed from the church courts, and the whole structure of presbyterian polity in Scotland was overturned. A royal mandate having been issued for the immediate introduction of the liturgy into the Church of Scotland, intimation was made from the pulpit, appointing it to be read in all churches the following Sunday. The liturgy, for the use of the Church of Scotland, was carefully revised, altered, and corrected by Charles; and where it differed in expression and form from that of England, it approached more nearly to popish tenets, and was therefore dreaded as an attempt, for the introduction of popery.

In conformity to this intimation, the dean of Edinburgh was to officiate in St. Giles's church. At the hour of the forenoon service, the novelty of the scene had collected together a large and indiscriminate concourse of people; among whom were two archbishops, several bishops, the lords chancellor and treasurer, privy-council, judges, and magistrates. The dean, arrayed in his surplice, had no sooner made his appearance, and opened the service book, than a tumult arose, and an old woman, named Janet Geddes, started up, and exclaimed, "*Out, out, does the false loon mean to say his black mass at my lug?*" and then threw her stool at the dean's head.

This was the signal for general uproar; and there immediately followed, wild clamours, clapping of hands, hisses, curses, and exclamations, which rendered every

31

sentence or attempt at speech unintelligible. Women rushed towards the desk; and the dean, disengaging himself from his surplice, with difficulty escaped from their hands. The bishop of Edinburgh, with a view of appeasing the tumult, ascended the pulpit, but had not a friendly hand averted a stool that was thrown at him, that member of the episcopal order would have been silenced for ever. He entreated the people to respect the sacredness of the place, and reminded them of their duty to God and the king. But the tumult was only increased by this address. Stones, and other missiles were thrown at the pulpit. The magistrates, at command of the lord chancellor, called the town guard, and drove the ringleaders out of the church.

Annals of Edinburgh

A HOT-BED OF GENIUS

Edinburgh is a hot-bed of genius. I have had the good fortune to be made acquainted with many authors of the first distinction; such as the two Humes, Robertson, Smith, Wallace, Blair, Ferguson, Wilkie, etc., and I have found them all as agreeable in conversation as they are instructive and entertaining in their writings. These acquaintances I owe to the friendship of Dr. Carlyle, who wants nothing but inclination to figure with the rest upon paper. The magistracy of Edinburgh is changed every year by election, and seems to be very well adapted both for state and authority. The *Lord Provost* is equal in dignity to the *Lord Mayor of London*: and the *four Bailies* are equivalent to the rank of Aldermen. There is a *Dean of Guild*, who takes cognisance of mercantile affairs; a Treasurer, a Town Clerk; and the Council is composed of Deacons, one of whom is returned every year in rotation, as representative of every company of artificers or handicraftsmen.

TOBIAS SMOLLETT (1721-71)
Humphry Clinker

DR. JOHNSON IN EDINBURGH
1773

We walked out, that Dr. Johnson, might see some of the things which we have to shew at Edinburgh. We went to the Parliament-House, where the Parliament of Scotland sat, and where the *Ordinary Lords* of Session hold their courts; and to the New Session-House adjoining to it, where our Court of Fifteen (the fourteen *Ordinaries*, with the Lord President at their head,) sit as a court of Review. We went to the Advocates' Library, of which Dr. Johnson took a cursory view, and then to what is called the ' Laigh ' (or under) Parliament-House, where the records of Scotland, which has an universal security by register, are deposited, till the great Register Office be finished. I was pleased to behold Dr. Samuel Johnson rolling about in this old magazine of antiquities. There was, by this time, a pretty numerous circle of us attending upon him. Somebody talked of happy moments for composition; and how a man can write at one time, and not at another.—"Nay (said Dr. Johnson) a man may write at any time, if he will set himself *doggedly* to it."

I here began to indulge old Scottish sentiments, and to express a warm regret, that, by our Union with England, we were no more;—our independent kingdom was lost.—JOHNSON. "Sir, never talk of your independency, who could let your Queen remain twenty years in captivity, and then be put to death, without even a pretence of justice, without your ever attempting to rescue her; and such a Queen too! as every man of any

33

gallantry of spirit would have sacrificed his life for."—
Worthy Mr. JAMES KERR, Keeper of the Records. "Half
our nation was bribed by English money."—JOHNSON.
"Sir, that is no defence: that makes you worse."—Good
Mr. Brown, Keeper of the Advocates' Library. "We had
better say nothing about it."—BOSWELL. "You would
have been glad, however, to have had us last war, sir,
to fight your battles!"—JOHNSON. "We should have had
you for the same price, though there had been no Union,
as we might have had Swiss, or other troops. No, no,
I shall agree to a separation. You have only to *go home*."
—Just as he had said this, I to divert the subject, shewed
him the signed assurances of the three successive Kings
of the Hanover family, to maintain the Presbyterian
establishment in Scotland.—"We'll give you that (said
he) into the bargain."

JAMES BOSWELL (1740-95)
Journal of a Tour to the Hebrides

EDINBURGH

A windy toon o cloods an' sunny glints;
pinnacled, turreted, stey an' steep grey toon;
her soughin' gables sing their norlan' rants
tae saut[1] an' caller blufferts on her croon.

Steeple an' toor an' battlement stand bauld,
an' gaze oot owre the kindly lands o' Forth
tae the braid seaward lift, far, clean an' cauld,
an' front her airt, the stern,[2] abidin' north.

Oh, I hae seen her leamin' frae afar,
bricht thro the fleetin' blatter o' the rain,
an' happed an' hidden, rowed in norsea haar,[3]
secret an' dour, loom grandly, prood an' lane.

[1] salt and fresh blasts of wind [2] star [3] fog

34

Tae stand an' watch frae oot the wooded west
the heich[1] ranks o her dignity gang by,
an' see it surgein' seaward, crest on crest,
her lang swell merchin' ridged against the sky.

GEORGE CAMPBELL HAY (b. 1915)

[1] high

AN AMERICAN LADY'S FAREWELL

I canna thole my ain town,
Sin' I have dwelt i' this;
To hide in Edinboro' reek,
Wad be the tap o' bliss.
Yon bonnie plaid aboot me hap,
The skirling pipes gae bring,
With thistle fair tie up my hair,
While I of Scotia sing.

The collops an' the Cairngorms,
The haggis an' the whin,
The Stablished, Free, an' U P kirks,
The hairt convinced o' sin,—
The parritch an' the heather bell,
The snawdrap on the shaw,
The bit lam's bleating on the braes,
How can I leave them a'!

How can I leave the marmalade
An' bonnets of Dundee?
The Haar, the haddies, and the brose,
The East win' blawing free!

How can I lay my sporran by,
An' sit me doun at hame,
Wi' oot a Hieland philabeg
Or hyphenated name?

I lo'e the gentry o' the North,
The Southern men I lo'e,
The canty people o' the West,
The Paisley bodies too.
The pawky folk o Fife are dear—
Sae dear are ane an' a',
That e'en to think that we maun pairt
Maist braks my heart in twa.

So fetch me tartan, heather, scones,
An' dye my tresses red;
I'd deck me like the unconquer'd Scots
Wha hae wi' Wallace bled.
Then bind my claymore to my side,
My kilt an' mutch gae bring;
While Scottish lays soun i' my lugs
M'Kinley's no my king,—

For Charlie, bonnie Stuart Prince,
Has turned me Jacobite;
I'd wear displayed the white cockade,
An' (whiles) for him I'd fight!
An' (whiles) I'd fight for a' that's Scotch
Save Whuskey an' oatmeal,
For wi' their ballads in my bluid
Nae Scot could be mair leal!

KATE DOUGLAS WIGGIN
Penelope in Scotland

ST. ANDREWS

St. Andrews by the Northern Sea,
A haunted town it is to me!
A little city, worn and grey,
The grey North Ocean girds it round,
And o'er the rocks, and up the bay,
The long sea-rollers surge and sound.
And still the thin and biting spray
Drives down the melancholy street,
And still endure, and still decay,
Towers that the salt winds vainly beat.
Ghost-like and shadowy they stand
Dim-mirrored in the wet sea-sand.

O broken minster, looking forth
Beyond the bay, above the town,
O, winter of the kindly North,
O, College of the scarlet gown,
And shining sands beside the sea,
And stretch of links beyond the sand,
Once more I watch you, and to me
It is as if I touched a hand !

ANDREW LANG (1844-1912)
Rhymes à la Mode

PEEBLES FOR PLEESURE

In the early years of the 19th century, Peebles was little advanced from the condition in which it had mainly rested for several hundred years previously. It was eminently a quiet place—"As quiet as the grave or as Peebles," is a phrase used by Cockburn. It was said to be a finished town, for no new houses (exceptions to be of course allowed for) were ever built in it. Situated,

37

however, among beautiful pastoral hills, with a singu-
larly pure atmosphere, and with the pellucid Tweed
running over its pebbly bed close beside the streets, the
town was acknowledged to be, in the fond language of
its inhabitants, a bonny place. An honest old burgher
was enabled by some strange chance to visit Paris, and
was eagerly questioned, when he came back, as to the
character of that capital of capitals; to which, it is said,
he answered that "Paris, a'thing considered, was a
wonderful place—but still, Peebles for pleesure!" and
this has often been cited as a ludicrous example of rustic
prejudice and narrowness of judgment. But, on a fair
interpretation of the old gentleman's words, he was not
quite so benighted as at first appears. The "pleesures"
of Peebles were the beauties of the situation and the
opportunities of healthful recreation it afforded, and
these were certainly considerable.

R. CHAMBERS (1802-71)

BY YARROW'S STREAM

My second tour with Irving had nothing of circuit in
it: a mere walk homeward through the Peebles-Moffat
moor country, and it is not worth going into any detail.
The region was without roads, often without foot-tracks,
had no vestige of an inn, so that there was a kind of
knight-errantry in threading your way through it; not
to mention the romance that naturally lay in its Ettrick
and Yarrow, and old melodious songs and traditions.
We walked up Meggat Water to beyond the sources,
emerged into Yarrow not far above St. Mary's Loch; a
charming secluded shepherd country, with excellent
shepherd population—nowhere setting up to be picturesque, but everywhere honest, comely, well done-to,
peaceable and useful. Nor anywhere without its solidly
characteristic features, hills, mountains, clear rushing

38

streams, cosy nooks and homesteads, all of fine rustic type; and presented to you *in natura*, not as in a Drury Lane with stagelights and for a purpose; the vast and yet not savage solitude as an impressive item, long miles from farm to farm, or even from one shepherd cottage to another. No company to you but the rustle of the grass underfoot, the tinkling of the brook, or the voices of innocent primaeval things. I repeatedly walked through that country up to Edinburgh and down by myself in subsequent years, and nowhere remember such affectionate, sad, and thoughtful, and in fact, interesting and salutary journeys. I have had days clear as Italy (as in this Irving case), days moist and dripping, over-hung with the infinite of silent grey—and perhaps the latter were the preferable in certain moods. You had the world and its waste imbroglios of joy and woe, of light and darkness, to yourself alone. You could strip barefoot if it suited better, carry shoes and socks over shoulder, hung on your stick; clean shirt and comb were in your pocket; *omnia mea mecum porto*. You lodged with shepherds who had clean solid cottages; wholesome eggs, milk, oatbread, porridge, clean blankets to their beds, and a great deal of human sense and unadulterated natural politeness. Canty, shrewd, and witty fellows, when you set them talking; knew from their hill tops every bit of country between Forth and Solway, and all the shepherd inhabitants within fifty miles, being a kind of confraternity of shepherds from father to son. No sort of peasant labourers I have ever come across seemed to me so happily situated, morally and physically well-developed, and deserving to be happy, as those shepherds of the Cheviots. *O fortunatos nimium!* But perhaps it is all altered not a little now, as I sure enough am who speak of it!

THOMAS CARLYLE (1795-1881)
Reminiscences

A BORDER BURN

Oh, Tam! Gie me a Border burn
That canna rin without a turn,
And wi' its bonnie babble fills
The glens among oor native hills.
How men that ance have ken'd aboot it
Can leeve their after-lives without it
I canna tell, for day and nicht
It comes unca'd for to my sicht.
I see't this moment, plain as day,
As it comes bickerin' ower the brae,
Atween the clumps o' purple heather
Glistenin' in the summer weather,
Syne drivin' in below the grun'
Where, hidden frae the sicht and sun,
It gibbers like a deid man's ghost
That clamours for the licht it's lost,
Till oot again the loupin' limmer,
Comes dancin' doon through shine and shimmer
At heidlang pace, till wi' a jaw
It jumps the rocky waterfa',
And cuts sic cantrips in the air,
The picter-pentin' man's despair;
A row'ntree bus' oot ower the tap o't,
A glassy pule—to kep the lap o't,
While on the brink the blue harebell
Keeks ower to see its bonny sel'.
And sittin' chirpin' a' its lane
A water-waggy on a stane,
Ay, penter lad, thraw to the wund
Your canvas, this is holy grund;
Wi' a' its higher airt acheevin',
That picter's deid, and this is leevin'!

J. B. SELKIRK

MELROSE ABBEY BY NIGHT

If thou wouldst view fair Melrose aright,
Go visit it by the pale moonlight;
For the gay beams of lightsome day
Gild, but to flout, the ruins grey.
When the broken arches are black in night,
And each shafted oriel glimmers white;
When the cold light's uncertain shower
Streams on the ruin'd central tower;
When buttress and buttress, alternately,
Seem framed of ebon and ivory;
When silver edges the imagery,
And the scrolls that teach thee to live and die;
When distant Tweed is heard to rave,
And the owlet to hoot o'er the dead man's grave,
Then go—but go alone the while—
Then view St. David's ruin'd pile;
And, home returning, soothly swear,
Was never scene so sad and fair!

SIR WALTER SCOTT (1771-1832)
The Lay of the Last Minstrel

ST. MARY'S LOCH

Oft in my mind such thoughts awake,
By lone Saint Mary's silent lake;
Thou know'st it well,—nor fen, nor sedge,
Pollute the pure lake's crystal edge;
Abrupt and sheer, the mountains sink
At once upon the level brink;
And just a trace of silver sand
Marks where the water meets the land.
Far in the mirror, bright and blue,

41

Each hill's huge outline you may view;
Shaggy with heath, but lonely bare,
Nor tree, nor bush, nor brake, is there,
Save where, of land, yon slender line
Bears thwart the lake the scatter'd pine.
Yet even this nakedness has power,
And aids the feeling of the hour. . . .
There's nothing left to fancy's guess,
You see that all is loneliness:
And silence aids—though the steep hills
Send to the lake a thousand rills;
In summer tide, so soft they weep,
The sound but lulls the ear asleep;
Your horse's hoof-tread sounds too rude,
So stilly is the solitude.

SIR WALTER SCOTT (1771-1832)
Marmion

THE HAMLET OF BIRGHAM

A mile below Edenmouth the Tweed swerves suddenly
from its north-easterly course, turns south-east, meets
English soil at Carham, and becomes the boundary
between the two countries. Opposite Carham, on the
Scottish bank, lies the hamlet of Birgham among its
green fields; to the eye—one of those tranquil scenes
where the concern of men seems wrapped up in the
favour of unkindness of the seasons, the rise and fall of
agricultural markets, and the incidence of rent: to the
understanding—a spot whereon the Muse of History has
set her seal. For it was out of an event at Birgham that
the long-drawn dispute between England and Scotland
took its rise, so that men say to this day, ' Go to Birgham
and buy bickers!' It was here that the treaty was struck
in the summer of 1290 which, if envious fate had not

interposed, should have knit together two nations which ought never to have been sundered.

> ' Quhen Alysandyr oure Kyng was dede
> That Scotland led in luve and lé,[1]
> Away wes sons[2] of Ale and Brede,
> Of wyne and war, of gamyn[3] and glé,
> Our gold wes changyd into lede.
> Chryst, born into Virgynité,
> Succour Scotland, and remede![4]
> That stad[5] is in perplexité.'

Alexander, last of the Kings of Peace, was dead. He had won the love of his subjects and the fear of his barons; the kindly heart, the wise head, the firm hand, were cold in death, and the governance of the realm had passed to his grandchild, the Maid of Norway, who now became, in right of her mother, Margaret, Queen of Scots. Not undisputed Queen, for the land was like to be rent in the interests of other claimants, and wavered on the brink of anarchy for two years, until King Edward opened negotiations for the marriage of his son, after-wards Edward II, with the child Queen. The Pope granted the necessary dispensation for cousins-german; and on 18th July 1290 the marriage-treaty was concluded at Birgham. Everybody knows how that fair and states-manlike project miscarried through the untimely death of the young Queen of Scots, how Edward's claim to be Lord-Paramount of Scotland was laid before the con-ference at Norham on 10th May 1291, and accepted by the eight competitors for the succession at the adjourned conference of Upsettlington on 2nd June, and how King Edward gave his final award in favour of John Baliol at the final conference at Berwick on 17th November 1292. All this, and many incidents in the three centuries of war which it entailed, take rank among the best-

[1] law [2] abundance [3] sport [4] remedy [5] fixed

known parts of the Scottish chronicle; reference to them would be superfluous, even impertinent, were it not that we are passing among the very scenes where these foundations of national history were laid. As the eye travels over the peaceful landscape, with its teeming fields, sloping woods, and gliding river, it is good to recall what fierce passions here were raised, what manful battle was done for either cause, and how happily all these wasteful disputes have been laid to rest.

SIR HERBERT MAXWELL
The Story of the Tweed

THE EXILED HEART

Two purple pigeons circle a London square
as darkness blurs and smudges the shadowless light
of a winter evening. I pause on the pavement and stare
at the restless flutter of wings as they gather flight,
like rustling silk, and move out to meet the night.

And my restless thoughts migrate to a Northern city—
fat pigeons stalking the dirty cobbled quays,
where a sluggish river carries the cold self-pity
of those for whom life has never flowed with ease,
from a granite bridge to the green Atlantic seas:

the bristling, rough-haired texture of Scottish manners;
the jostling clatter of crowded shopping streets
where lumbering tramcars squeal as they take sharp
    corners:
the boosy smell from lounging pubs that cheats
the penniless drunkard's thirst with its stale deceits:

where my heart first jigged to the harsh and steady
    sorrow

of those for whom mostly the world is seldom glad,
who are dogged by the flat-heeled, footpad steps of to-
    morrow;
for whom hope is a dangerous drug, an expensive fad
of the distant rich, or the young and lovesick mad:

where chattering women in tearooms, swaddled with
    furs,
pass knife-edged gossip like cakes, and another's skirt
is unstitched with sharp words, and delicate, ladylike
    slurs
are slashed on the not-quite-nice or the over-smart
till smoke to the eyes is a hazy, prickled hurt.

I remember Glasgow, where sordid and trivial breed
from the same indifferent father; his children side
with the mother whose sour breasts taught them first
    to feed
on her hot, caressing hates that sear and divide,
or swell the itching, distended bladder of pride.

Yet my guilty sneers are the tossed-down, beggar's penny
which the goaded heart throws out, in vain, to procure
the comfortable forgetfulness of the many
who lie in content's soft arms, and are safe and sure
in the fabled Grecian wanderers' lotus-lure:

who forget the sullen glare of the wet, grey skies,
and the lashing Northern wind that flicks the skin
like a whip, where poverty's dull and listless eyes
are pressed to the window, hearing the friendly din
of the party, watching the lights and laughter within.

But oh, I cannot forget, so I wait and wonder,
how long will the thinly dividing window hold,
how long will the dancing drown the terrible anger
of those, the unwanted, who peddle their grief in the cold,
wrapped in their own despair's thick and unkindly fold?

Yet evil is no pattern of places
varied, like terraces from town to town,
A city's charms and individual graces
are but the sculptors' bleak and basic stone,
the photographic face without a frown.

The wound is in this bewildered generation,
tossed on the swollen, analytic mood,
its compasspoint no longer veneration
of that lost God who rewarded the simple and good,
vivid and real, now, only in childhood.

For we, the children of this uncertain age,
breathing its huge disasters and sad airs,
have seen that our warm, humanitarian rage
is impotent to soothe war's animal fears,
can never quell the lonely exile's tears.

So the heart, like a wounded seabird, hungers home
to muffled memories on faintly-beating wings
which once climbed over history's clouded foam
to that clear sky where each new hero flings
the careful stone that fades in slow, concentric rings.

MAURICE LINDSAY (b. 1918)

GLASGOW

I am so far happy as to have seen Glasgow, which to the best of my recollection and judgment, is one of the prettiest towns in Europe; and, without all doubt, it is one of the most flourishing in Great Britain. In short, it is a perfect bee-hive in point of industry. It stands partly on a gentle declivity; but the greatest part of it is in a plain, watered by the river Clyde. The streets are straight, open, airy, and well paved; and the houses lofty and well built of hewn stone. . . .

. . . Glasgow is the pride of Scotland, and indeed it might very well pass for an elegant and flourishing city in any part of Christendom. There we had the good fortune to be received into the house of Mr. Moore, an eminent surgeon, to whom we were recommended by one of our friends at Edinburgh; and truly he could not have done us more essential service. Mr. Moore is a merry, facetious companion, sensible and shrewd, with a considerable fund of humour; and his wife an agreeable woman, well-bred, kind, and obliging. Kindness, which I take to be the essence of good nature and humanity, is the distinguishing characteristic of the Scotch ladies in their own country. Our landlord showed us everything, and introduced us to all the world at Glasgow, where, through his recommendation, we were complimented with the freedom of the town. Considering the trade and opulence of this place, it cannot but abound with gaiety and diversions. Here is a great number of young fellows that rival the youth of the capital in spirit and expense; and I was soon convinced, that all the female beauties of Scotland were not assembled at the hunter's ball in Edinburgh. The town of Glasgow flourishes in learning as well as in commerce.

Here is a university, with professors in all the different branches of science, liberally endowed and judiciously chosen.

TOBIAS SMOLLETT (1721-71)
Humphry Clinker

GLASGOW

City! I am true son of thine;
Ne'er dwelt I where great mornings shine
    Among the bleating pens;
Ne'er by the rivulets I strayed,
And ne'er upon my childhood weighed
    The silence of the glens.
Instead of shores where ocean beats,
I hear the ebb and flow of streets.

Black labour draws his weary waves
Into their secret moaning caves;
    But with the morning light
That sea again will overflow
With a long, weary sound of woe,
    Again to faint in night.
Wave am I in that sea of woes,
Which, night and morning, ebbs and flows.

Draw thy fierce streams of blinding ore,
Smite on thy thousands anvil, roar
    Down to the harbour bars;
Smoulder in smoky sunsets, flare
On rainy nights, when street and square
    Lie empty to the stars.
From terrace proud to alley base
I know thee as my mother's face.

ALEXANDER SMITH (1830-67)

LOCH LOMOND

Loch Lomond lies quite near to Glasgow. Nice Glaswegians motor out there and admire the scenery and calculate its horse-power and drink whisky and chaff one another in genteelly Anglicized Glaswegianisms. After a hasty look at Glasgow the investigator would do well to disguise himself as one of like kind, drive down to Loch Lomondside and stare across its waters at the sailing clouds that crown the Ben, at the flooding of colours changing and darkling and miraculously lighting up and down those misty slopes, where night comes over long mountain leagues that know only the paddings of the shy, stray hare, the whirr and cry of the startled pheasant, silences so deep you can hear the moon come up, mornings so greyly coloured they seem stolen from Norse myth. This is the proper land and stance from which to look at Glasgow, to divest onself of horror or shame or admiration or—very real—fear, and ask: Why? Why did men ever allow themselves to become enslaved to a thing so obscene and so foul when there was *this* awaiting them here—hills and the splendours of freedom and silence, the clean splendours of hunger and woe and dread in the winds and rains and famine-times of the earth, hunting and love and the call of the moon? Nothing endured by the primitives who once roamed those hills—nothing of woe or terror—approximated in degree or kind to that life that festers in the courts and wynds and alleys of Camlachie, Govan, the Gorbals.

LEWIS GRASSIC GIBBON (J. LESLIE MITCHELL, 1901-35)
Scottish Scene

LOCH LOMOND

There is an old Celtic belief that when a man meets with death in a foreign land, his spirit returns to the homeland by "The Low Road." This song, so dear to Scots throughout the world, is said to refer to two Scottish soldiers of the second Stuart rising (1745) made captive at Carlisle, one of whom was to be set free, the other executed. It is he who will take the low road of death and reach Loch Lomond before his friend, who must take the terrestrial high road across the Cheviots.

By yon bonnie banks, and by yon bonnie braes,
Where the sun shines bright on Loch Lomond;
Where me and my true love were ever wont to gae,
On the bonnie, bonnie banks o' Loch Lomond.

Chorus
And you'll tak' the high road and I'll tak' the low road,
And I'll be in Scotland afore ye;
But me and my true love will never meet again
On the bonnie, bonnie banks o' Loch Lomond.

'Twas there that we parted in yon shady glen,
On the steep, steep side o' Ben Lomond,
Where in purple hue the Hieland hills we view,
An' the moon coming out in the gloamin'.

The wee birdies sing and the wild flowers spring,
An' in sunshine the waters are sleepin';
But the broken heart it kens nae second spring again,
Tho' the waefu' may cease frae their greetin'.

Songs of the North

THE TROSSACHS AT SUNSET

The western waves of ebbing day
Rolled o'er the glen their level way;
Each purple peak, each flinty spire,
Was bathed in floods of living fire.
But not a setting beam could glow
Within the dark ravines below,
Where twined the path in shadow hid,
Round many a rocky pyramid,
Shooting abruptly from the dell
Its thunder-splintered pinnacle;
Round many an insulated mass,
The native bulwarks of the pass,
Huge as the tower which builders vain
Presumptuous piled on Shinar's plain.
The rocky summits, split and rent,
Formed turret, dome, or battlement,
Or seemed fantastically set
With cupola or minaret,
Wild crests as pagod ever decked,
Or mosque of Eastern architect.
Nor were these earth-born castles bare,
Nor lacked they many a banner fair;
For, from their shivered brows displayed,
Far o'er the unfathomable glade,
All twinkling with the dew-drops sheen,
The brier-rose fell in streamers green,
And creeping shrubs, of thousand dyes,
Waved in the west-wind's summer sighs.

SIR WALTER SCOTT (1771-1832)
The Lady of the Lake

LOCH KATRINE

And now, to issue from the glen,
No pathway meets the wanderer's ken,
Unless he climb, with footing nice,
A far projecting precipice.
The broom's tough roots his ladder made,
The hazel saplings lent their aid;
And thus an airy point he won,
Where, gleaming with the setting sun,
One burnished sheet of living gold,
Loch Katrine lay beneath him rolled,
In all her length far winding lay,
With promontory, creek, and bay,
And islands that, empurpled bright,
Floated amid the livelier light,
And mountains, that like giants stand,
To sentinel enchanted land.
High on the south, huge Benvenue
Down on the lake in masses threw
Crags, knolls, and mounds, confusedly hurled,
The fragments of an earlier world;
A wildering forest feathered o'er
His ruined sides and summit hoar,
While on the north, through middle air,
Ben-an heaved high his forehead bare.

SIR WALTER SCOTT (1771-1832)
The Lady of the Lake

STIRLING

From the field of Bannockburn you obtain the finest view of Stirling. The Ochils are around you. Yonder sleeps the Abbey Craig, where, on a summer day, Wight Wallace sat. You behold the houses climbing up, picturesque, smoke-feathered; and the wonderful rock, in which the grace of the lily and the strength of the hills are mingled, and on which the castle sits as proudly as ever did rose on its stem. Eastward from the castle ramparts stretches a great plain, bounded on either side by mountains, and before you the vast fertility dies into distance, flat as the ocean when winds are asleep. It is through this plain that the Forth has drawn her glittering coils—a silvery entanglement of loops and links— a watery labyrinth. Turn round, look in the opposite direction, and the aspect of the country has entirely changed. It undulates like a rolling sea. Heights swell up into the blackness of pines, and then sink away into valleys of fertile green. At your feet the Bridge of Allan sleeps in azure smoke. Beyond are the classic woods of Keir; and ten miles farther, what see you? A multitude of blue mountains climbing the heavens! The heart leaps up to greet them—the ramparts of a land of romance, from the mouths of whose glens broke of old the foray of the freebooter; and with a chief in front, with banner and pibroch in the wind, the terror of the Highland war. Stirling, like a huge brooch, clasps Highlands and Lowlands together.

ALEXANDER SMITH (1830-67)
A Summer in Skye

STIRLING

Old Strevline,[1] thou stand'st beauteous on the height,
Amid thy peaceful vales of every dye,
Amid bewildered waves of silvery light
That maze the mind, and toil the raptured eye.
Thy distant mountains spiring to the sky
Seem blended with the mansions of the blest;
How proudly rise their gilded points on high
Above the morning cloud and man's behest
Like thrones of angels hung upon the welkin's breast!

For those I love thee; but I love thee more
For the grey relics of thy martial towers,
Thy mouldering palaces and ramparts hoar,
Throned on the granite pile that grimly lowers,
Memorial of the times, when hostile powers
So often proved thy steadfast patriot worth:
May every honour wait thy future hours,
And glad the children of thy kindred Forth!
I love thy very name, old bulwark of the North.

JAMES HOGG (1770-1835)

[1] Ancient name of Stirling.

THE WICKS OF BAIGLIE

One of the most beautiful points of view which
Britain, or perhaps the world, can afford, is, or rather
we may say was, the prospect from a spot called the
Wicks of Baiglie, being a species of niche at which the
traveller arrived, after a long stage from Kinross,
through a waste and uninteresting country, and from
which, as forming a pass over the summit of a ridgy
eminence which he had gradually surmounted, he

beheld, stretching beneath him, the valley of the Tay, traversed by its ample and lordly stream; the town of Perth, with its two large meadows, or Inches, its steeples, and its towers; the hills of Moncrieff and Kinnoul faintly rising into picturesque rocks, partly clothed with woods; the rich margin of the river, studded with elegant mansions; and the distant view of the huge Grampian mountains, the northern screen of this exquisite landscape. The alteration of the road, greatly, it must be owned, to the improvement of general intercourse, avoids this magnificent point of view, and the landscape is introduced more gradually and partially to the eye, though the approach must be still considered as extremely beautiful. There is still, we believe, a footpath left open, by which the station at the Wicks of Baiglie may be approached; and the traveller, by quitting his horse or equipage, and walking a few hundred yards, may still compare the real landscape with the sketch we have attempted to give. But it is not in our power to communicate, or in his to receive, the exquisite charm which surprise gives to pleasure, when so splendid a view arises when least expected or hoped for, and which Chrystal Croftangry experienced when he beheld, for the first time, the matchless scene.

Childish wonder, indeed, was an ingredient in my delight, for I was not above fifteen years old; and as this had been the first excursion which I was permitted to make on a pony of my own, I also experienced the glow of independence, mingled with that degree of anxiety which the most conceited boy feels when he is first abandoned to his own undirected counsels. I recollect pulling up the reins without meaning to do so, and gazing on the scene before me, as if I had been afraid it would shift like those in a theatre before I could distinctly observe its different parts, or convince myself that what I saw was real. Since that hour—and the period is now more than fifty years past,—the recollection of that inimitable landscape has possessed the strongest influence over my mind, and retained its place as a memorable thing, when much that was influential on my own fortunes has fled from my recollection.

SIR WALTER SCOTT (1771-1832)
The Fair Maid of Perth

THE STONE OF DESTINY

The Celtic name of the stone now in the Coronation Chair in Westminster Abbey is Lia Fàil, "the speaking stone," which named the king who should be chosen. Cambray in his *Monuments Celtiques* claims to have seen the stone when it still bore the inscription: *Ni fallat fatum, Scoti quocumque locatum Invenient lapidem, regnasse tenentur ibidem*: If Destiny prove true, then Scots are known to have been kings where'er men find this stone.

A few miles up the river from Perth is the site of the historic Abbey of Scone, where the kings of Scotland were crowned. But the glory of Scone has long departed, for, even in the time of the writing of the old *Statistical Account*, "on the spot where our ancient kings were crowned there now grows a clump of trees." At Scone the Coronation Stone or Stone of Destiny was "reverently kept for the consecration of the kings of Alba" and, according to an old chronicler, "no king was ever wont to reign in Scotland unless he had first, on receiving the royal name, sat upon this stone at Scone, which by the kings of old had been appointed the capital of Alba." The Stone of Destiny, now in Westminster Abbey, is an oblong block of red sandstone, some 26 inches long by 16 inches broad, and $10\frac{1}{2}$ inches deep: on the flat top of the stone are the marks of chiselling. Tradition affirms that it is the same stone which Jacob used as a pillow at Bethel and then set up as a pillar and anointed with oil: later, according to Jewish tradition, it became the pedestal of the ark in the Temple. The stone was brought from Syria to Egypt by Gathelus, who in order to escape the plague, sailed, on the advice of Moses, from the Nile with his wife and the Stone of Destiny, and landed in Spain. Gathelus sent the stone to Eire when he had invaded that country, and it was later brought to Scotland where it remained in the Abbey of Scone until, in the year 1296, Edward I of England carried it off to Westminster Abbey.

An interesting tradition has been given me by the Earl of Mansfield, whose family have owned the lands of Scone for more than three hundred years. The tradition, which has been handed down through several generations, is that, somewhere around the dates 1795-1820, a farm lad had been wandering with a friend on Dunsinnan, the site of MacBeth's castle, soon after a violent storm. The torrential rain had caused a small landslide, and as the result of this a fissure, which seemed to penetrate deep into the hillside, was visible. The two men procured some form of light and explored the fissure. They came at last to the broken wall of a subterranean chamber. In one corner of the chamber was a stair which was blocked with debris, and in the centre of the chamber they saw a slab of stone covered with hieroglyphics and supported by four short stone "legs." As there was no evidence of "treasure" in the subterranean apartment the two men did not realise the importance of their "find" and did not talk of what they had seen. Some years later one of the men first heard the local tradition, that on the approach of King Edward I the monks of Scone hurriedly removed the Stone of Destiny to a place of safe concealment and took from the Annety Burn a stone of similar size and shape, which the English king carried off in triumph. When he heard this legend, the man hurried back to Dunsinnan Hill, but whether his memory was at fault regarding the site of the landslide, or whether the passage of time, or a fresh slide of earth, had obliterated the cavity, the fact remains that he was unable to locate the opening in the hillside. It may be asked why the monks of Scone, after the English king had returned to London, did not bring back to the abbey the original Stone of Destiny, but the tradition accounts for this by explaining that it was not considered safe at the time to allow the English to know that they had been tricked, and that when the days of possible retribution were past, the monks who had known the secret were dead. This tradition, it is held, explains why the Coronation Stone in Westminster Abbey resembles geologically the stone commonly found in the neighbourhood of Scone.

SETON GORDON
Highways and Byways in the Central Highlands

THE BIRKS OF INVERMAY

The smiling morn, the breathing spring,
Invite the tuneful birds to sing;
And while they warble from each spray,
Love melts the universal lay.
Let us, Amanda, timely wise,
Like them improve the hour that flies,
And in soft raptures waste the day
Among the birks of Invermay.

For soon the winter of the year,
And age, life's winter, will appear;
At this, thy living bloom will fade,
As that will strip the verdant shade:
Our taste of pleasure then is o'er;
The feathered songsters love no more;
And when they droop, and we decay,
Adieu the birks of Invermay.

DAVID MALET (1700-65)

BALMORAL CASTLE

Immediately after lunch on that first day, September 8th, 1848, Victoria and Albert went for a walk on a wooded hill, revelling in the solitude and the pure mountain air. Next day the royal pair, mounted on ponies and attended by Highland gillies, picnicked on Lochnagar. The legend of Balmoral had been born.

Even in those first days Albert was dreaming of the new Balmoral, making rough sketches of its granite towers as he sat by the open windows of the little old castle in the evenings.

Five years later Victoria laid the foundation stone of the new castle at a ceremony which Albert had planned. Coins were buried, and a bottle containing a parchment signed by the Queen, the Prince Consort, and all the other important personages present, in strict order of precedence. The Rev. Mr Anderson, minister of Crathie, prayed. The pipes were played.

In two more years the royal holiday was spent in the new home, though the Gentlemen of the Household were still accommodated in the old one. But when the royal party arrived in 1851 they found everything finished and "the poor old house gone."

Not that Victoria gave it more than a passing thought. "Every year," she confided to her journal, "my heart becomes more fixed in this dear paradise, and so much more so now that *all* has become dearest Albert's *own* creation, own work, own building, own laying out, as at Osborne; and his great taste and the impress of his dear hand have been stamped everywhere."

The Victoria and Albert tartans, each named after their designers, were to be seen in every room—in hangings, chair-covers, even linoleums. Water-colours by the Queen's own hand, and the Prince's stags' heads, accumulated on the walls.

The simple life begun in the old castle went on. Parents and children went searching for cairngorms on the hillsides. Vicky sat on a wasps' nest. Alfred fell downstairs. The grown-ups played a quiet rubber of whist in the evenings. Mama went visiting the cottage women, making them presents of red flannel petticoats.

On September 8, 1855, news of the fall of Sebastopol reached Balmoral, and everyone climbed the hill to see the bonfire lit, and the Highlanders played the pipes and danced wildly round the flames. Then it seemed as if the two lives—the life of State and the simple country life—had merged, if only for a moment into a single great happiness.

For Victoria the Golden Age of Balmoral ended with the Prince Consort's death in 1861. She had spent the happiest days of her life there. The castle and the dear hills would go on being a solace to her right to the end; but they would never again glow in the celestial light shed on them by Albert's presence.

ISABEL ADAM

LOCHNAGAR

Away ye gay landscapes, ye gardens of roses,
In you let the minions of luxury rove!
Restore me the rock where the snowflake reposes,
If still they are sacred to freedom and love.
Stern Caledonia, beloved are thy mountains,
Round their wild summits though elements war,
Though cataracts foam 'stead of smooth flowing
    fountains,
I sigh for the valley of dark Lochnagar!

Oh there my young footsteps in infancy wandered,
My cap was the bonnet, my cloak was the plaid;
On chieftains long perished my memory pondered

As daily I strode through the pine-covered glade.
I sought not my home till the day's dying glory
Gave place to the rays of the bright polar-star;
And fancy was cheered by traditional story
Disclosed by the natives of dark Lochnagar.

Years have rolled on, Lochnagar, since I left you,
Years must elapse, ere I tread thee again:
Nature of verdure and flowers has bereft you,
Yet still are you dearer than Albion's plain.
England, thy beauties are tame and domestic
To one who has roamed o'er the mountains afar!
O for the crags that are wild and majestic,
The steep, frowning glories of dark Lochnagar!

LORD BYRON (1788-1824)
Hours of Idleness

THE BULLER OF BUCHAN

We soon turned our eyes to the Buller[1] or Bouilloir
of Buchan, which no man can see with indifference, who
has either sense of danger, or delight in variety. It is a
rock perpendicularly tubulated, united on one side with
a high shore, and on the other rising steep to a great
height above the main sea. The top is open, from which
may be seen a dark gulf of water, which flows into the
cavity through a breach made in the lower part of the
enclosing rock. It has the appearance of a vast well
bordered with a wall. The edge of the Buller is not wide,
and to those that walk round, appears very narrow. He
that ventures to look downward, sees that if his foot
should slip, he must fall from his dreadful elevation
upon stones on one side, or into the water on the other.

[1] Natural rocky cauldron 6 miles south of Peterhead, Aberdeenshire.

We, however, went round, and were glad when the circuit was completed.

When we came down to the sea, we saw some boats and rowers, and resolved to explore the Buller at the bottom. We entered the arch, which the water had made, and found ourselves in a place, which, though we could not think ourselves in danger, we could scarcely survey without some recoil of the mind. The basin in which we floated was nearly circular, perhaps thirty yards in diameter. We were enclosed by a natural wall, rising steep on every side to a height which produced the idea of insurmountable confinement. The interception of all lateral light caused a dismal gloom. Round us was a perpendicular rock, above us the distant sky, and below us an unknown profundity of water. If I had any malice against a walking spirit, instead of laying him in the Red Sea, I would condemn him to reside in the Buller of Buchan.

DR. SAMUEL JOHNSON (1709-84)
A Journey to the Western Isles

SEAS BUAN, CREAG EILEACHAIDH!
Stand Fast, Craigellachie!

In one of the loneliest districts of Scotland, where the peat cottages are darkest, just at the western foot of that great mass of the Grampians which encircles the sources of the Spey and the Dee, the main road which traverses the chain winds round the foot of a broken rock called the Crag, or Craig Ellachie. There is nothing remarkable in either its height or form; it is darkened with a few scattered pines, and touched along its summit with a flush of heather; but it constitutes a kind of headland, or leading promontory, in the group of hills to which it belongs—a sort of initial letter of the mountains;

and thus stands in the mind of the inhabitants of the district, the Clan Grant, for a type of their country, and of the influence of that country upon themselves.

Their sense of this is beautifully indicated in the war-cry of the clan—' Stand fast, Craig Ellachie.' You may think long over those few words without exhausting the deep wells of feeling and thought contained in them —the love of the native land, and the assurance of their faithfulness to it. . . . You could not but have felt, had you passed beneath it at the time when so many of England's dearest children were being defended by the strength of heart of men born at its foot, how often among the delicate Indian palaces, whose marble was pallid with horror, and whose vermilion was darkened with blood, the remembrance of its rough grey rocks and purple heaths must have risen before the sight of the Highland soldier; how often the hailing of the shot and the shriek of battle would pass away from his hearing, and leave, only the whisper of the old pine branches—' Stand fast, Craig Ellachie.'

JOHN RUSKIN (1819-1900)
The Two Paths

BURNING OF ELGIN CATHEDRAL

The foundation stone of The Church of the Holy Trinity at Elgin, the most magnificent of the Scottish Cathedrals, was laid by Bishop Andrew Moray on July 19th, 1224. According to Fordun the building was destroyed by fire in 1270, whether by accident or design is not known. However, the circumstances of its second burning in 1390 have been fully authenticated.

Alexander Stewart, the "Wolfe of Badenoch," third son of Robert II and Earl of Buchan (whose Gallic title was Alasdair Mór Mac an Righ—Big Alexander the King's son), was excommunicated by his brother-in-law, John Dunbar, Earl of Moray, for offences against ecclesiastical property. In revenge he collected a band of his savage followers (" wyld, wykked Heland men," as Wynton calls them), came down from the western braes upon the fertile Vale of Moray, and burned the Cathedral, the College and houses of the Canons, and the greater part of the town of Elgin. For this act of vandalism and his flouting of ecclesiastical authority the "wolfe" had, by order of the king, to do penance at the door of the Church of the Blackfriars at Perth. Then, in the presence of his father the king and a great concourse of nobles, bishops and canons, he was received back into the Church, and, having solemnly promised to make reparation for his deeds, given absolution at the altar by Walter Trail, Archbishop of St. Andrews.

The vesper hymn had died away through the lengthened aisles of the venerable Cathedral; every note of labour or of mirth was silenced within the town. The weary burghers were sunk in sleep, and even the members of the various holy fraternities had retired to their repose. No eye was awake save those of a few individuals among the religious, who, having habits of more than ordinary severity of discipline, had doomed themselves to wear the hard pavement with their bare knees, and the hours in endless repetition of penetential prayers before the shrine of the Virgin, or the image of some favourite saint. . . .

Suddenly, the sound of a large body of horsemen was heard entering the town from the west. The dreams of the burghers were broken, and they were roused from their slumbers; the casements were opened, one after another, as the band passed along, and many a curious head was thrust out. They moved on alertly without talking; but, although they uttered no sound, and were but dimly seen, the clank of their weapons and of their steel harness told well enough that they were no band of vulgar, peace-loving merchants, but a troop of stirring men-at-arms; and many was the cheek that blanched, and many was the ejaculation that escaped the shuddering lips of the timid burghers, as they shrank within their houses at the alarming conviction. They crossed and blessed themselves after the warriors had passed by, and each again sought his bed.

But the repose of the inhabitants was for that night doomed to be short. Distant shrieks of despair, mingled with shouts of exultation, began to arise in the neighbourhood of the Cathedral and the College, in which all the houses of the canons were clustered, and soon the town was alarmed from its centre to its suburbs by the confused cries of half-naked fugitives, who hurried along into the country as if rushing from some dreadful danger. ' Fire, fire!—murder!—fire, fire! the Wolfe of Badenoch! '

Those who were most timorous halted not until they had hid themselves in the neighbouring woods; others, whose curiosity was in some degree an equipoise to their fears, stopped to look behind wherever a view of the town could be obtained. Already they could see that the College, the Church of St. Giles, and the Hospital of the *Maison Dieu* were burning; but these were all forgotten as they beheld the dire spectacle of the Cathedral illuminated throughout all the rich tracery of its Gothic windows by a furious fire that was already raging high within it. Groans and lamentations burst from their hearts, and loud curses were poured out on the impious heads of those whose fury had led them to destroy so glorious a fabric—an edifice which they had been taught to venerate from their earliest infancy, and to which they were attached by every association, divine and human, that could possibly bind the heart of man. In the midst of their wailings the pitchy vault of heaven began to be reddened by the glare of the spreading conflagration; and the loud and triumphant shouts that now arose, mingled with those cries of terror which had at first blended with them, too plainly told that the power of the destroyer was resistless.

SIR THOMAS DICK LAUDER (1784-1848)
The Wolfe of Badenoch

CROMARTY FIRTH

All the workmen rested at midday, and I went to enjoy my half-hour alone on a mossy knoll in the neighbouring wood, which commands through the trees a wide prospect of the bay and the opposite shore. There was not a wrinkle on the water, nor a cloud in the sky, and the branches were as moveless in the calm as if they had been traced on canvas. From a wooded promontory that stretched half-way across the frith there ascended a thin column of smoke. It rose straight as the line of a plummet for more than a thousand yards, and then, on reaching a thinner stratum of air, spread out equally on every side, like the foliage of a stately tree. Ben Wyvis rose to the west, white with the yet unwasted snows of winter, and as sharply defined in the clear atmosphere as if all its sunny slopes and blue retiring hollows had been chiselled in marble. A line of snow ran along the opposite hills: all above was white, and all below was purple.

HUGH MILLER (1802-56)
The Old Red Sandstone

THE LOCH NESS MONSTER

From the neighbourhood of Urquhart Castle of recent years the strange but now well-attested creature, the Loch Ness monster, has on a number of occasions been seen. There is in my mind no doubt that such a creature —there may be more than one—does exist in Loch Ness. Among a number of reliable witnesses who told me that they saw the monster was the late Captain Grant, of the MacBrayne paddle steamer *Pioneer*, which regularly plies on Loch Ness during the summer months. From Captain Grant's observations—and from the observations of other reputable witnesses—it would seem that the strange creature is timid, and that the sound, or vibration, of a steamer's screw or paddles causes it to submerge while the ship is yet a considerable distance off. Mr. Goodbody of Invergarry House and his daughter watched the creature for forty minutes through a stalking-glass. The Loch Ness Monster is indeed no recent "find," although at the present day it is known to a much larger number of people than ever before. The chief reason, I believe, why many more people now see it is that the new high-road along the north shore of Loch Ness gives a much better view of the loch. But there is another reason. Before the monster became, so to speak, public property, those who saw the "unchancy" creature decided that the less said about it the better. They realised that they would be laughed at, or pitied, or would be set down as addicted to a "dram." So long as half a century ago, to my own knowledge, children were told by their nurses that if they persisted in naughtiness the loch monster would take them. I heard of a well-known resident on Loch Ness-side who one day, after rowing down the loch in his small boat, appeared at a friend's house white and shaken, and asked for brandy. His friend for some time vainly endeavoured to ascertain the cause of his distress, to receive as answer, "It is no use my telling you, for even if I did you would not believe me." But in the end, when prevailed upon to unburden himself of his secret, he said to his friend, "As I was rowing down the loch some creature came to the surface beside me—and all I can say is that I hope I may never see the like again."

Most of the large and deep Highland lochs harbour, in the legends of the country, creatures which, as described in old books and writings, in their appearance resemble the Loch Ness monster. A peculiarity common to them all would appear to be their humps. The monster of Loch Morar, deepest loch in Scotland with a depth of 1,080 feet, and a floor no less than 1,050 below sea level, had a special name; it was known to the Gaelic-speaking Highlanders of the district as Mhorag (pronounced Vorag), and appeared only before a death in the family of MacDonell of Morar. May it not be that in the monster of Loch Ness we have a survival of an ancient race which, living for the most part under water and being of a timid disposition, has existed in comparative obscurity during successive centuries?

SETON GORDON
Highways and Byways in the Central Highlands

FOR THE OLD HIGHLANDS

That old lonely lovely way of living
in Highland places,—twenty years a-growing,
twenty years flowering, twenty years declining—
father to son, mother to daughter giving
ripe tradition; peaceful bounty flowing;
one harmony all tones of life combining—
old, wise ways, passed like the dust blowing.

That harmony of folk and land is shattered,—
the yearly rhythm of things, the social graces,
peat-fire and music, candle-light and kindness.
Now they are gone it seems they never mattered,
much, to the world, those proud and violent races,
clansmen and chiefs whose passioned greed and blindness
made desolate these lovely lonely places.

DOUGLAS YOUNG (b. 1913)

FROM BEN NEVIS

Let the reader imagine himself on the highest peak of the British Isles, watching the shadows of an autumnal sky as they steal over the vast sea of mountains that lies spread out around him . . . let him try to analyse some of the chief elements of the landscape. It is easy to recognise the more marked heights and hollows. To the south, away down Loch Linnhe, he can see the hills of Mull and the Paps of Jura closing in the horizon. Westward Loch Eil seems to lie at his feet, winding up into the lonely mountains, yet filled twice a day with the tides of the salt sea. Far over the hills beyond the head of the loch, he looks across Arisaig, and can see the cliffs of the Isle of Eigg and the dark peaks of Rum, with the Atlantic gleaming below them. If the air be clear, as it often is in that climate towards sunset, he may even behold the long broken line of the Outer Hebrides, half sunk in the sea a hundred miles away. Farther to the north-west the blue range of the Cuillin Hills rises along the sky line, and then, sweeping over all the intermediate ground, through Arisaig and Knoydart and the Clan-ranald country, he can mark mountain beyond mountain, ridge beyond ridge, cut through by dark glens, and varied here and there with the sheen of lake and tarn. Northward runs the mysterious straight line of the Great Glen, with its chain of lochs. Thence to east and south the same billowy sea of mountain tops stretches out as far as the eye can follow it—the hills and glens of Lochaber, the wide green strath of Spean, the grey corries of Glen Treig and Glen Nevis, the distant sweep of the moors and mountains of Brae Lyon and the Perthshire Highlands, the spires of Glencoe, and thence round again to the blue waters of Loch Linnhe.

SIR A. GEIKIE (1835-1924)
Scenery of Scotland

GLENCOE

Here, on February 13th, 1692, because of the belated submission of their Chief to William and Mary, 88 members of the Clan MacDonald were treacherously slaughtered by a body of soldiers under Capt. Campbell, after 12 days of professed friendship.

In the Gaelic tongue, Glencoe signifies the Glen of Weeping; and in truth that pass is the most dreary and melancholy of all the Scottish passes—the very Valley of the Shadow of Death. Mists and storms brood over it through the greater part of the finest summer; and even on those rare days when the sun is bright, and when there is no cloud in the sky, the impression made by the landscape is sad and awful. The path lies along a stream which issues from the most sullen and gloomy of mountain-pools. Huge precipices of naked stone frown on both sides. Even in July the streaks of snow may often be discerned in the rifts near the summits. All down the sides of the crags heaps of ruin mark the head-long paths of the torrents. Mile after mile the traveller looks in vain for the smoke of one hut, or for one human form wrapped in a plaid, and listens in vain for the bark of a shepherd's dog, or the bleat of a lamb. Mile after mile the only sound that indicates life is the faint cry of a bird of prey from some storm-beaten pinnacle of rock. The progress of civilisation, which had turned so many wastes into fields yellow with harvests or gay with apple-blossoms, has only made Glencoe more desolate. All the science and industry of a peaceful age can extract nothing valuable from that wilderness; but in an age of violence and rapine, the wilderness itself was valued on account of the shelter it afforded to the plunderer and his plunder.

LORD MACAULAY (1800-59)
History of England

LOCH CORUISK

Picking your steps carefully over huge boulder and slippery stone, you come upon the most savage scene of desolation in Britain. Conceive a large lake filled with dark green water, girt with torn and shattered precipices; the bases of which are strewn with ruin since an earthquake passed that way, and whose summits jag the sky with grisly splinter and peak. There is no motion here save the white vapour steaming from the abyss. The utter silence weighs like a burden upon you; you feel an intruder in the place. The hills seem to possess some secret; to brood over some unutterable idea which you can never know. You cannot feel comfortable at Loch Coruisk, and the discomfort arises in a great degree from the feeling that you are outside everything—that the thunder-splitten peaks have a life with which you cannot intermeddle. The dumb monsters sadden and perplex. Standing there, you are impressed with the idea that the mountains are silent because they are listening so intently. And the mountains *are* listening, else why do they echo our voices in such a wonderful way? Shout here like an Achilles in the trenches. Listen! The hill opposite takes up your words, and repeats them one after another, and curiously tries them over with the gravity of a raven. Immediately after, you hear a multitude of skyey voices.

"Methinks that there are spirits among the peaks."

How strangely the clear strong tones are repeated by these granite precipices! Who could conceive that Horror had so sweet a voice! Fainter and more musical they grow; fainter, sweeter, and more remote, until at last they come on your ear as if from the blank of the sky itself. M'Ian fired his gun, and it reverberated in a whole battle of Waterloo. We kept the hills busy with shouts and the firing of guns, and then M'Ian led us

71

to a convenient place for lunching. As we trudge along something lifts itself off a rock—'tis an eagle. See how grandly the noble creature soars away. What sweep of wings! What a lord of the air! And if you cast up your eyes you will see his brother hanging like a speck beneath the sun. Under M'Ian's guidance, we reached the lunching-place, unpacked our basket, devoured our fare, and then lighted our pipes and smoked—in the strangest presence. Thereafter we bundled up our things, shouldered our guns, and marched in the track of ancient Earthquake towards our boat. Embarked once again and sailing between the rocky portals of Loch Scavaig, I said, "I would not spend a day in that solitude for the world. I should go mad before evening."

ALEXANDER SMITH (1830-67)
A Summer in Skye

AIGNISH ON THE MACHAIR

When day and night are over,
And the World is done with me,
Oh carry me West and lay me
In Aignish by the Sea.

And never heed me lying
Among the ancient dead,
Beside the white sea breakers,
With the sand-drift overhead.

And the grey gulls wheeling ever,
And the wide arch of sky,
Oh Aignish on the Machair,
And quiet there to lie.

AGNES MURE MACKENZIE

STAFFA

The old name was Uamh Binn, the musical cave. The modern one was bestowed on the cave on account of its great size and magnificence, rendering it worthy of association with Ossian's heroic King of Selma. The height of the mouth of the cave is 66 feet, of the pillars on the west 36 feet, of those on the east 18 feet. The breadth at the entrance is 42 and the extreme length 227 feet.

The shores of Mull on the eastward lay,
And Ulva dark and Colonsay,
And all the group of islets gay
That guard famed Staffa round.
Then all unknown its columns rose,
Where dark and undisturb'd repose
The cormorant had found,
And the shy seal had quiet home,
And welter'd in that wondrous dome,
Where, as to shame the temples deck'd
By skill of earthly architect,
Nature herself, it seem'd, would raise
A Minster to her Maker's praise !
Not for a meaner use ascend
Her columns, or her arches bend;
Nor of a theme less solemn tells
That mighty surge that ebbs and swells,
And still, between each awful pause,
From the high vault an answer draws,
In varied tone prolong'd and high,
That mocks the organ's melody.
Nor doth its entrance front in vain
To old Iona's holy fane,
That Nature's voice might seem to say,
"Well has thou done, frail Child of clay!
Thy humble powers that stately shrine
Task'd high and hard—but witness mine!"

SIR WALTER SCOTT (1771-1832)
The Lord of the Isles

IONA

We were now treading that illustrious island, which was once the luminary of the Caledonian regions, whence savage clans and roving barbarians derived the benefits of knowledge, and the blessings of religion. To abstract the mind from all local emotion would be impossible, if it were endeavoured, and would be foolish, if it were possible. Whatever withdraws us from the power of our senses; whatever makes the past, the distant, or the future predominate over the present, advances us in the dignity of thinking beings. Far from me and from my friends be such frigid philosophy, as may conduct us indifferent and unmoved over any ground which has been dignified by wisdom, bravery, or virtue. That man is little to be envied, whose patriotism would not gain force upon the plain of Marathon, or whose piety would not grow warmer among the ruins of Iona.

DR. SAMUEL JOHNSON (1709-84)
Journey to the Western Isles

The holiest place in Scotland belongs to Mull—Iona. All the world may buy a guide-book to the namely relics of Columba's Isle. But only love, memory, knowledge, and the mystic's vision can unlock the secret of this Isle of Dream. The spirit of Columba, that Saint of blessed memory and martial monk with the tender heart, still broods over the green machar lands, the old grey stones, and the pure white sands. Yonder the dreamer may see the holy men landing from the coracles at the little bay—that navy of heaven which brought from Ireland more wealth of Christ than all the greatest ships of war. Here were set up the little cells, the wattled huts, the tiny thatch-and-timber church, the grinding mill. By the shores of this iridescent strait, whose waters gleam in the sunlight with heavenly greens and blues, opals and amethysts, Columba spoke to the fishes of the sea. On a wintry morning he saw a vision of God's love as he threw crumbs to the starving birds, and when they flew away he cried, "Oh, little birds—if only you knew the thoughts and feelings of Columba's heart towards you, you would not have taken fright!" The street of the dead, the silent crosses, the four-square church, the limitless seas—how long it seems since these sands of Hy were drenched with the blood of the martyred monks by the fair-haired vikings who for 400 years ruled these Western Isles! And yet, as we sit alone and dream, the very winds that blow about the graves become Columba's voice calling us to worship God.

T. RATCLIFFE BARNETT (1868-1946)
The Road to Rannoch and the Summer Isles

MITHICH DOMH TRIALL GU TIGH PHARAIS

It is time for me to go up unto the House of Paradise

An I mo chridhe, I mo gràidh
An àit' guth manaich bidh geum bà;
Ach mu'n tig an Saoghal gu crìch
Bithidh I mar a bha.

In Iona of my heart, Iona of my love
Instead of monks' voices shall be lowing of cattle;
But ere the world shall come to an end
Iona shall be as it was.

TRADITIONAL

75

THE DEATH OF ST. COLUMBA

As the happy hour of his departure gradually approached, the saint became silent. Then as soon as the bell tolled out midnight, he rose hastily, and went to the church; and running more quickly than the rest, he entered it alone, and knelt down in prayer beside the altar. At the same time his attendant, Diormit, who more slowly followed him, saw from a distance that the whole interior of the church was filled with a heavenly light in the direction of the saint. And as he drew near the door, the same light he had seen, and which was also seen by a few more of the brethren standing at a distance, quickly disappeared. Diormit therefore entering the church, cried out in a mournful voice, "Where art thou, father?" And feeling his way in the darkness, as the brethren had not yet brought in the lights, he found the saint lying before the altar; and raising him up a little, he sat down beside him, and laid his holy head on his bosom. Meanwhile the rest of the monks ran in hastily in a body with their lights, and beholding their dying father, burst into lamentations. And the saint, as we have been told by some who were present, even before his soul departed, opened wide his eyes and looked round him from side to side, with a countenance full of wonderful joy and gladness, no doubt seeing the holy angels coming to meet him. Diormit then raised the holy right hand of the saint, that he might bless his assembled monks. And the venerable father himself moved his hand at the same time, as well as he was able —that as he could not in words, while his soul was departing, he might at least, by the motion of his hand, be seen to bless his brethren. And having given them his holy benediction in this way, he immediately breathed his last. After his soul had left the tabernacle of the body, his face still continued ruddy, and brightened in a wonderful way by his vision of the angels, and that to such a degree that he had the appearance, not so much of one dead, as of one in a quiet slumber.

ST. ADAMNAN (d. 704)
Life of St. Columba

THE COMING OF QUEEN MARGARET

So Edgar Atheling, seeing that everywhere things went not smoothly with the English, went on board ship with his mother and sisters, and tried to get back to the land where he was born. But the Sovereign Ruler, who ruled the winds and waves, troubled the sea, and the billows thereof were upheaved by the breath of the gale; so, while the storm was raging, they all, losing all hope of life, commended themselves to God, and left the vessel to the guidance of the waves. At length, tossed on the countless dangers of the deep, they were forced to bring up in Scotland. So that holy family brought up in a certain spot which was thenceforth called St. Margaret's Bay by the inhabitants. While then the aforesaid family tarried in that bay, and were all awaiting in fear the upshot of the matter, news of their arrival was brought to King Malcolm, who at that time was, with his men, staying not far from that spot; so he sent off messengers to the ship to inquire into the truth of the matter. When the meessengers came there, they were astonished at the unusual size of the ship, and hurried back to the King as fast as they could, to state what they had seen. On hearing these things the King sent off thither, from among his highest lords, a larger embassy of men more experienced than the former. So these, being welcomed as ambassadors from the King's

77

majesty, carefully noted, not without admiration, the lordliness of the men, the beauty of the women, and the good-breeding of the whole family; and they had pleasant talk thereon among themselves. To be brief— the ambassadors chosen for this duty plied them with sweet words and dulcet eloquence, as to how the thing began, went on, and ended; while they, on the other hand, humbly and eloquently unfolded to them in simple words, the cause and manner of their arrival. So the ambassadors returned. When they had informed the King of the stateliness of the older men, and the good sense of the younger, the ripe womanhood of the matrons and the loveliness of the young girls, one of them went on to say, "We saw a lady there—whom, by the bye, from the matchless beauty of her person, and the ready flow of her pleasant eloquence, teeming, moreover, as she did with all other qualities, I declare to thee, O King, that I suspect, in my opinion, to be the mistress of that family—whose admirable loveliness and gentleness one must admire, as I deem, rather than describe." The King hearing they were English and were there present, went in person to see them and talk with them . . .

The King therefore, when he had seen Margaret and learnt she was begotten of royal, and even imperial, seed, sought to have her to wife and got her: for Edgar Atheling gave her away to him, rather through the wish of his friends than his own—nay by God's behest. For as Hester of old was, through God's providence, for the salvation of her fellow-countrymen, joined in wedlock to King Ahasuerus, even so was this princess joined to the most illustrious King Malcolm. The wedding took place in the year 1070, and was held, with great magnificence, not far from the bay where she brought up, at a place called Dunfermline, which was then the King's town.

FORDUN'S *Chronicle*
translated by W. F. SKENE

MARTYRDOM OF WALLACE, 1270-1305

Sir William Wallace (second son of Sir Malcolm Wallace of Elderslie) the champion of Scottish independence, defied the authority of Edward I and eventually led a general revolt which culminated in the victorious Battle of Stirling, 1297. Wallace became Guardian of Scotland but was outnumbered and overwhelmingly defeated by the English at the Battle of Falkirk, 1298. On August 3rd, 1305, Sir John Menteith and a company of 60 men came to Robroystoun, having been apprised of the defenceless state of Wallace, and surprised him when asleep and unarmed. He was seized, bound and carried captive to Carlisle where he was handed over to the Earl of Pembroke. He was executed in London on Black Wednesday, August 22nd, 1305.

Bound with cords and chains, as a malefactor of the first rank, Wallace was led through the streets of London to the place of execution at Westminster amid the scoffs and revilings of the rabble. His last moments were troubled by the pertinacity of one of the English priests who urged him repeatedly to confess his errors, and especially his sins against the king of England. The discussion betwixt the patriot and the priest is recited in detail by Blind Harry, and he shows how boldly and sternly the imprisoned warrior rebuked the officious cleric. One special grace was granted to him at the request of Lord Clifford. From his childhood Wallace had kept a psalter which his mother had given him, and which he had carried with him safely through all his devious wanderings. He besought that this should be borne before him open in the hands of one of the priests whilst on his way to execution, and thus he marched undauntedly to his lamentable end. Firmly, but without boastfulness, he met his fate, suffering his captors to do with him as they chose and keeping his eye steadfastly fixed on the psalter which had been so long his faithful companion until the headsman's weapon did its fatal work. The prevalent opinion amongst the spectators was, that he did not suffer at the last, his mind being absorbed in spiritual devotion. His body was divided into five portions, which were sent severally to the five principal burghs in Scotland, as a warning to the inhabitants who had so frequently regarded Wallace as their deliverer.

A. H. MILLAR
Sir William Wallace

LORD PROVOST OF EDINBURGH
The First on Record, 1296

The office of chief magistrate is synonymous with that of the Lord Mayor of London. Previous to this date the chief magistrate of Edinburgh was styled *Alderman* but he is now honoured with the title of *Lord Provost*. John de Quhitness is the first on record, who filled the office of chief magistrate, under the title of *provost*. He, this year, together with eleven burgesses of the city, signed the Ragman Roll, and swore allegiance to Edward I of England, as superior lord of the kingdom of Scotland. Within the bounds of the city, he has the precedency of all the great officers of state, and the nobility; walking on the right hand of the king, or of his majesty's commissioner and representative. He had a jurisdiction in matters of life and death, now in desuetude, and previous to the union, was an officer in the Scottish parliament, colonel of the city regiment of trained bands, and captain of the city company of fuzileers, while in existence. He is high sheriff, coroner, and admiral, within the city and liberties, and in the town, harbour, and roadstead of Leith. He is president of the convention of royal burghs, and of the town council, a justice of peace for the county, &c., and enjoys the privileges of having a sword and mace carried before him, while walking in any procession.

Annals of Edinburgh

VALIANT IN DEFENCE OF FREEDOM

An excerpt from a translation of the *Declaration of Arbroath*, the letter sent by the Council to Pope John XXII, 1320.

... So under the protection of these (your predecessors) our nation lived in freedom and peace until the Mighty Prince Edward, King of England, the father of the present king, aggressively attacked our kingdom, while it was without a head, and our people, who were both guiltless of any wrong doing or perfidy and at the time unaccustomed to wars or invasions. No one who did not know them from experience could describe or fully appreciate all his outrages, massacres, violence, plunder and burning, the imprisoning of prelates, the firing of monasteries, the robbing and murdering of religious persons, and other atrocities as well which he perpetrated against the said people, sparing neither age nor sex, religion nor order.

But with the help of Him who after injuries gives healing and health we have been liberated from these countless evils by our valiant Prince and Sovereign Lord, Robert, who, like a second Maccabaeus or Joshua, has cheerfully endured exertion and fatigue, hunger and danger, in order to deliver his people and his inheritance out of the hands of their enemies. Now the will of God, and the right of succession in accordance with our laws and traditions, which we mean to uphold to the death, and the due agreement and consent of all of us have appointed him our Prince and King. To him, as the author of our people's deliverance, we are bound both by law and by his own gallantry for the defence of our freedom, and we are determined to be loyal to him in everything. But if he were to abandon the cause by being ready to make us or our kingdom subject to the King of England or to the English, we should at once do our utmost to expel him as our enemy and the betrayer of his own rights and ours, and should choose some other man to be our king, who would be ready to defend us. For so long as a hundred of us remain alive, we are resolved never to submit to the domination of the English. It is not for glory, wealth or honour that we are fighting, but for freedom, and freedom only, which no true man ever surrenders except with his life. . . .

translated from the Latin by
DOUGLAS A. KIDD

BRUCE AND THE BLOODHOUND

About the time when the Bruce was yet at the head of but few men, Sir Aymer de Valence, who was Earl of Pembroke, together with John of Lorn, came into Galloway, each of them being at the head of a large body of men. John of Lorn had a bloodhound with him, which it was said had formerly belonged to Robert Bruce himself; and having been fed by the King with his own hands, it became attached to him, and would follow his footsteps anywhere, as dogs are well known to trace their master's steps, whether they be bloodhounds or not. By means of this hound, John of Lorn thought he should certainly find out Bruce, and take revenge on him for the death of his relation Comyn.

When these two armies advanced upon King Robert, he at first thought of fighting the English Earl; but becoming aware that John of Lorn was moving round with another large body to attack him in the rear, he resolved to avoid fighting at that time, lest he should be oppressed by numbers. For this purpose, the King divided the men he had with him into three bodies, and commanded them to retreat by three different ways, thinking the enemy would not know which party to pursue. He also appointed a place at which they were to assemble again. But when John of Lorn came to the place where the army of Bruce had been thus divided, the bloodhound took his course after one of these divisions, neglecting the other two, and then John of Lorn knew that the King must be in that party; so he also made no pursuit after the two other divisions of the Scots, but followed that which the dog pointed out, with all his men.

The King again saw that he was followed by a large body, and being determined to escape from them if possible, he made all the people who were with him disperse themselves different ways, thinking thus that the enemy must needs lose trace of him. He kept only one man along with him, and that was his own foster-brother, or the son of his nurse. When John of Lorn came to the place where Bruce's companions had dispersed themselves, the bloodhound, after it had snuffed up and down for a little, quitted the footsteps of all the other fugitives, and ran barking upon the track of two men out of the whole number. Then John of Lorn knew that one of these two must needs be King Robert. Accordingly, he commanded five of his men that were speedy of foot to chase after him, and either make him prisoner or slay him. The Highlanders started off accordingly, and ran so fast, that they gained sight of Robert and his foster-brother. The King asked his companion what help he could give him, and his foster-brother answered he was ready to do his best. So these two turned on the five men of John of Lorn, and killed them all. It is to be supposed they were better armed than the others were, as well as stronger and more desperate.

But by this time Bruce was very much fatigued, and yet they dared not sit down to take any rest; for whenever they stopt for an instant, they heard the cry of the bloodhound behind them, and knew by that, that their enemies were coming up fast after them. At length, they came to a wood, through which ran a small river. Then Bruce said to his foster-brother, "Let us wade down this stream for a great way, instead of going straight across, and so this unhappy hound will lose the scent; for if we were once clear of him, I should not be afraid of getting away from the pursuers." Accordingly, the King and his attendant walked a great way down the stream, taking care to keep their feet in the water, which could not retain any scent where they had stepped. Then they came ashore on the further side from the enemy, and went deep into the wood before they stopped to rest themselves. In the meanwhile, the hound led John of Lorn straight to the place where the King went into the water, but there the dog began to be puzzled, not knowing where to go next; for you are well aware that the running water could not retain the scent of a man's foot, like that which remains on turf. So, John of Lorn seeing the dog was at fault, as it is called, this is, had lost the track of that which he pursued, he gave up the chase, and returned to join with Aymer de Valence.

SIR WALTER SCOTT (1771-1832)
Tales of a Grandfather

THE TOMB OF BRUCE

In the year 1818, the workmen engaged in clearing the foundations for a new church among the ruins of Dunfermline Abbey, came upon the tomb of Robert the Bruce. . . . Men looked with wonder and awe upon the skull where once had dwelt counsel so sage and high, and upon the mouldering bone which had once been the strong right arm that struck down the fierce de Bohun.

MACKENZIE
History of Scotland

ROBERT THE BRUCE STRICKEN
WITH LEPROSY: TO DOUGLAS

' My life is done, yet all remains,
    The breath has vanished, the image not,
The furious shapes once forged in heat
    Live on, though now no longer hot.

' Steadily the shining swords
    In order rise, in order fall,
In order on the beaten field
    The faithful trumpets call.

' The women weeping for the dead
    Now are not sad but dutiful,
The dead men stiffening in their place
    Proclaim the ancient rule.

' Great Wallace's body hewn in four,
    So altered, stays as it must be.
O Douglas, do not leave me now,
    For by your side I see

' My dagger sheathed in Comyn's heart,
    And nothing there to praise or blame,
Nothing but order which must be
    Itself and still the same.

' But that Christ hung upon the Cross,
    Comyn would rot until Time's end
And bury my sin in boundless dust,
    For there is no amend.

' In order; yet in order run
    All things by unreturning ways.

If Christ live not, nothing is there
   For sorrow or for praise.'

So the King spoke to Douglas once
   A little time before his death,
Having outfaced three English kings
   And kept a people's faith.

EDWIN MUIR (b. 1887)

BRUCE BEFORE BANNOCKBURN

Scots, wha hae wi' Wallace bled,
Scots, wham Bruce has aften led,
Welcome to your gory bed,
    Or to victorie.

Now's the day, and now's the hour;
See the front of battle lour;
See approach proud Edward's power—
    Chains and slaverie!

Wha will be a traitor knave?
Wha can fill a coward's grave?
Wha sae base as be a slave?
    Let him turn and flee!

Wha for Scotland's King and Law
Freedom's sword will strongly draw,
Free-man stand, or free-man fa'?
    Let him follow me!

By Oppression's woes and pains!
By your sons in servile chains!
We will drain our dearest veins,
    But they shall be free!

Lay the proud usurpers low!
Tyrants fall in every foe!
Liberty's in every blow!
Let us do, or die!

ROBERT BURNS (1759-96)

BEFORE BANNOCKBURN

Bannockburn, a village (now a small town with various industries, chiefly textile) 3 miles south-east of Stirling, is celebrated for the decisive battle in which Robert the Bruce defeated Edward II's attempt to relieve the English garrison at Stirling and secured the independence of Scotland. It was fought on June 24th, 1314. The exact site of the battle is doubtful. Recent research tends to show that the engagement took place about 2 miles east of the traditional Field of Bannockburn, the site of which was acquired for a national park in 1929.

On Sunday then, in the morning,
Weil soon after the son rising,
They heard their mass commonaly;
And mony them shrave full devoutly,
That thocht to die in that melée,
Or then to make their country free! . . .
Troughout the host then gart he cry
That all should arm them hastily,
And busk them on their best manner;
And when they assembled were,
He gart array them for the fight:
And syne gart cry oure all on height,
That wha soever he were that fand
His heart nocht sicker for to stand
To win all or die with honour,
For to maintain that stalwart stour,
That he betime should hald his way;
And nane should dwell with them but they
That would stand with him to the end,
And tak the ure that God would send.

Then all answered with a cry,
And with a voice said generally,
That nane for doubt of deid should fail,
Quhill discomfit were the great battaile.

JOHN BARBOUR (*c.* 1316-95)
The Bruce

RESTRICTIONS ON DRESS
1457

The Scottish Parliament conceiving that the kingdom suffered greatly at this period, by the sumptuous dress both of men and women, passed the following act, regulating the dress of persons according to their station in life.

"That sen the realme in ilk estaite is greatumlie pured throwe sumptuous claithing, baith of men and women, and in special within burrowes and commouns of landwart: The lordes thinkis speidful, that restriction be thereof in this manner: That na man within burgh that livis be merchandice, bot gif hee be a person constitute in dignitie, as alderman, baillie, or uther gude worthy men, that ar of the councel of the toune, and their wives, weare claithes of silk, nor costly scarletts in gownes, or furringes with mertrickes. And that they make their wives and dauchters in like manner be abuilzied, gangand and correspondant for their estaite, that is to say, on their heads short curches with little hudes, as ar used in Flanders, England, and uther cuntries.

And as to their gownes, that na women weare mertricks nor letteis, nor tailes unfit in length, nor furred under, bot on the halie-days. And in like manner, the barronnes and uther puir gentlemen, and their wives, that ar within fourtie pund of auld extent. And as anent the commouns, that na laborers nor husbandmen, weare

on the warke daye, bot gray and quhite, and on the halie-
daye, bot light blew, greene, redde, and their wives right
swa, and courchies of their awin making, and that it
exceed not the price of xl. pennyes the elne.

And that na woman cum to kirk, nor mercat, with her
face mussalled or covered that sche may not be kend,
under the paine of escheit of the courchie. And as to the
clerkes, that nane weare gownes of scarlet, nor furring
of mertricks, bot gif he be ane person constitute in
dignitie, in cathedral or colledge kirk: or else, that he
may spende two hundreth markes, or greate nobiles, or
doctoures. And this to be now proclaimed, and put to
execution, be the first day of Maij, under the paine of
escheit of the habite, that is to say, of the clerkes be the
ordinar judge, and the lave be the kinges officiares."

Annals of Edinburgh

BLUEBONNETS OVER THE BORDER

The Scots are bold, hardy, and much inured to war.
When they make their invasions into England, they
march from twenty to four-and-twenty leagues without
halting, as well by night as day; for they are all on
horseback, except the camp-followers, who are on foot.
The knights and esquires are well mounted on large bay
horses, the common folk on little Galloways. They
bring no carriages with them on account of the
mountains they have to pass in Northumberland; neither
do they carry with them any provisions of bread or
wine; for their habits of sobriety are such, in time of
war, that they will live for a long time on flesh half
sodden, without bread, and drink the river water without
wine. They have, therefore, no occasion for pots or
pans; for they dress the flesh of their cattle in the skins,
after they have taken them off; and being sure to find

plenty of them in the country which they invade, they carry none with them. Under the flaps of his saddle, each man carries a broad plate of metal; behind the saddle a little bag of oatmeal. When they have eaten too much of the sodden flesh, and their stomach appears weak and empty, they place this plate over the fire, mix with water their oatmeal, and when the plate is heated, they put a little of the paste upon it, and make a thin cake, like a cracknel or biscuit, which they eat to warm their stomach; it is therefore no wonder that they perform a longer day's march than other soldiers.

FROISSART
translated by JOHNES

BORDER KEEPS

The policy of the Scots deterred them from erecting upon the Borders buildings of such extent and strength, as, being once taken by the foe, would have been capable of receiving a permanent garrison. To themselves the woods and hills of their country were pointed out by the Great Bruce as their safest bulwarks; and the maxim of the Douglases, that "it was better to hear the lark sing than the mouse cheep," was adopted by every Border chief. For these combined reasons the residence of the chieftain was commonly a large square battle-mented tower, called a *keep*, or *peel*, placed on a precipice, or on the banks of a torrent, and, if the ground would permit, surrounded by a moat. In short, the situation of a Border house, surrounded by woods, and rendered almost inaccessible by torrents, by rocks, or by morasses, sufficiently indicated the pursuits and apprehensions of its inhabitant.

No wonder, therefore, that James V. on approaching the castle of Lochwood, the ancient seat of the Johnstones, is said to have exclaimed, " that he who built it must have been a knave in his heart." An outer wall, with some slight fortifications, served as a protection for the castle at night. The walls of the fortresses were of immense thickness, and they could easily be defended against any small force; more especially as, the rooms being vaulted, each story formed a separate lodgment, capable of being held out for a considerable time. On such occasions, the usual mode adopted by the assailants, was to expel the inhabitants by setting fire to wet straw in the lower apartments. But the Border chieftains seldom choose to abide in person a siege of this nature. The common people resided in paltry huts, about the safety of which they were little anxious, as they contained nothing of value. On the approach of a superior force, they unthatched them, to prevent their being burned, and then abandoned them to the foe. Their only treasures were a fleet and active horse, with the ornaments which their rapine had procured for the females of their family, of whose gay appearance the Borderers were vain.

SIR WALTER SCOTT (1771-1832)
The Border Minstrelsy

THE BORDER LAW

'Hout, there's nae great skill needed; just put a lighted peat on the end of a spear, or hayfork, or siclike, and blaw a horn, and cry the gathering-word, and then it's lawful to follow gear into England, and recover it by the strong hand, or to take gear frae some other Englishman, providing ye lift nae mair than's been lifted frae you. That's the auld Border Law, made at Dundrennan in the days of the Black Douglas. Deil ane need doubt it. It's as clear as the sun.'

SIR WALTER SCOTT (1771-1832)
The Black Dwarf

MARCH, MARCH,
ETTRICK AND TEVIOTDALE

March, march, Ettrick and Teviotdale,
  Why the deil dinna ye march forward in order?
March, march, Eskdale and Liddesdale,
  All the Blue Bonnets are bound for the Border.
     Many a banner spread,
     Flutters above your head,
  Many a crest that is famous in story.
     Mount and make ready then,
     Sons of the mountain glen,
  Fight for the Queen and the old Scottish glory.

Come from the hills where your hirsels are grazing,
  Come from the glen of the buck and the roe;
Come to the crag where the beacon is blazing,
  Come with the buckler, the lance, and the bow.
     Trumpets are sounding,
     War-steeds are bounding,
  Stand to your arms then, and march in good order;
     England shall many a day
     Tell of the bloody fray,
  When the Blue Bonnets came over the Border.

SIR WALTER SCOTT (1771-1832)
The Monastery

A SEA FIGHT
1490

But soon after the King of England heard tell of this
news, and how his ships were so fought and taken by
Sir Andrew Wood as aforesaid. He was greatly discon-
tented therewith, and made proclamation through all

England who would pass to the sea and fight with Sir Andrew Wood; and if he happened to take him prisoner, and bring him to him, he should have for his reward £1000 to spend yearly. There was many that refused, because they knew Sir Andrew Wood to be such a captain upon the sea, and also so chancey (skilful) in battle, that ofttimes (he) obtained the victory; therefore they had the less will to assail him.

Notwithstanding, a captain of war, a gentleman named Stephen Bull, took in hand to the King of England's majesty to pass to the sea, and fight with Sir Andrew Wood, and bring him to the King of England, either dead or quick. Upon this the King of England was right rejoiced and gart (made) provide the Captain Stephen Bull three great ships well manned, well victualled, and artilleried.

Soon after this the said captain passed to the sea, and sailed till he came to the Scottish Firth, that is to say, at the back of May (Island), and there lay and waited Sir Andrew Wood's homecoming, who was then in Flanders for the time, trusting then nothing but peace. Yet, notwithstanding, this Captain Stephen Bull waiting his time at the back of May, took many of the boats who was travelling in the Firth for fish to win their living; notwithstanding the said Stephen Bull ransomed the skippers, and held many of the mariners prisoners to that effect that they should give him knowledge of Sir Andrew Wood, when he came in the Firth. Till at the last, upon a summer morning a little after the day breaking, one of the English ships perceived two ships coming under sail by St. Abb's Head.

Then this English captain caused some of the Scottish prisoners to pass to the top of the ships that they might see and spy if it was Sir Andrew Wood or not; but the Scotsmen had no will to show the verity, but feigned, and said they knew them not. But at last the captain promised them their freedom, if they would tell him if it was Sir Andrew Wood or not, who certified that it was he indeed. Then the captain was blithe and gart broach the wine, and drank about to all his skippers and captains that was under him, praying them to take good courage for the enemy was at hand. For the which cause he gart order his ships in order of battle, and set his quartermasters and captains every man in his own station, then caused his gunners to charge the artillery and put all in order, and left nothing undone pertaining to a good captain.

On the other side Sir Andrew Wood came boldly forward, knowing no impediment of enemies to be in his way, till at last he perceived these three ships making under sail and coming fast toward them in fighting trim. Then Andrew Wood seeing this exhorted his men to battle, beseeching them to take courage against their enemies of England who had sworn and made their vows "that they should make us prisoners to the King of England, but, God willing, they shall fail of their purpose. Therefore set yourselves in order every man in his own station, let the gunners charge their artillery, and the cross-bows, and make them ready, with their lime-pots and fireballs in our tops, and two-handled swords in your fore-rooms and let every man be diligent and stout for his own part, and for the honour of his realm." And thereupon he made them fill the wine, and each drank to the other.

By this time the sun began to rise, and shone bright on the sails. So the Englishmen appeared very awful in the sight of the Scots, by reason that their ships were very great and strong, and well furnished with greater artillery: yet, notwithstanding, the Scots feared nothing, but cast them to windward of the Englishmen, who, seeing that, shot a great cannon or two at the Scots, thinking that they should have struck sails at their challenge. But the Scotsmen nothing afraid thereat came swiftly on the windward upon Captain Stephen

Bull, and closed together and fought from the sun-rising till the sun went down, a long summer day, while that all the men and women that dwelt near the coast came and beheld the fighting that was very terrible to see. Yet, notwithstanding, the night sundered them, that they were fain to depart from one another, till on the morn that the day began to break fair, and their trumpets blew on every side, and made quickly to battle; who clapped to, and fought so cruelly that neither the shippers nor mariners took heed of their ships, but fought till the ebb-tide. A wind bore them to Inchcape, opposite the mouth of Tay. The Scotsmen seeing this took such courage and daring, that they doubled their strokes upon the Englishmen, and there took Stephen Bull and his three ships, and had them up the Tay to the town of Dundee, and there remained till their hurt men were cured and the dead buried.

LINDSAY OF PITSCOTTIE (d. *c.* 1565)
History of Scotland (*modernised*)

SOMETHING TO FIGHT FOR

"I would not have thought you, Edie, had so much to fight for?"

"*Me* no muckle to fight for, sir? Isna there the country to fight for, and the burnsides that I gang daundering beside, and the hearths o' the gudewives that gie me ma bit bread, and the bits o' weans that come toddling to play wi' me when I come about a landward town?" Deil!" he continued, grasping his pikestaff with great emphasis, "an had I as gude pith as I hae gude-will, and a gude cause, I should gie some o' them a day's kemping."

SIR WALTER SCOTT (1771-1832)
The Antiquary

FLODDEN

The battle of Flodden, perhaps the most disastrous event in Scottish history, was fought on Flodden hill, Northumberland, a low spur of the Cheviots six miles south of Coldstream, between the armies of James IV of Scotland and the English under the Earl of Surrey, on September 9th, 1513. It resulted in the crushing defeat of the Scots, who lost their king and the flower of their nobility.

Often as I have wished for your company, I never did it more earnestly than when I rode over Flodden Edge. I know your taste for these things, and could have undertaken to demonstrate that never was an affair more completely bungled than that day's work was. Suppose one army posted upon the face of a hill, and secured by high grounds projecting on each flank, with the river Till in front, a deep and still river, winding through a very extensive valley called Milfield Plain, and the only passage over it by a narrow bridge, which the Scots artillery, from the hill, could in a moment have demolished. Add that the English must have hazarded a battle while their troops, which were tumultuously levied, remained together; and that the Scots, behind whom the country was open to Scotland, had nothing to do but to wait for the attack as they were posted. Yet did two thirds of the army, actuated by the perfervidum ingenium Scotorum, rush down and give an opportunity to Stanley to occupy the ground they had quitted, by coming over the shoulder of the hill, while the other third, under Lord Home, kept their ground, and having seen their king and about 10,000 of their countrymen cut to pieces, retired into Scotland without loss.

SIR WALTER SCOTT (1771-1832)
to William Clerk, *August 26th*, 1791

THE LAST STAND AT FLODDEN

But as they left the dark'ning heath,
More desperate grew the strife of death.
The English shafts in volleys hail'd,
In headlong charge their horse assail'd;
Front, flank, and rear, the squadrons sweep
To break the Scottish circle deep,
　　That fought around their King.
But yet, though thick the shafts as snow,
Though charging knights like whirlwinds go,
Though bill-men ply the ghastly blow,
　　Unbroken was the ring;
The stubborn spear-men still made good
Their dark impenetrable wood,
Each stepping where his comrade stood,
　　The instant that he fell.
No thought was there of dastard flight;
Link'd in the serried phalanx tight,
Groom fought like noble, squire like knight,
As fearlessly and well;
Till utter darkness closed her wing
O'er their thin host and wounded King.
Then skilful Surrey's sage commands
Led back from strife his shatter'd bands;
　　And from the charge they drew,
As mountain-waves, from wasted lands,
　　Sweep back to ocean blue.
Then did their loss his foemen know;
Their King, their Lords, their mightiest low,
They melted from the field, as snow,
When streams are swoln, and south winds blow,
　　Dissolves in silent dew.
Tweed's echoes heard the ceaseless plash,
　　While many a broken band,
Disorder'd, through her currents dash,

To gain the Scottish land;
To town and tower, to down and dale,
To tell red Flodden's dismal tale,
And raise the universal wail.
Tradition, legend, tune, and song,
Shall many an age that wail prolong:
Still from the sire the son shall hear
Of the stern strife, and carnage drear,
 Of Flodden's fatal field,
Where shiver'd was fair Scotland's spear,
And broken was her shield!

SIR WALTER SCOTT (1771-1832)
Marmion

EDINBURGH AFTER FLODDEN

When news of the tragic defeat of Flodden reached the capital, the remaining men and most of the women were impressed into service to strengthen the city's defences. The following is a transcript of the Municipal Proclamation issued on September 10th, 1513.

Forasmuch as there is a great rumour now lately risen within this town, touching our Sovereign Lord and his army, of which we understand there is come no verity as yet; wherefore we charge strictly and command in our said Sovereign Lord the King's name, and in that of the Presidents, for the Provosts and Baillies within the burgh, that all manner of persons, townsmen within the same, have ready their arms of defence and weapons for war, and appear therewith before the said Presidents at the tolling of the common bell, for the keeping and defence of the town against them that would invade the same. And we also charge that all women, and especially vagabonds, that they pass to their labours, and be not seen upon the streets clamouring and crying, upon the pain of banishing of their persons without favour, and that the other women of the better sort pass to the kirk and pray, when time requires, for our Sovereign Lord and his army, and the townsmen who are with the army: and that they hold them at their private labours off the streets within their houses as becometh.

THE FLOWERS OF THE FOREST

The version by Miss Jane Elliot, second daughter of Sir Gilbert Elliot, second baronet of Minto.

I've heard them lilting at our yowe[1]-milking—
  Lasses a-lilting before dawn of day;
But now they are moaning on ilka[2] green loaning[3]—
  The Flowers of the Forest are a' wede away.

At buchts,[4] in the morning, nae blythe lads are scorning;
  Lasses are lonely, and dowie[5] and wae[6];—
Nae daffin',[7] nae gabbin'[8] but sighing and sabbing[9]
  Ilk[10] ane lifts her leglin[11] and hies her away.

In hairst, at the shearing, nae youths now are jeering—
  Bandsters are runkled and lyart[12] or grey:
At fair or at preaching, nae wooing, nae fleeching[13]:
  The Flowers of the Forest are a' wede away.

At e'en, in the gloaming,[14] nae swankies[15] are roaming,
  'Bout stacks with the lasses at bogle[16] to play;
But ilk[17] ane sits drearie, lamenting her dearie—
  The Flowers of the Forest are a' wede away.

Dool[18] and wae for the order sent our lads to the Border!
  The English, for ance, by guile wan the day;—

[1] ewe [2] every [3] avenue [4] sheep folds [5] drooping [6] sad [7] romping
[8] chatting [9] sobbing [10] each [11] milk-pail [12] faded [13] flattering
[14] twilight [15] smart young fellows [16] hide-and-seek [17] each
[18] sorrow

The Flowers of the Forest, that foucht aye the foremost—
  The prime o' our land—are cauld in the clay.

We'll hear nae mair lilting at the yowe-milking;
  Women and bairns are heartless and wae,
Sighing and moaning on ilka green loaning—
  The Flowers of the Forest are a' wede away.

JANE ELLIOT (1727-1805)

LADY GLAMMIS BURNED ALIVE
1539

Joan Douglas sister of the earl of Angus, and widow of John Lyon Lord Glammis, her son, Gillespie Campbell, her second husband, Lord Lyon, a relation of her first husband, and an old priest, were accused of attempting to poison the king. All these, although they lived constantly in the country at a distance from court, and though nothing to their disadvantage could be extorted from their relatives and servants, even when examined by torture, were nevertheless condemned and confined in Edinburgh castle. Lady Glammis was burnt alive on the castle hill, greatly pitied by the spectators; her rank, blooming youth and uncommon beauty, affected them so deeply that they burst into tears and loud lamentations for her untimely end. The next day, her husband in endeavouring to escape from the castle, fell, the rope being too short, and was dashed to pieces among the rocks.

The accuser William Lyon, a relation, when he saw the ruin in which his calumnious falsehood had involved a noble family, repented when too late, and confessed his offence to the king, but could neither obtain from him any alteration of the punishment to the accused, nor the restoration of any of the estates. The son of

Lord Glammis being too young to be suspected of any crime, was confined in the castle till the king's death, when he was liberated, and put in possession of his hereditary estates, which had been confiscated.

Annals of Edinburgh

KNOX AND QUEEN MARY

Placeboes and flatterers posted to the court, to give advertisement, that John Knox had spoken against the queen's marriage. The provost of Glencudan, Douglas by sirname, of Drumlanerk, was the man that gave the charge, that the said John should present himself before the queen; which he did immediately after dinner. The lord Ochiltrie, and divers of the faithful, bare him company to the abbey; but none past with him into the cabinet to the queen, but John Erskine of Dun, then superintendant of Angus and Mearns.

Then queen, in a vehement rage, began to cry out, That never prince was used as she was. "I have," said she, "borne with you in all your rigorous manner of speaking, both against myself and against my uncles; yea, I have sought your favour by all possible means: I offered unto you presence and audience, whensoever it pleased you to admonish me, and yet I cannot be quit of you; I vow to God I shall be once revenged." And with these words scarce could Marnock, one of her pages, get handkerchiefs to hold her eyes dry, for the tears and weeping staid her speech. The said John did patiently abide all this fume, and at opportunity answered, "True it is, madam, your majesty and I have had divers controversies, and I never perceived your majesty to be offended at me; but when it shall please God to deliver you from that bondage of darkness and error, wherein ye have been nourished, for the want of true doctrine, your majesty will find the liberty of my tongue nothing offensive. Without the preaching-place, madam, I think few have occasion to be offended at me, and there, madam, I am not master of myself, but must obey him who commands me to speak plain, and to flatter no flesh upon the face of the earth."

"But what have you to do," said she, " with my marriage?"

"If it please your majesty," said he, "patiently to hear me, I shall shew the truth in plain words. I grant your majesty offered unto me more than ever I required; but my answer was then, as it is now, that God hath not sent me to wait upon the courts of princes, or upon the chamber of ladies; but I am sent to preach the gospel of Jesus Christ, to such as please to hear: it hath two points, *repentance* and *faith*. Now, madam, in preaching repentance, of necessity it is, that the sins of men be noted, that they may know wherein they offend; but so it is, that the most part of your nobility are so addicted to your affections, that neither God's word, nor yet their commonwealth, are rightly regarded; and therefore it becometh me to speak, that they may know their duty."

"What have you to do," said she, " with my marriage? Or what are you in this commonwealth?"

"A subject born within the same," said he, "madam, and albeit I be neither earl, lord, nor baron within it, yet hath God made me (how abject so ever I be in your eyes) a profitable and useful member within the same; yea, madam, to me it appertaineth, no less to forewarn of such things as may hurt it, if I foresee them, that it doth to any one of the nobility; for both my vocation and office craveth plainness of me; and therefore, madam, to yourself I say, that which I spake in public, Whensoever the nobility of this realm shall consent, that you be subject to an unlawful husband, they do as much as in them lieth to renounce Christ, to banish the truth, to betray the freedom of this realm, and perchance shall in the end do small comfort to yourself."

At these words complaining was heard and tears might have been seen in greater abundance than the matter required. John Erskine of Dun, a man of meek and gentle spirit, was present, and did what he could to mitigate her anger, and gave unto her many pleasant words, of her beauty, of her excellency; and how that all the princes in Europe would be glad to seek her favour. But all that was to cast oil into the flaming fire. The said John stood still, without any alteration of countenance for a long time, till the queen gave place to her inordinate passion; and, in the end, he said, "Madam, in God's presence I speak, I never delighted in the weeping of any of God's creatures; yea, I can scarcely well abide the tears of mine own boys, when my hands correct them, much less can I rejoice in your majesty's weeping: but seeing I have offered unto you no just occasion to be offended, but have spoken the truth, as my vocation craves of me, I must sustain your majesty's tears rather than I dare hurt my conscience, or betray the commonwealth, by silence." Herewith was the queen more offended, and commanded the said John to go out of the cabinet, and wait her further pleasure in the chamber.

The laird of Dun tarried, and lord John of Coldingham came into the cabinet; and so they both remained with her near the space of an hour. The said John stood in the chamber, as one whom men had never seen, so were all afraid, except that the lord Ochiltrie bore him company; and therefore he began to discourse with the ladies, who were there sitting in all their gorgeous apparel: which when he espied, he merely said, "Fair ladies, how pleasant were this life of yours, if it should ever abide; and then in the end, that we might pass to heaven, with this gear? But fy upon that knave Death, who will come whether we will or not; and when he hath laid on the arrest, then foul worms will be busy with this flesh, be it never so fair and so tender; and the silly soul, I fear, shall be so feeble, that it can neither carry with it gold, garnishing, targating, pearl, nor precious stones." And by such discourse entertained he the ladies, and past the time, till that the laird of Dun desired him to go to his house, till new advertisement.

JOHN KNOX (c. 1505-1572)
History of the Reformation

ALAS! POOR QUEEN

She was skilled in music and the dance
And the old arts of love
At the court of the poisoned rose
And the perfumed glove,
And gave her beautiful hand
To the pale Dauphin
A triple crown to win—
And she loved little dogs
        And parrots
      And red-legged partridges
And the golden fishes of the Duc de Guise
And a pigeon with a blue ruff
She had from Monsieur d'Elbœuf.

Master John Knox was no friend to her.
She spoke him soft and kind,
Her honeyed words were Satan's lure
The unwary soul to bind.
' Good sir, doth a lissome shape
And a comely face
Offend your God His Grace
Whose Wisdom maketh these
Golden fishes of the Duc de Guise? '

She rode through Liddesdale with a song;
' Ye streams saw wondrous strang,
Oh, mak' me a wrack as I come back
But spare me as I gang.'
While a hill-bird cried and cried
Like a spirit lost
By the grey storm-wind tost.

Consider the way she had to go,
Think of the hungry snare,
The net she herself had woven,
Aware or unaware,
Of the dancing feet grown still,
The blinded eyes—
Queens should be cold and wise,
And she loved little things,
   Parrots
  And red-legged partridges
And the golden fishes of the Duc de Guise
And the pigeon with the blue ruff
She had from Monsieur d'Elbœuf.

MARION ANGUS (1866-1946)

MARRIAGE OF
MARY AND DARNLEY
1565

Let no man grudge the beautiful Queen of Scots the
rapture of those fleeting summer days. If there was more
than indiscretion, it was to be atoned for bitterly. If
Darnley and she had gone through a secret form of
marriage, it was not legally done, for the Papal dispensation did not come to hand till 22nd July, on which day
the banns were proclaimed; and at 6 a.m. on Sunday
the 29th, the marriage ceremony was performed by the
Bishop of Brechin according to the Roman ritual in the

Queen's private chapel in Holyroodhouse. According to Randolph, who, though in Edinburgh, was not present, the Queen wore

"the greate mourninge gowne of blacke, with the great wyde mourninge hoode, not unlyke unto that which she wore the dolefull daye of the buriall of her husbande [the Dauphin]. . . . She was ledde unto the chappell by the Erles of Lenox and Athol, and there she was lefte untyll her housband came, who was also conveide by the same lords. . . . The words were spoken; the rings, which were three, the middle a riche diamonde, were put upon her finger, theie kneel together, and manie prayers saide over them. She tarrieth owte the masse, and he taketh a kysse and leaveth her there and wente to her chamber, whither in a space she followeth; and there being required, accordinge to the solemnitie, to cast off her care, and lay asyde those sorrowfull garments, and give herself to a pleasanter lyfe, after some prettie refusall, more I believe for manner sake than greef of harte, she suffreth them that stood by, everie man that coulde approche to take owte a pyn, and so being commytted unto her ladies changed her garments. . . . After the marriage followeth commonly cheere and dancinge. To their dynner theie were conveide by the whole nobles. The trompets sounde, a larges [largesse] cried, and monie thrown abowte the howse in greate abundance to suche as were happie to gete anye parte. . . . After dyner theie dance awhyle, and retire themselves tyll the hower of supper, and as theie dyned so do theie suppe. Some dancing ther was, and so theie go to bedd."

Next morning the heralds proclaimed Darnley as Henry, King of Scots, in presence of the lords who happened to be in Edinburgh—an act of doubtful legality without the concurrence of Parliament. When it was declared that all letters henceforth should be set forth in the names conjointly of King Henry and Queen Mary, none responded save Lennox, who cried, "God save his Grace!"

SIR HERBERT MAXWELL
Holyroodhouse

QUEEN MARY AT LOCHLEVEN

The Lords of the Congregation visit Queen Mary at Lochleven Castle to demand her resignation of the crown.

"We come, madam," said the Lord Ruthven, "to request your answer to the proposal of the Council."

"Your final answer," said Lord Lindesay; "for with a refusal you must couple the certainty that you have precipitated your fate, and renounced the last opportunity of making peace with God, and ensuring your longer abode in the world."

"My lords," said Mary, with inexpressible grace and dignity, "the evils we cannot resist we must submit to —I will subscribe these parchments with such liberty of choice as my condition permits me. Were I on yonder shore, with a fleet jennet and ten good and loyal knights around me, I would subscribe my sentence of eternal condemnation as soon as the resignation of my throne. But here, in the castle of Lochleven, with deep water around me—and you, my lords, beside me,—I have no freedom of choice.—Give me the pen, Melville, and bear witness to what I do, and why I do it."

"It is our hope your Grace will not suppose yourself compelled, by any apprehensions from us," said the Lord Ruthven, "to execute what must be your own voluntary deed."

The Queen had already stooped towards the table, and placed the parchment before her, with the pen between her fingers, ready for the important act of signature. But when Lord Ruthven had done speaking, she looked up, stopped short, and threw down the pen. "If," she said, "I am expected to declare I give away my crown of free will, or otherwise than because I am compelled to renounce it by the threat of worse evils to myself and my subjects, I will not put my name to such an untruth —not to gain full possession of England, France, and Scotland!—all once my own, in possession, or by right."

"Beware, madam," said Lindesay, and snatching hold of the Queen's arm, with his own gauntleted hand, he pressed it, in the rudeness of his passion, more closely perhaps, than he was himself aware of,—"beware how you contend with those who are the stronger, and have the mastery of your fate!"

He held his grasp on her arm, bending his eyes on her with a stern and intimidating look, till both Ruthven and Melville cried shame! and Douglas, who had hitherto remained in a state of apparent apathy, had made a stride from the door, as if to interfere. The rude Baron then quitted his hold, disguising the confusion which he really felt at having indulged his passion to such extent, under a sullen and contemptuous smile.

The Queen immediately began, with an expression of pain, to bare the arm which he had grasped, by drawing up the sleeve of her gown, and it appeared that his gripe had left the purple mark of his iron fingers upon her flesh—"My lord," she said, "as a knight and gentleman, you might have spared my frail arm so severe a proof that you have the greater strength on your side, and are resolved to use it—But I thank you for it—it is the most decisive token of the terms on which this day's business is to rest.—I draw you to witness, both lords and ladies," she said, showing the marks of the grasp on her arm, "that I subscribe these instruments in obedience to the sign manual of my Lord of Lindesay, which you may see imprinted on mine arm."

Lindesay would have spoken, but was restrained by his colleague Ruthven, who said to him, "Peace, my lord. Let the Lady Mary of Scotland ascribe her signature to what she will, it is our business to procure it, and carry it to the Council. Should there be debate hereafter on the manner in which it was adhibited, there will be time enough for it."

Lindesay was silent accordingly, only muttering within his beard, "I meant not to hurt her; but I think women's flesh be as tender as new-fallen snow."

The Queen meanwhile subscribed the rolls of parchment with a hasty indifference, as if they had been matters of slight consequence, or of mere formality. When she had performed this painful task, she arose, and, having curtsied to the lords, was about to withdraw to her chamber. Ruthven and Sir Robert Melville made, the first a formal reverence, the second an obeisance, in which his desire to acknowledge his sympathy was obviously checked by the fear of appearing in the eyes of his colleagues too partial to his former mistress. But Lindesay stood motionless, even when they were preparing to withdraw. At length, as if moved by a sudden impulse, he walked round the table which had hitherto been betwixt them and the Queen, kneeled on one knee, took her hand, kissed it, let it fall, and arose—"Lady," he said, "thou art a noble creature, even though thou hast abused God's choicest gifts. I pay that devotion to thy manliness of spirit, which I would not have paid to the power thou hast long undeservedly wielded—I kneel to Mary Stewart, not to the Queen."

"The Queen and Mary Stewart pity thee alike, Lindesay," said Mary—"alike they pity, and they forgive thee. An honoured soldier hadst thou been by a king's side—leagued with rebels, what art thou but a good blade in the hands of a ruffian?—Farewell, my Lord Ruthven, the smoother but the deeper traitor.—Farewell, Melville—Mayst thou find masters that can understand state policy better, and have the means to reward it more richly, than Mary Stewart!—Farewell, George of Douglas—make your respected grand-dame comprehend that we would be alone for the remainder of the day—God wot, we have need to collect our thoughts."

SIR WALTER SCOTT (1771-1832)
The Abbot

A BOND OF ASSOCIATION

Upon Mary Queen of Scot's resigning the Crown in favour of her son, 1567

WWe quhiks has subscrivit the underwritten Bond, understanding that the Queenis Majesty willing nathing mair earnestlie, nor that in her Lifetime her Majesties Dear Son, our Native Prince, be placit and inaugurat in the Kindom of this his Native Cuntre and Realm, and be obeyit as King be us, and uthers his subjects: And being wearit of the great Pains and Travels taken be her in her Government thereof, hes be her Letters demittit and renderit, and given power thairby to demit and renunce the said Government of this Realm, Liegis and Subjectis thairof, in Favours of her said Son, our Native Prince: To the effect he may be inaugurat thairin, the Crown Royal put upon his Head, and be obeyit in all Things as King and Native Prince thairof, as her Hieness Letters past thairupon bears. Thairfore, and because it is ane of the maist happy Things that can come to any Pepill or Cuntre, to be governit and rulit by their awn Native King; We, and ilk ane of us, quhilk hes subscrivit thir Presents, be the Tenor heirof, promitties, binds, and oblissis us, faithfully to convene and assembil our selfs at the Burgh of Sterling, or any other Place to be appointit, to the Effect foresaid; and thair concur, assist and fortify our said Native King and Prince, to the

Establishing, Planting and Placing of him in his Kingdom, and Putting of the Crown Royal thairof upon his
Head, and in the Fear of our God being instructit and
teichit be his and all other Laws, sall giff our Aith of
Fidelity and Homage, and lawfull and dutiful Obedience,
to be made by us to him during his Graces Lifetime, as it
bedomes faithfull, Christian, and true Subjects to do to
thair Native King and Prince. And farther, that we sall
with all our Strength and Forcis promote, concurre,
fortifie and assist, to the Promoteing and Establishing
of him in his Kingdom and Government, as becumis
faithfull and true Subjects to do to thair Prince, and to
resist all sick as wald oppon them thairto, or make any
Trouble or Impediment to him thairin, and sall do all
uther Things, that becomis faithfull and Christian
Subjects to do to thair Native King and Prince. In
Witness of the quhilk Thing, we haif subscrivit thir
Presents with our Handis, at Edinburgh, the day of . . . ,
the Year of God 1567 Years.

James Regent. *Huntley. Archibald Argyle. Athol.
Mortoun. Mar. Glencairn. Errol. Buchan.
Graham. Alexander* Lord *Home. William* Lord
Ruthven. Lord *Sanquhar. Ihon* Lord *Glamis.
Patrick* Lord *Lindsey. Michael* Lord *Carlisle*:
With my Hand at the Pen, *Alexander Hay*,
Notarius. *William* Lord *Borthwick.* Lord *Inner-
maith. Ucheltrie. Sempill.* Henry Lord *Methven.
Allan* Lord *Cathcart. Patrick* Lord *Gray. Robert*
Com. of *Dumferling. James Stuart. Alexander*
Com. of *Culross. Adam* Com. of *Cambuskenneth.
Dryburgh.* Master of *Montrose. Alexander* Bishop
of *Galoway. Caprington. Blairquhan. Tullibarden,*
Comptroller; with Eighteen more.

SIR JAMES MELVILLE INTERVIEWS QUEEN ELIZABETH

She (Queen Elizabeth) desired to know of me what colour of hair was reputed best; and whether my queen's (Queen Mary) hair or hers was best, and which of them two was fairest. I answered, the fairness of them both was not their worst faults. But she was earnest with me to declare which of them I judged fairest. I said, she was the fairest queen in England, and mine in Scotland. Yet she appeared earnest. I answered, they were both the fairest ladies in their countries; that her majesty was whiter, but my queen was very lovely. She inquired which of them was of highest stature. I said: "My queen." "Then," saith she, "she is too high, for myself am neither too high nor too low." Then she asked what exercises she used. I answered, that when I received my dispatch, the queen was lately come from the Highland hunting; that when her more serious affairs permitted, she was taken up with reading of histories; that sometimes she recreated herself in playing upon the lute and virginals. She asked if she played well. I said reasonably, for a queen.

That same day after dinner, my Lord of Hunsdon drew me up to a quiet gallery that I might hear some music; but he said he durst not avow it, where I might hear the queen play upon the virginals. After I had hearkened awhile, I took by the tapestry that hung before the door of the chamber, and seeing her back was toward the door, I ventured within the chamber, and stood a pretty space hearing her play excellently well; but she left off immediately, as soon as she turned about and saw me. She appeared to be surprised to see me, and came forward, seeming to strike me with her hand; alleging that she used not to play before men but when she was solitary, to shun melancholy. She asked how I came there. I answered: "As I was walking with my Lord of Hunsdon, as we passed by the chamber-door, I heard such melody as ravished me, whereby I was drawn in ere I knew how;" excusing my fault of homeliness as being brought up in the court of France, where such freedom was allowed; declaring myself willing to endure what kind of punishment her majesty should be pleased to inflict upon me, for so great an offence. Then she sat down low upon a cushion, and I upon my knees by her, but with her own hand she gave me a cushion to lay under my knee, which at first I refused, but she compelled me to take it. She then called for my Lady Strafford out of the next chamber, for the queen was alone. She inquired whether my queen or she played best. In that I found myself obliged to give her the praise. She said my French was very good, and asked if I could speak Italian, which she spoke reasonably well. I told her majesty I had no time to learn the language, not having been above two months in Italy. Then she spake to me in Dutch, which was not good; and would know what kind of books I most delighted in—whether theology, history, or love matters. I said I liked well of all the sorts. Here I took occasion to press earnestly my dispatch; she said I was sooner weary of her company than she was of mine. I told her majesty, that though I had no reason of being weary, I knew my mistress her affairs called me home; yet I was stayed two days longer, that I might see her dance, as I was afterwards informed. Which being over, she inquired of me whether she or my queen danced best. I answered the queen danced not so high or disposedly as she did. Then again she wished that she might see the queen at some convenient place of meeting. I offered to convey her secretly to Scotland by post, clothed like a page, that under this disguise she might see the queen: as James V. had gone in disguise with his own ambassador to see the Duke of Vendome's sister, who should have been his wife. Telling her that her chamber might be kept in her absence, as though she were sick; that none need be privy thereto except Lady Strafford and one of the grooms of her chamber. She appeared to like that kind of language, only answered it with a sigh, saying: "Alas! if I might do it thus!"

SIR JAMES MELVILLE (1535-1617)
Memoirs

THE DEATH OF QUEEN MARY

Fotheringay, February 8th, 1587

The warrant and sentence the Earl of Kent held in his hand. The Great Seal of the Crown of England was thereon. Then the Queen replied that she would as lief die as live any longer. As she turned round she perceived her most distinguished servitor, Melville, and said to him: "My faithful servant Melville, though thou art a Protestant and I a Catholic, there is nevertheless but one Christendom and I am thy Queen. . . . And so I adjure thee before God that thou give this command to my son: I beg him to serve God, and the Catholic Church, and to rule and keep his country in peace and to submit (as I have done) to no other Master. Although I had the right good will to unite the kingdoms of this island, I renounce this. May he do likewise; and do not let him put overmuch trust in the presumptions of the world. . . . Let him speak no evil of the Queen of England; and thou, Melville, art my witness that I die like a true Scotswoman, Frenchwoman, and Catholic, which belief has ever been mine." These words and such like did she repeat. . . . When the executioner wished to assist her, she said to him that it was not her wont to be disrobed in the presence of such a crowd, nor with the help of such handmaidens. She herself took off her robe and pushed it down as far as the waist. . . . As she knelt down she repeated the 70th Psalm. . . . When she had said this to the end, she full of courage, bent down with her body and laid her head on the block, exclaiming: "*In manus tuas, Domine, commendo spiritum meum.*" Then one of the executioners held down her hands, and the other cut off her head with two strokes of the chopper. Thus ended her life. The executioner took the head and showed it to the people, who cried: "God spare our Queen of England!"

SAMUEL TOMASCON
The Fugger News Letters

THE RESTLESS GHOST

Wae's me, wae's me!—
The acorn's no' yet
Fa'en frae the tree
That's to grow the wood,
That's to mak the creddle,
That's to rock the bairn
That's to grow a man
That's to lay me.

TRADITIONAL

RESTRICTIONS ON EATING, DRINKING AND DRESS
1581

At this period, people went to so great an excess in eating, drinking, and banqueting, at marriages, baptisms, night wakings, and funerals, that it required the interference of an act of the legislature to repress on these occasions, so extraordinary a consumption, not only of articles of home produce, but also of "drogges, confectoures, and spiceries," brought from foreign countries and sold at dear prices "to monie folkes, that were very unabill to sustein that coaste." To put a stop to such abuses and disorders, parliament ordained, "That na maner of persones under the degree of prelates, earles, lordes, barronnes, landed gentil-men or utheris, that are worth and may spende in zeirlie frie rent, twa thousand markes money, or fifteen chalders victuall, all charges deduced, sall presume, to have at their bridelles, or uther banquettes, or at their tables in dayly cheare, onie drogges or confectoures, brocht from the pairtes bezond sea; and that na banquettes sall be at onie upsittinges, nor after baptizing of bairnes, in time cumming, under the paine of twentie pund, to be payed be everie persone doer in the contrair; asweill of the maister of the house, quhair the effect of this act is contravened, as of all uther persones, that sall be found or tryed partakeris of sik superfluous banquetting, and escheitting of the drogges and confectoures apprehended."

Provosts of burghs, sheriffs of counties, etc., were authorised by this act to appoint searchers, and empower them to make open doors, in any house they pleased to search, and apprehend offenders and put them in prison until they paid their fines, which were divided equally between the searchers and the poor of the parish in which the defaulter resided.

At this period, the common people had grown so extravagant in their dress, that they presumed to imitate the king and his nobility in the use and wearing of costly clothing made and brought from foreign countries, in consequence of which so exorbitant prices were charged for wearing apparel that the legislature interfered and passed the following regulations:—"That na man or woman, being under the degrees of dukes, earles, lordes of parliament, knichtes, or landed gentil-men, that hes or may spend of frie zearly rent, twa thousand markes, or fiftie chalders of victuall at least, or their wives, sonnes or dauchteris, sall use or weare in their cleithing, or apparell, or lyning thereof, onie claith of gold or silver, velvot, satine, damask, taffataes, or ony begairies, frenzies, pasments, or broderie of gold, silver, or silk, not zit layne, cammerage, or woollen claith, maid and brocht from onie foreine cuntries, under the paine of ane hundreth pundes, of every gentil-man landed, ane hundred markes, of every gentil-man unlanded, and fourtie pundes for ilk zeaman, for every day that he, his wife, his sonne, or dauchter, transgressis this present act." All judges and other officers belonging to the court, were exempted from the terms of this act, and servants were allowed to wear the old clothes of their master or mistress.

Annals of Edinburgh

WITCHCRAFT

The commissioners appointed to try witches, eagerly seized upon the report of James VI's bride having been driven back to Norway by the influence of witchcraft; and had a few unfortunate beings tried for that crime, which common sense might have taught them it was impossible for any human being to commit.

It was proved against John Cunningham, that the devil appeared to him in white raiment, and promised that, if he would become his servant, he would never want, and should be revenged of all his enemies. It was further proved, that he (the prisoner) *raised the wind on the king's passage to Denmark: that he met with Satan on the king's return from Denmark, and Satan promised to raise a mist, by which his majesty should be thrown up on the coast of England; and thereupon threw something like a football into the sea, which raised a vapour.* He was condemned and burned.

Agnes Sampson, in Keith, a grave matron-like woman, of a rank and comprehension above the vulgar, was accused of having renounced her baptism, and of having received the devil's mark, and of raising storms to prevent the queen's coming from Denmark; as also, of being at *the famous* meeting at North Berwick, where six men and ninety women, witches, were present, dancing to one of their number, who played to them on a Jew's harp. It was charged in the indictment, that the devil was present at this meeting, and started up in the pulpit, which was hung round with black candles: that he called them all by their names, and asked them if they had kept their promises, and been good servants, and what they had done since the last meeting: that they opened up three graves, and cut off the joints from the dead bodies' fingers; *and that the prisoner got for her share, two joints, and a winding sheet to make powder of, to do mischief*: that the devil was dressed in a black gown and hat, and that he ordered them to keep his commandments, which were to do all the ill they could. She was condemned and burned.

Euphan M'Calzeane, daughter of Lord Cliftonhall, one of the senators of the college of justice (his death, in 1581, spared him the disgrace and misery of seeing his daughter fall by the hands of the executioner), who was married to a gentleman, by whom she had three children, was accused of treasonably conspiring the king's death by enchantments; particularly by framing a waxen picture of the king; *of raising storms to hinder his return from Denmark;* and of various other articles of witchcraft. She possessed a considerable estate in her own right; was heard by counsel in her defence; was found guilty by the jury, which consisted of landed gentlemen of note; and was *burnt alive*, and her estate confiscated. Her children, however, after being thus barbarously robbed of their mother, were restored by act of parliament, against the forfeiture. The act does not say the sentence was unjust, but that the king was *touched in honour and conscience* to restore the children. But, to move his majesty's conscience, the children had to pay five thousand merks to the donator of escheat, and relinquish the estate of Cliftonhall, which the king gave to Sir James Sandilands of Slamanno.

Annals of Edinburgh

EXTRAVAGANCE OF THE TABLE
1581

The sumptuousness of the table, both of rich and poor, was considered to be such at this period, as to cause a dearth in the kingdom, therefore, "to stanch sik ex-orbitant dearth risen in this realme of victualles and uther stuffe, for the sustentation of mankinde, and quhilk is dailie increassand, to the great hurte of the common weill of the samin, and damnage to the bodie, quhilkis makis ane man unable to exerce all leifful and gude warkes necessar," for remedy thereof, parliament ordained: "That na arch-bishops, bishops, nor earls, have at his meate bot aucht dishes of meate; nor na abbot, lord, priour, nor deane, have at his meate bot sex dishes; nor na barronne, nor free-halder, have bot foure dishes of meate at his messe; nor na burgess nor uther sub-stantious man, spiritual nor temporal, bot three dishes and bot ane kinde of meate in everie dish."

Those who did not regulate their tables in conformity to this act, were fined as follows, viz.: An arch-bishop, &c. £100; a lord, &c. 100 merks; a baron, £40; a burgess, &c. 20 merks; and "gif ony uther small person or persones wauld presume to break this present acte, he sall be taken and punished in his person and gudes at the lorde governours will for their contemption; and he that falzies and breakis this ordinance, sall be repute, and halden as ane man given to his volumtuousnes."

Annals of Edinburgh

WEARING OF PLAIDS PROHIBITED
1636

The Act of 1631 having been honoured more in the breach than in the observance the town council seemed determined to enforce their ruling by the following thundering enactment. A further enactment was made in 1648.

"Forasmeikell as notwithstanding of divers and sundrie laudabill actes and Statutis maid be the Proveist, Baillies and Counsall of this Burgh in former tymes, discharging that barbarous and uncivill Habitte of womens wearing of plaids; zit such hes bein the impudencie of manie of them, that they have continewit the foresaid barbarous habitte, and hes added thairto the wearing of thair Gownes and Petticottes about thair heads and faces, so that the same has becum the ordinar habitte of all women within the Cittie to the general imputation of thair sex, Matrones not being abill to be discerned from Strumpettis and lowse living women, to thair awne dishonour, and scandal of the cittie; which the Proveist, Baillies, and Counsall have taken into thair serious consideration; thairfore have Statute and ordaynit and by thir presentis Statutis and ordaynis that none of whatsomever degrie or qualitie persume, after this day, under the payne of escheitt of the said plaids, not onlie be such as shall be appoyntit for that effect, but be all persones who sall challange the same.

"And that nae women weir thair Gownes or Petticottes about thair heads and faces, under the payne of ten pundis to be payit by women of qualitie for the first falt, twenty pundis for the second; and under such farder paynes as sall pleas the Counsall to inflict upon them for the third falt, and under the payne of fourtie shillings to be payit be servandis and uthers of lower degrie for the first falt, five pundis for the second, and banishment from the Cittie for the third falt; and ordaynes this present Statute to be intimate throwgh this Burgh be sound of drum, that nane pretend ignorance hereof."

Annals of Edinburgh

SCOTLAND'S HIGH NOON
1650

Scotland hath been, even by emulous foreigners, called Philadelphia; and now she seemed to be in her flower. Every minister was to be tried five times a year, both for his personal and ministerial behaviour; every congregation was to be visited by the presbyterie that they might see how the vine flourished, and how the pomegranate budded. And there was no case nor question in the meanest family in Scotland, but it might become the object of the deliberation of the General Assembly, for the congregational session's book was tried by the presbyterie, the presbyterie's book by the synod, and the synod's book by the General Assembly. Likewayes, as the bands of the Scottish Church were strong, so her beauty was bright; no error was so much as named, the people were not only sound in the faith, but innocently ignorant of unsound doctrine, no scandalous person could live, no scandal could be concealed in all Scotland, so strict a correspondence there was betwixt ministers and congregations. The General Assembly seemed to be the priest with Urim and Thumim, and there were not ane 100 person in all Scotland to oppose their conclusions; all submitted, all learned, all prayed; most part were really godly, or at least counterfeited themselves Jews. Then was Scotland a heap of wheat set about with lilies, uniform, or a palace of silver beautifully proportioned; and this seems to me to have been Scotland's high noon. The only complaint of prophane people was that the government was so strict that they hade not liberty enough to sin. I confess I thought at that time, the common sort of ministers strained too much at the sin which in these dayes was called Malignancie (and I should not paint the moon faithfully if I marked not her spots), otherwayes think if church officers could polish the saints on earth as bright as they are in heaven, it were their excellencie and the churches happiness. But this season lasted not long.

JAMES KIRKTON (1620-99)
History of the Church of Scotland

DUNBAR
1650

The small Town of Dunbar stands, high and windy, looking down over its herring-boats, over its grim old Castle now much honeycombed,—on one of those projecting rock-promontories with which that shore of the Firth of Forth is niched and vandyked, as far as the eye can reach. A beautiful sea; good land too, now that the plougher understands his trade; a grim niched barrier of whinstone sheltering it from the chafings and tumblings of the big blue German Ocean. Seaward St. Abb's Head, of whinstone, bounds your horizon to the east, not very far off; west, close by, is the deep bay, and fishy little village of Belhaven: the gloomy Bass and other rock-islets, and farther the Hills of Fife, and foreshadows of the Highlands, are visible as you look seaward. From the bottom of Belhaven bay to that of the next seabight St. Abbsward, the Town and its environs form a peninsula. Along the base of which peninsula, "not much above a mile, and a half from sea to sea," Oliver Cromwell's Army, on Monday 2nd of

September, 1650, stands ranked, with its tents and Town behind it,—in very forlorn circumstances. This now is all the ground that Oliver is lord of in Scotland. His Ships lie in the offing, with biscuit and transport for him; but visible elsewhere in the Earth no help.

Landward as you look from the Town of Dunbar there rises, some short mile off, a dusky continent of barren heath Hills; the Lammermoor, where only mountain-sheep can be at home. The crossing of *which*, by any of its boggy passes, and brawling stream-courses, no Army, hardly a solitary Scotch Packman could attempt, in such weather. To the edge of these Lammermoor Heights, David Lesley has betaken himself; lies now along the outmost spur of them,—a long Hill of considerable height, which the Dunbar people call the Dun, Doon, or sometimes for fashion's sake the Down, adding to it the Teutonic *Hill* likewise, though *Dun* itself in old Celtic signifies Hill. On this Doon Hill lies David Lesley with the victorious Scotch Army, upwards of Twenty-thousand strong; with the Committees of Kirk and Estates, the chief Dignitaries of the Country, and in fact the flower of what the pure Covenant in this the Twelfth year of its existence can still bring forth. There lies he since Sunday night, on the top and slope of this Doon Hill, with the impassable heath-continents behind him; embraces, as within outspread tiger-claws, the base-line of Oliver's Dunbar peninsula; waiting what Oliver will do. Cockburnspath with its ravines has been seized on Oliver's left, and made impassable; behind Oliver is the sea; in front of him Lesley, Doon Hill, and the heath-continent of Lammermoor. Lesley's force is of Three-and-twenty-thousand, in spirits as of men chasing, Oliver's about half as many, in spirits as of men chased. What is to become of Oliver?

THOMAS CARLYLE (1795-1881)
Letters and Speeches of Oliver Cromwell

SCOTLAND'S FIRST NEWSPAPER

The first newspaper supposed to have been printed in Scotland, was entitled, "*Mercurius Scoticus, or a true character of affairs in England, Ireland, Scotland, and other foreign parts, collected for publicque satisfaction,*" which was published weekly, and consisted of eight pages small quarto. The first number was issued on 5th August, 1651, but neither the place where it was printed, nor the name of the printer are mentioned in it, however, it is supposed to have been printed at Leith. It was but a short-lived publication, having, in November, 1652, given place to a paper published at London, and reprinted at Leith, entitled, "*A Diurnal of some passages and affairs.*" This paper was also of short duration, it having been superseded in less than a year by another, entitled, "*Mercurius Politicus,* comprising the sum of intelligence, with the affairs and designs now on foot in the three nations of England, Ireland, and Scotland, in defence of the commonwealth, and for information of the people. *Ita vertere seria, Hor. de art poet.* Printed at London, and reprinted at Leith." This paper generally consisted of from eight to sixteen pages, and was, in 1655, reprinted in Edinburgh, which is said to have been the first time that a newspaper was put to press in the city.

Annals of Edinburgh

THE MURDER OF JOHN BROWN

In the beginning of May, 1685, Mr. Alexander Peden came to the house of John Brown and Isabel Weir, whom he married before he went back to Ireland, where he stayed all night; and on the morning, when he took his farewell, he came to the door saying to himself, "Poor woman, a fearful morning!" twice over, "A dark misty morning!" The next morning between five and six hours, the said John Brown, having performed the worship of God in his family, was going with a spade in his hand to make ready some peat-ground; the mist being very dark (he) knew not until bloody, cruel Claverhouse compassed him with three troops of horses, brought him to his house, and there examined him; who, though he was a man of a stammering speech, yet answered him distinctly and solidly; which made Claverhouse to examine these whom he had taken to be his guides thorow the muirs, if they had ever heard him preach; they answered "No, no, he never was a preacher." He said, "If he had never preached, meikle has he prayed in his time." He said to John, "Go to your prayers, for you shall immediately die." When he was praying, Claverhouse interrupted him three times. One time that he stopt him, he was pleading that the Lord would spare a remnant, and not make a full end in the day of his anger. Claverhouse said, "I gave you time to pray, and ye've begun to preach"; he turned about upon his knees, and said, "Sir, you know neither the nature of preaching or praying, that calls this preaching"; then continued without confusion. When ended, Claverhouse said, "Take good-night of your wife and children." His wife was standing by, with her child in her arms which she had brought forth to him, and another child of his last wife's; he came to her and said, "Now, Isabel, the day is come, that I told you would come, when I spake first to you of marrying me." She said, "Indeed, John, I can willingly part with you." Then he said, "That's all I desire. I have no more to do but die. I have been in case to meet with death for so many years." He kissed his wife and bairns, and wished purchased and promised blessing to be multiplied upon them, and his blessing. Claverhouse ordered six soldiers to shoot him; the most part of the bullets came upon his head, which

scattered his brains upon the ground. Claverhouse said
to his wife, "What thinkest thou of thy husband now,
woman?" She said, "I thought ever much good of him,
and as much now as ever." He said, "It were but justice
to lay thee beside him." She said, "If ye were permitted,
I doubt not but your cruelty would go that length; but
how will ye make answer for this morning's work?"
He said, "To man I can be answerable; and for God, I
will take him in my own hand." Claverhouse mounted
his horse, and marched, and left her with the corps of
her dead husband lying there. She set the bairn upon
the ground, and gathered his brains, and tied up his
head, and straighted his body, and covered him with her
plaid, and sat down and wept over him; it being a very
desert place, where never victual grew, and far from
neighbours. It was some time before any friends came
to her. . . . The said Isabel Weir, sitting upon her
husband's gravestone, told me, that, before that, she
could see no blood but she was in danger to faint, and
yet she was helped to be a witness to all this without
either fainting or confusion, except, when the shotts
were let off, her eyes dazled. His corps was buried at
the end of his house where he was slain, with this
inscription on his gravestone:

> In earth's cold bed the dusty part here lies
> Of one who did the earth as dust despise.
> Here in that place from earth he took departure,
> Now he has got the garland of the martyre.

PATRICK WALKER (1666-1745)
Life of Peden

KIRKBRIDE

Bury me in Kirkbride,
  Where the Lord's redeemed anes lie,
The auld kirkyard on the green hillside,
    Under the open sky—
    Under the open sky,
On the briest o' the brae sae steep,
  And side by side wi' the banes that lie
Streikit there in their hinmost sleep.
    This puir dune body maun sune be dust,
    But it thrills wi' a stound o' pride,
To ken it will mix wi' the great and just
    That are buried in thee—Kirkbride.

Wheesht! Did the saft wind speak?
  Or a yammerin' nicht bird cry?
Did I dream that a warm hand touched my cheek,
    And a winsome face gaed by?—
    And a winsome face gaed by?
Wi' a far-aff licht in its een—
  A light that bude come frae the dazzlin' sky,
For it spak' o' the sternies sheen.
    Age may be donnert and dazed and blin',
    But, I'll warrant, whate'er betide,
A true heart there made tryst wi' my ain,
    And the tryst word was—Kirkbride!

Hark! Frae the far hill-taps,
  And laigh frae the lanesome glen,
A sweet psalm tune, like a late dew, draps
    Its wild notes doon the wind:—
    Its wild notes doon the wind,
Wi' a kent soun' ower my mind,
  For we sang 't on the muir—a wheen huntit men
Wi' our lives in our hand lang syne;

But naething on earth can disturb this sang,
   Were it Clavers in a' his pride,
For it's raised by the Lord's ain ransomed thrang
   Foregathered abune Kirkbride.

I hear May Moril's tongue
   That I wisna to hear again,
And there 'twas the Black Macmichael's sang
    Clear in the closin' strain—
    Clear in the closin' strain,
Frae his big heart bauld and true;
   It stirs my soul as in days bygane,
When his guid braidsword he drew:
I needs maun be aff to the moors once mair,
   For he'll miss me by his side;
In the thrang o' the battle I aye was there,
   And sae maun it be in Kirkbride.

Rax me my staff and plaid,
   That in readiness I may be,
And dinna forget that *The Book* be laid
    Open across my knee—
    Open across my knee,
And a text close by my thoom;
   And tell me true, for I scarce can see,
That the words are "Lo, I come!"
Then carry me through at the Cample Ford,
   And up the lang hillside;
And I'll wait for the comin' o' God the Lord
   In a neuk o' the auld Kirkbride.

R. WANLOCK REID

BONNY DUNDEE

To the Lords of Convention 'twas Claver'se who spoke,
"Ere the King's crown shall fall there are crowns to be
    broke;
So let each Cavalier who loves honour and me
Come follow the bonnet of Bonny Dundee.

  Come fill up my cup, come fill up my can,
  Come saddle your horses, and call up your men;
  Come open the West Port, and let me gang free,
  And it's room for the bonnets of Bonny Dundee!"

Dundee he is mounted, he rides up the street,
The bells are rung backward, the drums they are beat;
But the Provost, douce man, said, "Just e'en let him be,
The Gude Town is weel quit of that Deil of Dundee."

As he rode down the sanctified bends of the Bow,
Ilk carline was flyting and shaking her pow;
But the young plants of grace they looked couthie and
    slee,
Thinking, luck to thy bonnet, thou Bonny Dundee!

"There are hills beyond Pentland, and lands beyond
    Forth,
If there's lords in the Lowlands, there's chiefs in the
    North;
There are wild Duniewassals three thousand times three,
Will cry *hoigh*! for the bonnet of Bonny Dundee.

"Away to the hills, to the caves, to the rocks,—
Ere I own an usurper, I'll couch with the fox;
And tremble, false Whigs, in the midst of your glee,
You have not seen the last of my bonnet and me!"

SIR WALTER SCOTT (1771-1832)

BATTLE OF KILLIECRANKIE

A Pass in Perthshire, some two miles long, through which go a
road and the River Garry. Here, on July 17th, 1689, Viscount Claverhouse and his Highlanders defeated General Mackay and an English
force 4000 strong. Dundee was killed in the fight.

Soon we heard a challenge-trumpet
   Sounding in the Pass below,
And the distant tramp of horses,
   And the voices of the foe:
Down we crouched amid the bracken,
   Till the Lowland ranks drew near,
Panting like the hounds in summer,
   When they scent the stately deer.
From the dark defile emerging,
   Next we saw the squadrons come,
Leslie's foot and Leven's troopers
   Marching to the tuck of drum;
Through the scattered wood of birches,
   O'er the broken ground and heath,
Wound the long battalion slowly,
   Till they gained the plain beneath;
Then we bounded from our covert.—
   Judge how looked the Saxons then,
When they saw the rugged mountain
   Start to life with arméd men !

Like a tempest down the ridges
   Swept the hurricane of steel,
Rose the slogan of Macdonald—
   Flashed the broadsword of Lochiel!
Vainly sped the withering volley
   'Mongst the foremost of our band—
On we poured until we met them,
   Foot to foot. and hand to hand.

Horse and man went down like drift-wood
  When the floods are black at Yule,
And their carcasses are whirling
  In the Garry's deepest pool.
Horse and man went down before us—
  Living foe there tarried none
On the field at Killiecrankie,
  When that stubborn fight was done!

And the evening star was shining
  On Schehallion's distant head,
When we wiped our bloody broadswords,
  And returned to count the dead.
There we found him gashed and gory,
  Stretched upon the cumbered plain,
As he told us where to seek him,
  In the thickest of the slain.
And a smile was on his visage,
  For within his dying ear
Pealed the joyful note of triumph,
  And the clansmen's clamorous cheer:
So, amidst the battle's thunder,
  Shot, and steel, and scorching flame,
In the glory of his manhood
  Passed the spirit of the Græme!

W. E. AYTOUN (1813-65)
Lays of the Scottish Cavaliers

THE MASSACRE OF GLENCOE

"O tell me, Harper, wherefore flow
Thy wayward notes of wail and woe
Far down the desert of Glencoe,
  Where none may list their melody?
Say, harp'st thou to the mists that fly,

Or to the dun deer glancing by,
Or to the eagle that from high
 Screams chorus to thy minstrelsy?"—

"No, not to these, for they have rest,—
The mist-wreath has the mountain-crest,
The stag his lair, the erne her nest,
 Abode of lone security.
But those for whom I pour the lay,
Not wildwood deep, nor mountain gray,
Not this deep dell, that shrouds from day,
 Could screen from treach'rous cruelty.

"Their flag was furl'd, and mute their drum,
The very household dogs were dumb,
Unwont to bay at guests that come
 In guise of hospitality.
His blithest notes the piper plied,
Her gayest snood the maiden tied,
The dame her distaff flung aside,
 To tend her kindly housewifery.

"The hand that mingled in the meal,
At midnight drew the felon steel,
And gave the host's kind breast to feel
 Meed for his hospitality!
The friendly hearth which warm'd that hand,
At midnight arm'd it with the brand,
That bade destruction's flames expand-
 Their red and fearful blazonry.

"Then woman's shriek was heard in vain,
Nor infancy's unpitied plain,
More than the warrior's groan, could gain
 Respite from ruthless butchery!
The winter wind that whistled shrill,
The snows that night that cloked the hill,

Though wild and pitiless, had still
 Far more than Southron clemency.

"Long have my harp's best notes been gone,
Few are its strings, and faint their tone,
They can but sound in desert lone
 Their grey-hair'd master's misery
Were each grey hair a minstrel string,
Each chord should imprecations fling,
Till startled Scotland loud should ring,
 'Revenge for blood and treachery!'"

SIR WALTER SCOTT (1771-1832)

THE MASSACRE OF GLENCOE
February 13th, 1692

To Captain Robert Campbell of Glenlyon
'For Their Majesties' Service'

BALLACHOLIS,
12th February, 1692.

Sir,
 You are hereby ordered to fall upon the rebels, the M'Donalds, of Glencoe, and putt all to the sword under seventy. You are to have special care that the old fox and his sons doe upon no account escape your hands. You are to secure all the avenues, that no man escape. This you are to put in execution att five o'clock in the morning precisely, and by that time, or very shortly after it, I'll strive to be att you with a stronger party. If I doe not come to you att five, you are not to tarry for me, but to fall on. This is by the [1]king's special command, for the good and safety of the country, that

[1] William, Prince of Orange

these miscreants be cutt off root and branch. See that this be putt in execution without feud or favour, else you may expect to be treated as not true to the king's government, nor a man fitt to carry a commission in the king's service. Expecting you will not faill in the fulfilling hereof as you love yourself, I subscribe these with my hand.

ROBERT DUNCANSON

THE STATE OF SCOTLAND
1698

There are at this day in Scotland—besides a great many poor families very meanly provided for by the church-boxes, with others who, by living on bad food, fall into various diseases—*two hundred thousand people begging from door to door*. These are not only no way advantageous, but a very grievous burden to so poor a country. And though the number of them be perhaps double to what it was formerly, by reason of this present great distress, yet in all times there have been about one hundred thousand of those vagabonds, who have lived without any regard or subjection either to the laws of the land, or even those of God and nature. No magistrate could ever be informed, or discover, which way one in a hundred of these wretches died, or that ever they were baptised. Many murders have been discovered among them; and they are not only a most unspeakable oppression to poor tenants—who, if they give not bread, or some kind of provision, to perhaps forty such villains in one day, are sure to be insulted by them—but they rob many poor people who live in houses distant from any neighbourhood. In years of plenty, many thousands of them meet together in the mountains, where they feast and riot for many days; and at country-weddings, markets, burials, and the like public occasions, they are to be seen, both men and women, perpetually drunk, cursing, blaspheming, and fighting together. These are such outrageous disorders, that it were better for the nation they were sold to the galleys or West Indies, than that they chould continue any longer to be a burden and curse upon us.

FLETCHER OF SALTOUN (1655-1716)

PRINCE CHARLES AND LOCHIEL

It is impossible to imagine an abode more suitable to the circumstances and designs of Charles than Boradale, which is one of the most remote and inaccessible places in the Highlands of Scotland, surrounded on every side by the territories of those chiefs, who, in former times, had fought the battles of the family of Stuart. From this retreat, Charles dispatched messengers to the chiefs from whom he expected assistance. The first chief that came to Charles at Boradale, was Cameron of Lochiel.

He was no sooner arrived at Boradale, than Charles and he retired by themselves. The conversation began on the part of Charles, with bitter complaints of the treatment he had received from the ministers of France, who had so long amused him with vain hopes, and deceived him with false promises; their coldness in his cause, he said, but ill agreed with the opinion he had of his own pretensions, and with that impatience to assert them, with which the promises of his father's brave and faithful subjects had inflamed his mind. Lochiel acknowledged the engagements of the chiefs, but observed that they were no way binding, as he had come over without the stipulated aid; and therefore, as there was not the least prospect of success, he advised his Royal Highness to return to France, and to reserve himself and his faithful friends for a more favourable opportunity. Charles refused to follow Lochiel's advice, affirming that a more favourable opportunity than the present would never come: that almost all the British troops were abroad, and kept at bay by Marshal Saxe, with a superior army: that in Scotland there were only a few new raised regiments, that had never seen service, and could not stand before the Highlanders: that the very first advantage gained over the troops would encourage his father's friends at home to declare themselves: that his friends abroad would not fail to give their assistance: that he only wanted the Highlanders to begin the war.

Lochiel still resisted, entreating Charles to be more temperate, and consent to remain concealed where he was, till he (Lochiel) and his other friends should meet together, and concert what was best to be done. Charles, whose mind was wound up to the utmost pitch of impatience, paid no regard to this proposal, but answered, that he was determined to put all to the hazard. "In a few days," said he, "with the few friends that I have, I will erect the royal standard, and proclaim to the people of Britain, that Charles Stuart is come over to claim the crown of his ancestors; to win it, or to perish in the attempt; Lochiel, who, my father has often told me, was our firmest friend, may stay at home, and learn from the newspapers the fate of his prince." "No," said Lochiel, "I'll share the fate of my prince; and so shall every man over whom nature or fortune hath given me any power." Such was the singular conversation, on the result of which depended peace or war. For it is a point agreed among the Highlanders, that if Lochiel had persisted in his refusal to take arms, the other chiefs would not have joined the standard without him, and the spark of rebellion must have instantly expired.

JOHN HOME (1722–1808)
History of the Rebellion of 1745

SKYE BOAT SONG

Chorus

Speed bonnie boat like a bird on the wing,
*   "Onward" the sailors cry;*
Carry the lad that's born to be king
*   Over the sea to Skye.*

Loud the winds howl, loud the waves roar,
    Thunderclaps rend the air;
Baffled our foes stand by the shore,
    Follow they will not dare.

Chorus

Though the waves leap, soft shall ye sleep,
    Ocean's a royal bed.
Rocked in the deep Flora will keep
    Watch by your weary head.

Chorus

Many's the lad fought on that day
    Well the claymore could wield
When the night came silently lay
    Dead on Culloden's field.

Chorus

Burned are our homes, exile and death
    Scatter the loyal men;
Yet, ere the sword cool in the sheath,
    Charlie will come again.

Chorus

HAROLD BOULTON

PRINCE CHARLIE IN FLIGHT

When the Prince came to Kingsburgh's house (Sunday, June 29, 1746) it was between ten and eleven at night: and Mrs. MacDonald, not expecting to see her husband that night, was making ready to go to bed. One of her servant maids came and told her that Kingsburgh was come home, and had brought some company with him. "What company?" says Mrs. MacDonald. "Milton's daughter, I believe," says the maid, "and some company with her." "Milton's daughter," replies Mrs. MacDonald, "is very welcome to come here with any company she pleases to bring. But you'll give my service to her, and tell her to make free of anything in the house: for I am very sleepy and cannot see her this night."

In a little her own daughter came and told her in a surprise, "O mother, my father has brought in a very odd, ill-shaken-up wife as ever I saw! I never saw the like of her, and he has gone into the hall with her." She had scarce done when Kingsburgh came and desired his lady to fasten her bucklings again, and to get some supper for him and the company he had brought with him. "Pray, goodman," says she, "what company is this you have brought with you?" "Why, goodwife," said he, "you shall know that in due time: only make haste and get some supper in the meantime."

Mrs. MacDonald desired her daughter to go and fetch the keys she had left in the hall. When the daughter came to the door of the hall, she started back, ran to her mother, and told her she could not go in for the keys, for the muckle wife was walking up and down in the hall, and she was so frighted at seeing her that she could not have the courage to enter. Mrs. MacDonald went herself to get the keys, and I heard her more than once declare that upon looking in at the door she had not the courage to go forward. "For," said she, "I saw such an odd muckle trallop of a carlin, making lang wide steps through the hall that I could not like her appearance at all."

Mrs. MacDonald called Kingsburgh, and very seriously begged to know what a lang odd hussie was this he had brought to the house; for that she was so frighted at the sight of her that she could not go into the hall for her keys. "Did you never see a woman before," said he, "goodwife? What frights you at seeing a woman? Pray, make haste, and get us some supper." Kingsburgh would not go for the keys, and therefore his lady behoved to go for them.

When she entered the hall the Prince happened to be sitting; but immediately he arose, went forward, and saluted Mrs. MacDonald, who, feeling a long stiff beard, trembled to think that this behoved to be some distressed nobleman or gentleman in disguise, for she never dreamed it to be the Prince, though all along she had been seized with a dread she could not account for from the moment she had heard that Kingsburgh had brought company with him. She very soon made out of the hall with her keys, never saying a word. Immediately she importuned Kingsburgh to tell her who the person was, for she was sure by the salute that it was some distressed gentleman. Kingsburgh smiled at the mention of the bearded kiss, and said, "Why, my dear, it is the Prince. You have the honour to have him in your house."

"The Prince!" said she. "O Lord, we are a' ruined and undone for ever! We will a' be hanged now!" "Hout, goodwife!" says the honest stout soul, "we will die but ance; and if we are hanged for this, I am sure we die in a good cause. Pray, make no delay; go, get some supper. Fetch what is readiest. You have eggs and butter and cheese in this house, get them as quickly as possible." "Eggs and butter and cheese!" said Mrs. MacDonald, "what a supper is that for a Prince?" "O goodwife!" said he, "little do you know how this good

Prince has been living for some time past. Make haste and see that you come to supper." "I come to supper!" says Mrs. MacDonald, "how can I come to supper? I know not how to behave before Majesty." "You must come," says Kingsburgh, "for he will not eat a bit till he see you at the table; and you will find it no difficult matter to behave before him, so obliging and easy as he is in conversation."

The Prince ate of our roasted eggs, some collop, plenty of bread and butter, etc., and (to use the words of Mrs. MacDonald) "the deil a drap did he want in's wame of twa bottles of sma' beer. God do him good o't: for, weel I wat, he had my blessing to gae down wi't." After he had made a plentiful supper, he called for a dram; and when the bottle of brandy was brought, he said he would fill a glass for himself; "for," said he, "I have learned in my skulking to take a hearty dram." He filled a bumper and drank it to the happiness and prosperity of his landlord and landlady. Then taking a cracked and broken pipe out of his pouch, wrapt about with thread, he asked Kingsburgh if he could furnish him with some tobacco: for that he had learned likewise to smoke in his wanderings. Kingsburgh took from him the broken pipe and laid it carefully up with the brogs, and gave him a new clean pipe and plenty of tobacco.

The Lyon in Mourning

CUIMHNE MACH TEID AS
A Memory that will not fade

For though it were in Paradise
or the far islands of the blest,
the sound of water down a glen
would come between me and my rest.

If only over sleeping seas
one breath of wind should wander there,
straying from off the hills I knew,
I'd think upon a land more fair.

There is not Lethe that would drown
the longing or the memory,
whose kindly stream would bear away
my tears, if that wind blew on me.

For if I thought on sea and wind
and Sleea under rainy skies,
and minded of another land,
little to me were Paradise.

GEORGE CAMPBELL HAY (b. 1915)

CULLODEN MOOR

Here on April 16th, 1746, on a day of bitter cold and snow, the gallant Highlanders, weary and hungry after an all-night march, did battle for Scotland and Prince Charlie against a Hanoverian force twice their number. The victorious enemy was commanded by William Augustus Duke of Cumberland (1721-65) a son of George II. Culloden, an eye-witness account of which is given below, brought irretrievable disaster to the Jacobite cause.

The right of our army, commanded by Lord George Murray, had made a furious attack, cut their way through Barrel's and Munro's regiments, and had taken possession of two pieces of cannon; but a reinforcement of Wolfe's regiment, etc. coming up from the Duke's second line, our right wing was obliged to give way, being at the same time flanked with some pieces of artillery, which did great execution. Towards the left the attack had been less vigorous than on the right, and of course had made but little impression on the Duke's

141

army; nor was it indeed general, for the centre, which had been much galled by the enemy's artillery, almost instantly quitted the field. The scene of confusion was now great; nor can the imagination figure it. The men in general were betaking themselves precipitately to flight; nor was there any possibility of their being rallied. Horror and dismay were painted in every countenance. It now became time to provide for the Prince's safety: his person had been abundantly exposed. He was got off the field and very narrowly escaped falling in with a body of horse which, having been detached from the Duke's left, were advancing with incredible rapidity, picking up the stragglers, and, as they gave no quarter, were levelling them with the ground. The greater numbers of the army were already out of danger, the flight having been so precipitate. We got upon a rising ground, where we turned round and made a general halt. The scene was, indeed, tremendous. Never was so total a rout—a more thorough discomfiture of an army. The adjacent country was in a manner covered with its ruins. The whole was over in about twenty-five minutes. The Duke's artillery kept still playing, though not a soul upon the field. His army was kept together, all but the horse. The great pursuit was upon the road towards Inverness. Of towards six thousand men, which the Prince's army at this period consisted of, about one thousand were asleep in Culloden parks, who knew nothing of the action till awaked by the noise of the cannon. These in general endeavoured to save themselves by taking the road towards Inverness; and most of them fell a sacrifice to the victors, for this road was in general strewed with dead bodies. The Prince at this moment had his cheeks bedewed with tears; what must not his feelings have suffered!

Memoirs of Sir Robert Strange

JOHN O' LORN

My plaid is on my shoulder and my boat is on the shore,
 And it's all bye wi' auld days and you;
Here's a health and here's a heartbreak, for it's hame, my
 dear, no more,
 To the green glens, the fine glens we knew!

'Twas for the sake o' glory, but oh! woe upon the wars,
 That brought my father's son to sic a day;
I'd rather be a craven wi' nor fame nor name nor scars,
 Than turn an exile's heel on Moidart Bay.

And you, in the daytime, you'll be here, and in the mirk,
 Wi' the kind heart, the open hand and free;
And far awa' in foreign France, in town or camp or kirk,
 I'll be wondering if you keep a thought for me.

But never more the heather nor the bracken at my knees,
 I'm poor John o' Lorn, a broken man;
For an auld Hielan' story I must sail the swinging seas,
 A chief without a castle and a clan.

My plaid is on my shoulder and my boat is on the shore,
 And it's all bye wi' auld days and you;
Here's a health and here's a heartbreak, for it's hame, my
 dear, no more,
 To the green glens, the fine glens we knew!

NEIL MUNRO (1864-1930)

143

THE·SUTHERLAND CLEARANCES

In order that the county of Sutherland might be turned from its native state into more profitable sheep-runs, the inhabitants were, in March, 1814, warned out of their holdings, and ordered to migrate to the coast to earn their living as fishermen. Failing to obey the proprietors' orders they were summarily ejected.

The work of devastation was begun by setting fire to the houses of the small tenants in extensive districts— Farr, Rogart, Golspie, and the whole parish of Kildonan. I was an eye-witness of the scene. The calamity came on the people quite unexpectedly. Strong parties for each district, furnished with faggots and other combustibles, rushed on the dwellings of the devoted people, and immediately commenced setting fire to them, proceeding in their work with the greatest rapidity, till about three hundred houses were in flames. Little or no time was given for the removal of persons or property—the consternation and confusion were extreme—the people stirring to remove the sick and helpless before the fire should reach them—next struggling to save the most valuable of their effects—the cries of the women and children—the roaring of the affrighted cattle, hunted by the dog of the shepherds amid the smoke and the fire—altogether composed a scene that completely baffled description. A dense cloud of smoke enveloped the whole country by day, and even extended far on the sea. At night, an awfully grand but terrific scene presented itself—all the houses in an extensive district in flames at once. I myself ascended a height about eleven o'clock in the evening, and counted two hundred and fifty blazing houses, many of the owners of which were my relations, and all of whom I personally knew, but whose present condition I could not tell. The conflagration lasted six days, till the whole of the dwellings were reduced to ashes or smoking ruins. During one of these days a boat lost her way in the dense smoke as she approached the shore, but at night she was enabled to reach a landing-place by the light of the flames.

DONALD M'LEOD

WHO KILLED THE RED FOX?

I am never in Appin but I try to fathom the Appin Mystery—"Who killed the Red Fox?" It is an over-adventurous question. For the shooting of Campbell of Glenure in the Wood of Lettermore yonder is still the hundred-and-fifty-year-old Mystery of Appin. I tried again this year. But in every case the man interrogated smiled and said he did not know. It was Andrew Lang who said that the tragedy remains as fresh as if it were an affair of yesterday, and he adds—"I have had the secret—the secret which I may not tell." And one of the latest historians of the affair tells us that the true story of the Appin Murder is known to at least one family, who have preserved their secret inviolate. Certain it is—that Alan Breck, "the pock-marked," did not fire the shot: that James Stewart of Acharn, or Seumas a Ghlinne, did not commit the murder for which he was hanged; that several were in the planning of the affair; and that a man with a short dark-coloured coat was seen escaping along the hillside carrying a gun. This man in the short coat—the mysterious other man —escaped. There, you have the mystery of the Appin murder, which still is expressed in this single question —"Who killed the Red Fox?"

As I was wandering in a place of Appin I met an old man with the Gaelic tradition in his soul, and the Celt's long memory that never forgets—and, at long last, he told me the secret. I now know the name of the man who killed the Red Fox. I know the house where, until

145

recently, there lay the *gunne dubh a mhi-fhortain*—the black gun of the misfortune. I know, also, why and where the fatal gun will never now be found. But, strangest of all, I too, when asked for the secret, can only smile like the men of Lochaber and the men of Appin, and say, "I may not tell!"

T. RATCLIFFE BARNETT (1868-1946)
The Road to Rannoch and the Summer Isles

THE DISRUPTION

The law-courts of Scotland having invaded the spiritual independence of the Church of Scotland, the Evangelical party of the Church seceded, and formed the Free Church of Scotland.

8th June, 1843. The crash is over!
Dr. Welsh, Professor of Church History in the University of Edinburgh, having been Moderator last year, began the proceedings by preaching a sermon before his Grace the Commissioner in the High Church, in which what was going to happen was announced and defended. The Commissioner then proceeded to St. Andrew's Church, where the Assembly was to be held. The streets, especially those near the place of meeting, were filled, not so much with the boys who usually gaze at the annual show, as by grave and well-dressed grown people of the middle rank. According to custom, Welsh took the chair of the Assembly. Their very first act ought to have been to constitute the Assembly of this year by electing a new Moderator. But before this was done, Welsh rose and announced that he and others who had been returned as members held this not to be a free Assembly—that, therefore, they declined to acknowledge it as a Court of the Church—that they meant to leave the very place, and, as a consequence of this, to abandon the Establishment. In explanation of the grounds of

this step he then read a full and clear protest. It was read as impressively as a weak voice would allow, and was listened to in silence by as large an audience as the church could contain.

As soon as it was read, Dr. Welsh handed the paper to the clerk, quitted the chair, and walked away. Instantly, what appeared to be the whole left side of the house rose to follow. Some applause broke from the spectators, but it checked itself in a moment. 193 members moved off, of whom about 123 were ministers, and about 70 elders. Among these were many upon whose figures the public eye had been long accustomed to rest in reverence. They all withdrew slowly and regularly amidst perfect silence, till that side of the house was left nearly empty. They were joined outside by a large body of adherents, among whom were about 300 clergymen. As soon as Welsh, who wore his Moderator's dress, appeared on the street, and people saw that principle had really triumphed over interest, he and his followers were received with the loudest acclamations. They walked in procession down Hanover Street to Canonmills, where they had secured an excellent hall, through an unbroken mass of cheering people, and beneath innumerable handkerchiefs waving from the windows. But amidst this exultation there was much sadness and many a tear, many a grave face and fearful thought; for no one could doubt that it was with sore hearts that these ministers left the Church, and no thinking man could look on the unexampled scene and behold that the temple was rent, without pain and sad forebodings. No spectacle since the Revolution reminded one so forcibly of the Covenanters.

HENRY, LORD COCKBURN (1779-1854)
Journal

Pastoral

HAME, HAME, HAME

Hame, hame, hame, O hame fain wad I be—
O hame, hame, hame, to my ain countree!

When the flower is i' the bud and the leaf is on the tree,
The larks shall sing me hame in my ain countree;
Hame, hame, hame, O hame fain wad I be—
O hame, hame, hame, to my ain countree!

The green leaf o' loyaltie's beginning for to fa',
The bonnie White Rose it is withering an' a';
But I'll water 't wi' the blude of usurping tyrannie,
An' green it will graw in my ain countree.

O, there's nocht now frae ruin my country can save,
But the keys o' kind heaven, to open the grave;
That a' the noble martyrs wha died for loyaltie
May rise again an' fight for their ain countree.

The great now are gane, a' wha ventured to save,
The new grass is springing on the tap o' their grave;
But the sun through the mirk blinks blythe in my e'e,
' I'll shine on ye yet in your ain countree.'

Hame, hame, hame, O hame, fain wad I be—
O hame, hame, hame, to my ain countree!

ALLAN CUNNINGHAM (1784-1842)

IN THE HIGHLANDS

In the highlands, in the country places,
Where the old plain men have rosy faces,
And the young fair maidens
Quiet eyes;
Where essential silence cheers and blesses,
And for ever in the hill-recesses
Her more lovely music
Broods and dies.

O to mount again where erst I haunted;
Where the old red hills are bird-enchanted,
And the low green meadows
Bright with sward;
And when even dies, the million-tinted,
And the night has come, and planets glinted,
Lo, the valley hollow
Lamp-bestarred.

O to dream, O to awake and wander
There, and with delight to take and render,
Through the trance of silence,
Quiet breath;
Lo! for there, among the flowers and grasses,
Only the mightier movement sounds and passes;
Only winds and rivers,
Life and death.

R. L. STEVENSON (1850-94)

A SYLVAN REPAST

Much nearer to the mouth of the cave, he heard the
notes of a lively Gaelic song, guided by which, in a
sunny recess, shaded by a glittering birch-tree, and

149

carpeted with a bank of firm white sand, he found the damsel of the cavern, whose lay had already reached him, busy, to the best of her power, in arranging to advantage a morning repast of milk, eggs, barley-bread, fresh butter, and honey-comb. The poor girl had already made a circuit of four miles that morning in search of the eggs, of the meal which baked her cakes, and of the other materials of the breakfast, being all delicacies which she had to beg or borrow from distant cottagers. The followers of Donald Bane Lane used little food except the flesh of the animals which they drove away from the Lowlands; bread itself was a delicacy seldom thought of, because hard to be obtained, and all the domestic accommodations of milk, poultry, butter, etc., were out of the question in this Scythian camp. Yet it must not be omitted, that, although Alice had occupied a part of the morning in providing those accommodations for her guest which the cavern did not afford, she had secured time also to arrange her own person in her best trim. Her finery was very simple. A short russet-coloured jacket, and a petticoat, of scanty longitude, was her whole dress; but these were clean, and neatly arranged. A piece of scarlet embroidered cloth, called the *snood*, confined her hair, which fell over it in a profusion of rich dark curls. The scarlet plaid, which formed part of her dress, was laid aside, that it might not impede her activity in attending the stranger. I should forget Alice's proudest ornament, were I to omit mentioning a pair of gold ear-rings, and a golden rosary, which her father (for she was the daughter of Donald Bane Lane) had brought from France, the plunder, probably, of some battle or storm.

Her form, though rather large for her years, was very well proportioned, and her demeanour had a natural and rustic grace, with nothing of the sheepishness of an ordinary peasant. The smiles, displaying a row of teeth of exquisite whiteness, and the laughing eyes, with which, in dumb show, she gave Waverley that morning greeting which she wanted English words to express, might have been interpreted by a coxcomb, or perhaps by a young soldier, who, without being such, was conscious of a handsome person, as meant to convey more than the courtesy of an hostess. Nor do I take it upon me to say, that the little wild mountaineer would have welcomed any staid old gentleman advanced in life with the cheerful pains which she bestowed upon Edward's accommodation. She seemed eager to place him by the meal which she had so sedulously arranged, and to which she now added a few bunches of cranberries, gathered in an adjacent morass. Having had the satisfaction of seeing him seated at his breakfast, she placed herself demurely upon a stone at a few yards' distance, and appeared to watch with great complacency for some opportunity of serving him.

Evan and his attendant now returned slowly along the beach, the latter bearing a large salmon-trout, the produce of the morning's sport, together with the angling-rod, while Evan strolled forward, with an easy, self-satisfied, and important gait, towards the spot where Waverley was so agreeably employed at the breakfast-table. After morning greetings had passed on both sides, and Evan, looking at Waverley, had said something in Gaelic to Alice, which made her laugh, yet colour up to her eyes, through a complexion well embrowned by sun and wind, Evan intimated his commands that the fish should be prepared for breakfast. A spark from the lock of his pistol produced a light, and a few withered fir branches were quickly in flame, and as speedily reduced to hot embers, on which the trout was broiled in large slices. To crown the repast, Evan produced from the pocket of his short jerkin, a large scallop of shell, and from under the folds of his plaid, a ram's horn full of whisky. Of this he took a copious dram, observing he had already taken his *morning* with Donald Bane Lane, before his departure; he offered the same cordial to Alice and to Edward, which they both declined. With the bounteous air of a lord, Evan then proferred the scallop to Dugald Mahony, his attendant, who, without waiting to be asked a second time, drank it off with great gusto. Evan then prepared to move towards the boat, inviting Waverley to attend him. Meanwhile, Alice had made up in a small basket what she thought worth removing, and flinging her plaid around her, she advanced up to Edward, and, with the utmost simplicity, taking hold of his hand, offered her cheek to his salute, dropping, at the same time, her little courtesy. Evan, who was esteemed a wag among the mountain fair, advanced, as if to secure a similar favour; but Alice, snatching up her basket, escaped up the rocky bank as fleetly as a roe, and turning round and laughing, called something out to him in Gaelic, which he answered in the same tone and language; then, waving her hand to Edward, she resumed her road, and was soon lost among the thickets, though they continued for some time to hear her lively carol, as she proceeded gaily on her solitary journey.

SIR WALTER SCOTT (1771-1832)
Waverley

DAMON AND SYLVIA

Yon wandering rill that marks the hill,
    And glances o'er the brae, Sir,
Slides by a bower, where mony a flower
    Sheds fragrance on the day, Sir;
There Damon lay with Sylvia gay,
    To love they thought no crime, Sir,
The wild birds sang, the echoes rang,
    While Damon's heart beat time, Sir.

ROBERT BURNS (1759-96)

152

THE SOLITARY REAPER

Behold her, single in the field,
Yon solitary Highland Lass !
Reaping and singing by herself;
Stop here, or gently pass !
Alone she cuts and binds the grain,
And sings a melancholy strain;
Oh listen ! for the Vale profound
Is overflowing with the sound.

No nightingale did ever chaunt
    More welcome notes to weary bands
Of travellers in some shady haunt
Among Arabian sands !
A voice so thrilling ne'er was heard
In spring-time from the Cuckoo-bird
Breaking the silence of the seas
Among the farthest Hebrides.

Will no one tell me what she sings?—
Perhaps the plaintive numbers flow
For old, unhappy, far-off things,
And battles long ago:
Or is it some more humble lay,
Familiar matter of to-day?
Some natural sorrow, loss, or pain,
That has been, and may be again?

What'er the theme, the Maiden sang
As if her song could have no ending;
I saw her singing at her work,
And o'er the sickle bending;—

I listened, motionless and still ;
And as I mounted up the hill
The music in my heart I bore
Long after it was heard no more.

WILLIAM WORDSWORTH (1770-1850)

A HEALING WELL

There are many such wells throughout Scotland. That of St.
Fillan of Loch Earn is to be found near Dùn Fhaolain (which rises
at the east end of the loch) and is said to possess miraculous properties.
Pilgrims visited the well twice yearly (on May 1st and August 1st)
in bygone centuries.

The invalids, whether men, women or children walk,
or are carried, round the well, three times, in a direction
Deishal, that is from E. to W. according to the course
of the Sun. They also drink of the water, and bathe in
it. These operations are accounted a certain remedy for
various diseases. They are particularly efficacious for
curing barrenness; on which account it is frequently
visited by those who are very desirous of offspring. All
the invalids throw a white stone on the Saint's cairn,
and leave behind, as tokens of their confidence and
gratitude, some rags of linen or woollen cloth. The rock
on the summit of the hill, formed, of itself, a chair for
the Saint, which still remains. Those who complain of
rheumatism in the back, must ascend the hill, sit in the
chair, then lie down on their back, and be pulled by the
legs to the bottom of the hill. This operation is still
performed and reckoned very efficacious. At the foot of
the hill, there is a basin, made by the Saint, on the top
of a large stone, which seldom wants water even in the
greatest drought: and all who are distressed with sore
eyes must wash them three times with this water.

Statistical Account

KILMENY

Bonny Kilmeny gaed up the glen;
But it wasna to meet Duneira's men,
Nor the rosy monk of the isle to see,
For Kilmeny was pure as pure could be.
It was only to hear the yorlin sing,
And pu' the cress-flower round the spring;
The scarlet hypp and the hind-berrye,
And the nut that hung frae the hazel tree;
For Kilmeny was pure as pure could be.
But lang may her minny look o'er the wa';
And lang may she seek i' the greenwood shaw;
Lang the laird o' Duneira blame,
And lang, lang greet or Kilmeny come hame!

When many lang day had come and fled,
When grief grew calm, and hope was dead,
When mass for Kilmeny's soul had been sung,
When the bedesman had pray'd and the dead-bell rung,
Late, late in a gloaming, when all was still,
When the fringe was red on the westlin hill,
The wood was sere, the moon i' the wane,
The reek o' the cot hung o'er the plain,
Like a little wee cloud in the world its lane;
When the ingle lowed wi' an eiry leme—
Late, late in the gloaming Kilmeny came hame! . . .
And O, her beauty was fair to see,
But still and steadfast was her ee!
Such beauty bard may never declare,
For there was no pride nor passion there;
And the soft desire of maiden's een
In that mild face could never be seen.
Her seymar was the lily flower,
And her cheek the moss-rose in the shower;
And her voice like the distant melodye,

That floats along the twilight sea.
But she loved to raike the lanely glen,
And keep afar frae the haunts of men,
Her holy hymns unheard to sing,
To suck the flowers, and drink the spring;
But wherever her peaceful form appeared,
The wild beasts of the hill were cheered;
The wolf played blythely round the field,
The lordly byson lowed, and kneeled;
The dun deer wooed with manner bland,
And cowered beneath her lily hand.
And when at eve the woodlands rung,
When hymns of other worlds she sung
In ecstasy of sweet devotion,
O, then the glen was all in motion!
The wild beasts of the forest came,
Broke from their boughts and faulds the tame,
And goved around, charmed and amazed;
Even the dull cattle crooned and gazed,
And murmured, and looked with anxious pain
For something the mystery to explain.
The buzzard came with the throstle-cock;
The corby left her houf in the rock;
The blackbird alang wi' the eagle flew;
The hind came tripping o'er the dew;
The wolf and the kid their raike began,
And the kid and the lamb and the leveret ran;
The hawk and the hern attour them hung,
And the merle and the mavis forhooyed their young;
And all in a peaceful ring were hurled—
It was like an eve in a sinless world!
When a month and a day had come and gane,
Kilmeny sought the greenwood wene;
There laid her down on the leaves sae green,
And Kilmeny on earth was never mair seen.
But O! the words that fell frae her mouth
Were words of wonder, and words of truth!

But all the land were in fear and dread,
For they kendna whether she was living or dead.
It wasna her hame, and she couldna remain;
She left this world of sorrow and pain,
And returned to the land of thought again.

JAMES HOGG (1770-1835)
The Queen's Wake

THE TWA DOGS

'Twas in that place o' Scotland's Isle,
That bears the name o' Auld King Coil
Upon a bonnie day in June,
When wearing through the afternoon,
Twa dogs that were na thrang[1] at hame,
Forgather'd ance upon a time.

The first I'll name, they ca'd him Cæsar,
Was keepit for his Honour's pleasure;
His hair, his size, his mouth, his lugs,[2]
Show'd he was nane o' Scotland's dogs,
But whalpit[3] some place far abroad,
Where sailors gang to fish for cod.
His locked, letter'd, braw brass collar,
Shew'd him the gentleman and scholar;
But though he was o' high degree,
The fient[4] a pride, nae pride had he;
But wad hae spent an hour caressin'
E'en wi' a tinkler-gipsy's messin:[5]
At kirk or market, mill or smiddie,
Naw tawted[6] tyke, though e'er sae duddie,[7]
But he wad stan't as glad to see him,
And stroan't on stanes and hillocks wi' him.

[1] busy [2] ears [3] whelped [4] fiend [5] mongrel cur [6] matted
[7] ragged

157

The tither was a ploughman's collie,
A rhyming, ranting, raving billie;
Wha for his friend and comrade had him,
And in his freaks had Luath ca'd him,
After some dog in Highland sang,
Was made lang syne—Gude kens how lang!
He was a gash an' faithfu' tyke,
As ever lap a sheugh[1] or dyke ;[2]

His honest, sonsie,[3] bawsn't[4] face,
Aye gat him friends in ilka place.
His breast was white, his towzie[5] back
Weel clad wi' coat o' glossy black;
His gawcie[6] tail, wi' upward curl,
Hung o'er his hurdies[7] wi' a swirl.

Nae doubt but they were fain o' ither,
And unco pack and thick thegither;
Wi' social nose whyles[8] snuff'd[9] and snowkit;
Whyles mice and moudie[10] worts they howkit[11];
Whyles scour'd awa in lang excursion,
And worried ither in diversion;
Until wi' daffin[12] weary grown,
Upon a knowe[13] they sat them down,
And there began a lang digression,
About the lords of the creation.

ROBERT BURNS (1759-96)

[1] ditch [2] stone fence [3] jolly [4] having a white stripe down the
face [5] shaggy [6] large [7] hips [8] sometimes [9] snuffed and pryed
with the nose [10] moles [11] digged for [12] merriment [13] hillock

A TOAD FOUND IN THE HEART
OF A STONE
1769

I have my doubts whether it was in the beginning of
this year, or in the end of the last, that a very extraordinary thing came to light in the parish; but, howsoever that may be, there is nothing more certain than
the fact, which it is my duty to record. I have mentioned
already how it was that the toll, or trust-road, was set
a-going, on account of the Lord Eaglesham's tumbling
on the midden in the Vennel. Well, it happened to one
of the labouring men, in breaking the stones to make
metal for the new road, that he broke a stone that was
both large and remarkable, and in the heart of it, which
was boss, there was found a living creature, that jumped
out the moment it saw the light of heaven, to the great
terrification of the man, who could think it was nothing
but an evil spirit that had been imprisoned therein for
a time. The man came to me like a demented creature,
and the whole clachan gathered out, young and old,
and I went at their head to see what the miracle could
be, for the man said it was a fiery dragon, spewing
smoke and flames. But when we came to the spot, it
was just a yird toad, and the laddie weans nevelled it to
death with stones, before I could persuade them to give
over. Since then, I have read of such things coming to
light in the *Scots Magazine*, a very valuable book.

JOHN GALT (1779-1839)
Annals of the Parish

THE SHEPHERD'S LOT

Earlier than wont along the sky,
Mix'd with the rack, the snow mists fly;
The shepherd who in summer sun,
Had something of our envy won,
As thou with pencil, I with pen,
The features traced of hill and glen;—
He who, outstretch'd the livelong day,
At ease among the heath-flowers lay,
View'd the light clouds with vacant look,
Or slumber'd o'er his tatter'd book,
Or idly busied him to guide
His angle o'er the lessen'd tide;—
At midnight now, the snowy plain
Finds sterner labour for the swain.

When red hath set the beamless sun,
Through heavy vapours dark and dun;
When the tired ploughman, dry and warm,
Hears, half asleep, the rising storm
Hurling the hail, and sleeted rain,
Against the casement's tinkling pane;
The sounds that drive wild deer, and fox,
To shelter in the brake and rocks,
Are warnings which the shepherd ask
To dismal and to dangerous task.
Oft he looks forth, and hopes, in vain,
The blast may sink in mellowing rain;
Till, dark above, and white below,
Decided drives the flaky snow,
And forth the hardy swain must go.
Long, with dejected look and whine,
To leave the hearth his dogs repine;
Whistling and cheering them to aid,
Around his back he wreathes the plaid:

His flock he gathers, and he guides,
To open downs, and mountain-sides,
Where fiercest though the tempest blow,
Least deeply lies the drift below.
The blast, that whistles o'er the fells,
Stiffens his locks to icicles;
Oft he looks back, while streaming far,
His cottage window seems a star,—
Loses its feeble gleam,—and then
Turns patient to the blast again,
And, facing to the tempest's sweep,
Drives through the gloom his lagging sheep.
If fails his heart, if his limbs fail,
Benumbing death is in the gale:
His paths, his landmarks, all unknown,
Close to the hut, no more his own,
Close to the aid he sought in vain,
The morn may find the stiffen'd swain:
The widow sees, at dawning pale,
His orphans raise their feeble wail;
And, close beside him, in the snow,
Poor Yarrow, partner of their woe,
Couches upon his master's breast,
And licks his cheek to break his rest
Who envies now the shepherd's lot,
His healthy fare, his rural cot,
His summer couch by greenwood tree,
His rustic kirn's loud revelry,
His native hill-notes, tuned on high
To Marion of the blithsome eye;
His crook, his scrip, his oaten reed,
And all Arcadia's golden creed?

SIR WALTER SCOTT (1771-1832)
Marmion

COLLIES

We quite well remember sitting on a dike by the road-side for nearly an hour with a shepherd of those parts, whilst, at our request, he despatched his dog over to the opposite hill, the face of which rose steeply backwards for nearly two miles, and stretched for double that space to right and left. The intelligence displayed by the creature was infinitely beyond anything we could previously have conceived. The moment he had compelled the brigade of bleaters to perform the evolution which his master's first signal had dictated, he sat down in his distant position with his eyes fixed on him; and, though certainly not nearer to us than half-a-mile to a mile, as the crow would fly, he at once caught up every successive signal, however slight, of his commanding officer, and put the troops into active motion, to carry the wished-for manœuvre into effect. In this manner, they were made to visit every part of the hill-face in succession—at one time keeping in compact phalanx, as if prepared to receive cavalry, and at another scouring away and scattering themselves over the mountain, as if skirmishing, like *tirailleurs* against some unseen enemy advancing from over the hill-top beyond; and it appeared to us that, great as we had always considered the talents of Lieutenant Lightbody, the able adjutant of the distinguished corps we had then recently left, we must feel ourselves compelled to declare that he was a mere tyro compared to this wonderful canine tactician.

And then, as to council, as well as war, we have seen some half-dozen of these highly gifted animals meet together from different parts of the mountains and glens, as if by appointment, at a sunny nook of some *fauld dike*, and then, seated on their haunches, hold a conference in which we, who were watching them, could have no doubt matters of vital importance to the collie population

of the parish were discussed. No body of bishops or Presbyterian elders of kirks could have behaved with greater
decorum, or could have shaken their heads more wisely;
and when the conference broke up, we had not a single
lingering doubt in our mind that the important business
which had been under discussion, had been temperately
settled in the wisest and most satisfactory manner. For
our part, we confess we should rather be put in possession
of a picture of such a canine conference, painted by the
wonderful pencil of Landseer, than that of any other
similar convocation of human beings that we know of.

SIR THOMAS DICK LAUDER (1784-1848)
Scottish Rivers

THE ANCIENT LAND

The wind blew steadily and, though the sky was
overcast, fanned the face with a fresh warmth. Very
soft it felt, like a petal between finger-tips. Reflective
finger-tips touched her cheeks. Eyes steadied on the far
sea, glimmered. North-west to north, to the Arctic. A
grey haze for horizon, for the illimitable. Space vast and
quiet and strong. The breasts of the hills about her
with the sea strip yonder like a shining doorstep to the
uttermost. Magnificent the sweep of the spirit from the
grey Arctic to the still, dark mountains, to the far cones
hazed in purple, south-west to west. Hazed sky, too, high
overhead; and passing from peak to sea, through corrie
and heather and myrtle, the wind, the soft, warm
August wind. Yet for all its breadth and sentinel
grandeur, this land was in some curious way intimate
and known of the spirit that swept and bathed.

NEIL M. GUNN (b. 1891)
The Lost Glen

TARRY WOO

Tarry woo, tarry woo,
Tarry woo is ill to spin,
Card it weel, card it weel,
Card it weel ere ye begin.

When 'tis carded, row'd and spun,
Then the work is hafflins done;
But when woven, drest and clean,
It may be cleeding for a queen.

Sing, my bonnie harmless sheep,
That feed upon the mountains steep,
Bleating sweetly as ye go
Through the winter's frost and snow;
Hart and hynd and fallow deer,
No by hauf so useful are;
Frae kings to him that hauds the ploo,
Are all obliged to tarry woo.

Up ye shepherds, dance and skip,
O'er the hills and valleys trip,
Sing the praise of tarry woo,
Sing the flocks that bear it too;
Harmless creatures without blame,
That cleed the back and cram the wame,
Keep us warm and hearty fou;
Leeze me on the tarry woo!

How happy is the shepherd's life,
Far frae courts and free o' strife,
While the gimmers bleat and bae,
And the lambkins answer mae.
No such music to his ear,
Of thief or fox he has no fear;

Sturdy kent and collie too
Will defend the tarry woo.

He lives content, and envies none;
Not even the monarch on his throne,
Though he the royal sceptre sways,
Has not sweeter holy days.
Who'd be a king, can ony tell,
When a shepherd sings sae well;
Sings sae well, and pays his due,
With honest heart and tarry woo?

ANONYMOUS
Herd's Scottish Songs

LEVEN WATER

On Leven's banks, while free to rove,
And tune the rural pipe to Love,
I envied not the happiest swain
That ever trod the Arcadian plain.
Pure stream, in whose transparent wave
My youthful limbs I wont to lave;
No torrents stain thy limpid source,
No rocks impede thy dimpling course,
That sweetly warbles o'er its bed,
With white, round, polished pebbles spread;
While, lightly poised, the scaly brood
In myriads cleave thy crystal flood;
Devolving from thy parent lake,
A charming maze thy waters make,
By bowers of birch and groves of pine,
And hedges flowered with eglantine.
Still on thy banks so gaily green,
May numerous herds and flocks be seen:
And lasses chanting o'er the pail,
And shepherds piping in the dale;

And ancient faith that knows no guile,
And industry embrowned with toil;
And hearts resolved, and hands prepared,
The blessings they enjoy to guard!

TOBIAS SMOLLETT (1721-71)

ALBANIA—THE PHANTOM HUNT

Ere since of old, the haughty thanes of Ross,
(So to the simple swain tradition tells,)
Were wont with clans, and ready vassals thronged,
To wake the bounding stag, or guilty wolf,
There oft is heard at midnight, or at noon,
Beginning faint, but rising still more loud,
And nearer, voice of hunters, and of hounds,
And horns hoarse-winded, blowing far and keen:
Forthwith, the hubbub multiplies, the gale
Labours with wilder shrieks, and rifer din
Of hot pursuit, the broken cry of deer
Mangled by throttling dogs, the shouts of men,
And hoofs thick beating on the hollow hill.
Sudden the grazing heifer in the vale
Starts at the noise, and both the herdsman's ears
Tingle with inward dread. Aghast he eyes
The mountain's height and all the ridges round,
Yet not one trace of living wight discerns!
Nor knows, o'erawed, and trembling as he stands,
To what, or whom, he owes his idle fear,
To ghost, to witch, to fairy, or to fiend,
But wonders, and no end of wondering finds.

AUTHOR UNKNOWN
The complete poem, which was a favourite
of Sir Walter Scott, is contained in
Scottish Descriptive Poems, 1803.

AN OCHIL FARMER

Abune the braes I see him stand,
The tapmost corner o' his land,
An' scan wi' care, owre hill an' plain,
A prospect he may ca' his ain.

His yowes ayont the hillocks feed,
Weel herdit in by wakefu' Tweed;
An' canny thro' the bent his kye
Gang creepin' to the byre doun-by.

His hayfields lie fu' smoothly shorn,
An' ripenin' rise his rigs o' corn;
A simmer's evenin' glory fa's
Upon his hamestead's sober wa's.

A stately figure there he stands
An' rests upon his staff his hands:
Maist like some patriarch of eld,
In sic an evenin's calm beheld.

A farmer he of Ochilside,
For worth respectit far an' wide;
A friend of justice and of truth,
A favourite wi' age an' youth.

There's no' a bairn but kens him weel,
And ilka collie's at his heel;
Nor beast nor body e'er had ocht
To wyte him wi', in deed or thocht.

Fu' mony a gloamin' may he stand
Abune the brae to bless the land!
Fu' mony a simmer rise an' fa'
In beauty owre his couthie ha'!

For peacefu' aye, as simmer's air,
The kindly hearts that kindle there;
Whase friendship, sure an' aye the same,
For me mak's Ochilside a hame.

J. LOGIE ROBERTSON (1849-1922)

A SONG IN WAR-TIME

By Logan's streams that rin sae deep,
Fu' aft, wi' glee, I've herded sheep;
Herded sheep, or gathered slaes,
Wi' my dear lad on Logan Braes.
But wae's my heart! thae days are gane,
And I, wi' grief, may herd alane;
While my dear lad maun face his faes,
Far, far frae me and Logan Braes.

Nae mair at Logan Kirk will he
Atween the preachings, meet wi' me;
Meet wi' me, or when it's mirk,
Convoy me hame frae Logan Kirk.
I weel may sing thae days are gane—
Frae kirk an' fair I come alane,
While my dear lad maun face his faes,
Far, far frae me and Logan Braes!

At e'en, when hope amaist is gane,
I dander out, or sit alane,
Sit alane beneath the tree
Where aft he kept his tryst wi' me.
O! could I see thae days again,
My lover skaithless, and my ain!
Belov'd by frien's, rever'd by faes,
We'd live in bliss on Logan Braes.

JOHN MAYNE (1759-1836)

THE COTTER'S SATURDAY NIGHT

November chill blaws loud wi' angry sough;
   The short'ning winter-day is near a close;
The miry beasts retreating frae the pleugh:
   The black'ning trains o' craws to their repose;
The toil-worn Cotter frae his labour goes,
   This night his weekly moil is at an end,
Collects his spades, his mattocks, and his hoes,
   Hoping the morn in ease and rest to spend,
And weary, o'er the moor, his course does hameward
     bend.

At length his lonely cot appears in view,
   Beneath the shelter of an aged tree.
Th' expectant wee things, toddlin' stacher thro'
   To meet their dad, wi' flichterin' noise an' glee.
His wee bit ingle, blinkin' bonnily,
   His clean hearth-stane, his thriftie wifie's smile,
The lisping infant prattling on his knee,
   Does a' his weary carking cares beguile,
And makes him quite forget his labour and his toil.

Belyve the elder bairns come drapping in,
   At service out amang the farmers roun',
Some ca' the pleugh, some herd, some tentie rin
   A cannie errand to a neebor town;
Their eldest hope, their Jenny, woman grown,
   In youthfu' bloom, love sparklin' in her e'e,
Comes hame, perhaps, to show a bra' new gown,
   Or deposite her sair-won penny fee,
To help her parents dear, if they in hardship be.

Wi' joy unfeign'd brothers and sisters meet,
   An' each for other's weelfare kindly spiers;
The social hours swift-wing'd unnotic'd fleet;

Each tells the uncos that he sees or hears;
The parents, pairtial, ee their hopfu' years:
  Anticipation forward points the view:
The Mother, wi' her needle and her shears,
  Gars auld claes look amaist as weel's the new;
The Father mixes a' wi' admonition due.

But, hark! a rap comes gently to the door,
  Jenny, wha kens the meaning o' the same,
Tells how a neebor lad came o'er the moor,
  To do some errands, and convoy her hame.
The wily mother sees the conscious flame
  Sparkle in Jenny's e'e, and flush her cheek;
With heart-struck anxious care inquires his name,
  While Jenny hafflins is afraid to speak:
Weel-pleas'd the mother hears it's nae wild worthless
  rake.

Wi' kindly welcome Jenny brings him ben:
  A strappan youth; he taks the mother's eye:
Blithe Jenny sees the visit's no ill-taen;
  The father cracks o' horses, pleughs, and kye.
The youngster's artless heart o'erflows wi' joy,
  But blate and laithfu', scarce can weel behave;
The mother wi' a woman's wiles, can spy
  What maks the youth sae bashfu' and sae grave:
Weel pleas'd to think her bairn's respectit like the lave.

But now the supper crowns their simple board,
  The halesome parritch, chief o' Scotia's food;
The soupe their only hawkie does afford,
  That 'yont the hallan snugly chows her cood;
The dame brings forth, in complimental mood,
  To grace the lad, her weel-hain'd kebbuck fell,
An' aft he's prest, an' aft hc ca's it guid;
  The frugal wifie, garrulous, will tell,
How 'twas a towmond auld, sin' lint was i' the bell.

The cheerfu' supper done, wi' serious face,
   They, round the ingle, form a circle wide;
The sire turns o'er, wi' patriarchal grace,
   The big ha' Bible, ance his father's pride:
His bonnet rev'rently is laid aside,
   His lyart haffets wearing thin an' bare:
Those strains that once did sweet in Zion glide,
   He wales a portion with judicious care;
And "Let us worship GOD!" he says with solemn air.

They chant their artless notes in simple guise;
   They tune their hearts, by far the noblest aim;
Perhaps Dundee's wild warbling measures rise,
   Or plaintive Martyrs, worthy of the name,
Or noble Elgin beets the heav'n-ward flame,
   The sweetest far of Scotia's holy lays:
Compar'd wi' these, Italian trills are tame;
   The tickled ears no heartfelt raptures raise;
Nae unison hae they wi' our Creator's praise.

Then kneeling down to HEAVEN'S ETERNAL KING,
   The saint, the father, and the husband prays:
Hope "springs exulting on triumphant wing,"
   That thus they all shall meet in future days;
There ever bask in uncreated rays,
   No more to sigh, or shed the bitter tear,
Together hymning their Creator's praise,
   In such society, yet still more dear,
While circling time moves round in an eternal sphere.

Then homeward all take off their several way;
   The youngling cottagers retire to rest:
The parent-pair their secret homage pay,
   And proffer up to Heav'n the warm request,
That He who stills the raven's clam'rous nest,
   And decks the lily fair in flow'ry pride,
Would, in the way His wisdom sees the best,

For them and for their little ones provide;
But chiefly, in their hearts with grace divine preside.

From scenes like these old Scotia's grandeur springs,
    That makes her loved at home, revered abroad;
Princes and lords are but the breath of kings,
    "An honest man's the noblest work of GOD!"
And certes, in fair virtue's heav'nly road,
    The cottage leaves the palace far behind:
What is a lording's pomp?—a cumbrous load,
    Disguising oft the wretch of human kind,
Studied in arts of hell, in wickedness refined!

Oh Scotia! my dear, my native soil!
    For whom my warmest wish to Heaven is sent!
Long may thy hardy sons of rustic toil
    Be blest with health, and peace, and sweet content!
And, Oh! may Heav'n their simple lives prevent
    From luxury's contagion, weak and vile!
Then, howe'er crowns and coronets be rent,
    A virtuous populace may rise the while,
And stand a wall of fire around their much-lov'd Isle.

ROBERT BURNS (1759-96)

STRIP THE WILLOW

But then Chae cried *Strip the Willow*, and they all
lined up, and the melodeon played bonnily in Chae's
hands, and Long Rob's fiddle-bow was darting and
glimmering, and in two minutes, in the whirl and go
of *Strip the Willow*, there wasn't a cold soul in Blawearie
barn, or a cold sole either. Then here, soon's they'd
finished, was Mistress Melon with a great jar of hot
toddy to drink, she set it on a bench between Chae and
Long Rob. And whoever wanted to drink had just to

go there, few were bashful in the going, too; and another dance started, it was a schottische, and Chris found herself in the arms of the minister, he could dance like a daft young lad. And as he swung her round and around he opened his mouth and cried *Hooch!* and so did the red Highlander, McIvor, *Hooch!* careering by with fat Kirsty Strachan, real scared-like she looked, clipped round the waist.

Then Chae and Long Rob hardly gave them a breather, they were at it dance on dance; and every time they stopped for a panting second, Chae would dip in the jar and give Rob a wink and cry *Here's to you, man!* and Rob would dip, solemn-like as well, and say *Same to you!* and off the fiddle and melodeon would go again, faster than ever.

LEWIS GRASSIC GIBBON (J. LESLIE MITCHELL, 1901-35)
Sunset Song

THE MUIRLAND FARMER

I'm now a gude farmer, I've acres o' land,
    And my heart aye loups light when I'm viewin' o't;
And I ha'e servants at my command,
    And twa dainty cowts for the pleughin' o't.
My farm is a snug ane, lies high on a muir,
The muircocks and plivers aft skirl at my door,
And whan the sky lowers I'm aye sure o' a shower
    To moisten my land for the pleughin' o't.

Leeze me on the mailin that's fa'en to my share;
    It tak's sax meikle bowes for the sawin' o't.
I've sax braid acres for pasture, and mair,
    And a dainty bit bog for the mawin' o't.
A spence and a kitchen my mansionhouse gi'es;
I've a canty wee wifie to daut when I please,
Twa bairnies, twa callans that skelp ower the leas,
    And they'll soon can assist at the pleughin' o't.

173

My biggin' stands sweet on this south-slopin' hill,
  And the sun shines sae bonnily beamin' on't,
And past my door trots a clear prattlin' rill,
    Frae the loch, whare the wild ducks are swimmin'
      on't.
And on its green banks, on the gay simmer days
My wifie trips barefit, a-bleachin' her claes,
And on the dear creature wi' rapture I gaze,
    While I whistle and sing at the pleughin' o't.

To rank amang farmers I ha'e meikle pride,
    But I maunna speak high when I'm tellin' o't.
How brawly I strut on my shelty to ride,
    Wi' a sample to show for the sellin' o't.
In blue worset boots that my auld mither span,
I've aft been fu' vaunty sin' I was a man,
But now they're flung by, and I've bought cordovan,
    And my wifie ne'er grudged me a shillin' o't.

Sae now whan to kirk or to market I gae,
    My weelfare what need I be hidin' o't?
In braw leather boots shinin' black as the slae,
    I dink me to try the ridin' o't.
Last towmond I sell't off four bowes o' gude bere,
And thankfu' I was, for the victual was dear,
And I cam' hame wi' spurs on my heels shinin'
      clear,
    I had sic gude luck at the sellin' o't.

Now hairst-time is ower, and a fig for the laird,
    My rent's now secure for the toilin' o't;
My fields a' are bare, and my craps in the yard,
    And I'm nae mair in doubts o' the spoilin' o't.
Now welcome gude weather, or wind, or come weet,
Or bauld ragin' Winter, wi' hail, snaw, or sleet;
Nae mair can he draigle my crap 'mang his feet,
    Nor wraik his mischief, and be spoilin' o't.

174

And on the dowf days, when loud hurricanes blaw,
   Fu' snug in the spence I'll be viewin' o't,
And jink the rude blast in my rush-theekit ha',
   When fields are sealed up frae the pleughin' o't.
My bonnie wee wifie, the bairnies, and me,
The peat-stack and turf-stack our Phœbus shall be,
Till day close the scowl o' its angry e'e,
   And we'll rest in gude hopes o' the pleughin' o't.

Nor need I to envy our braw gentlefolks,
   Wha fash na their thumbs wi' the sawin' o't,
Nor e'er slip their fine silken hands i' the pocks,
   Nor foul their black shoon wi' the pleughin' o't;
For, pleased wi' the little that fortune has lent,
The seasons row round us in rural content;
We've aye milk and meal, and our laird gets his rent,
   And I whistle and sing at the pleughin' o't.

ANDREW SCOTT (1757-1839)

DIALOGUE OF THE RIVERS

Tweed said to Till,
"What gars ye rin sae still?"
Till said to Tweed,
"Though ye rin wi' speed,
And I rin slaw,
Whar ye droon ae man,
I droon twa."

ANONYMOUS

WHAT THE AULD FOWK ARE THINKIN

The bairns i' their beds, worn out wi' nae wark,
 Are sleepin, nor ever an eelid winkin ;
The auld fowk lie still, wi' their een starin stark,
 An' the mirk pang-fou[1] o' the things they are thinkin.

Whan oot o' ilk[2] corner the bairnies they keek,[3]
 Lauchin an' daffin,[4] airms loosin an' linkin,
The auld fowk they watch frae the warm ingle-cheek,[5]
 But the bairns little think what the auld fowk are
 thinkin.

Whan the auld fowk sit quaiet at the reet[6] o' a stook,[7]
 I' the sunlicht their washt een blinterin and' blinkin,
Fowk scythin, or bin'in, or shearin wi' heuk
 Carena a strae what the auld fowk are thinkin.

At the kirk, whan the minister's dreich[8] an' dry,
 His fardens as gien[9] they war gowd guineas chinkin,
An' the young fowk are noddin, or fidgetin sly,
 Naebody kens what the auld fowk are thinkin.

Whan the young fowk are greitin[10] aboot the bed
 Whaur like water throu san' the auld life is sinkin,
An' some wud say the last word was said,
 The auld fowk smile, an' ken what they're thinkin.

GEORGE MACDONALD (1824-1905)

[1] dark stuffed full   [2] each   [3] peep   [4] teasing   [5] side of the fire
  [6] root, foot   [7] sheaf   [8] dreary   [9] if   [10] weeping

WITH ROD AND LINE

The stones of Banchory were not worth talking about; shooting and fishing made up for them. Those hours devoted to fly-fishing during the evenings under the beeches, with the brown stream rippling at my feet— they were sacred; how glad one was to escape after dinner to the Feugh! During a spate we generally fished in the pool below the bridge with a worm or minnow and watched the salmon leaping up; the maximum I remember counting was sixty-three in one minute. And the strangest fish I ever drew out of that pool was a flounder. "That's nothing," said a friend to whom I once related the fact. "I've caught a swordfish on the Bosphorous with a fly—I'll take my Bible oath on it. Can you beat that?" . . .

My thoughts often wander in the direction of Banchory. There are moments when I feel the need of that landscape, when I wonder whether I shall ever return to savour the charm of those long-drawn twilights and the perfume of its woodlands.

NORMAN DOUGLAS (1868-1952)
Looking Back

WITH THE HERRING FISHERS

"I see herrin'"—I hear the glad cry
An 'gainst the mune see ilka blue jowl
In turn as the fishermen haul on the nets
And sing: "Come, shove in your heids and growl."

"Soom on, bonnie herrin', soom on," they bawl,
And "Come in, O come in, and see me,"
"Come and gi'e the auld man something to dae;
It'll be a braw change frae the sea!"

177

O it's ane o' the bonniest sichts in the world
To watch the herrin' come walkin' on board
In the wee sma' 'oors o' a simmer's mornin'
As if o' their ain accord!

For this is the way that God sees life,
The haill jing-bank o's appearin'
Up owre frae the edge o' naethingness
—It's His happy cries I'm hearin'.

"Left, Right—O come in and see me,"
Reid and yellow and black and white,
Toddlin' up into Heaven thegither
At peep o' day frae the endless night!

HUGH MACDIARMID (C. M. GRIEVE, b. 1892)
Scottish Scene

HURLYGUSH

The hurlygush[1] and hallyoch[2] o the watter
a-skinklan i the moveless simmer sun,
harles aff the scaurie mountain wi a yatter
that thru ten-thoosan centuries has run.

Wi cheek agains the ash o wither't bracken,
I ligg at peace, an hear nae soun at aa
but yonder hurlygush that canna slacken,
thru time an space mak never-endan faa:

as if a volley o the soun had brought me
doun tae the pool whaur timeless things begin,
and e'en this endless faa'an that had caught me
wi ilka ither force was gether't in.

MAURICE LINDSAY (b. 1918)
[1] noise of running water [2] babble of unknown tongues

CALVINIST SANG

A Hunder pipers canna blaw
Wir trauchled[1] times awa,
Drams canna droun them oot, nor sang
Hap[2] their scarecraw heids for lang.

Gin as the warld was bleezan fou,[3]
Whit gowk[4] wad haud the plou?
Gin chiels were cowpan quines[5] aa day
Thy'd mak, bit never gaither, hay.

Pit by yir pipes[6] and brak yir gless,
Gie ower wi gallusness,[7]
The-day ye need a hert and harns[8]
Dour as the diamant, cauld as the starns.[9]

ALEXANDER SCOTT (b. 1920)

[1] troubled [2] cover [3] highly intoxicated [4] fool [5] embracing girls
[6] bagpipes [7] recklessness [8] a heart and brains [9] stars

LAST LAUCH

The Minister said it wald dee,
   the cypress buss I plantit.
But the buss grew til a tree,
   naething dauntit.

It's growan, stark and heich,
   derk and straucht and sinister,
kirkyairdie-like and dreich.
   But whaur's the Minister?

DOUGLAS YOUNG (b. 1913)

179

People, Great and Small

COLUMBA IN IONA

St. Columba, the apostle of Christianity to the Scots, was born in Donegal. He came to Scotland *circa* 563 when in his forty-second year, founded the monastery of Iona and made this the centre of his evangelical work in which he was occupied incessantly until shortly before his death in 597.

Columba's work in Iona looked to the care both of the place and the people. He conserved the forest. He introduced the culture of fruit trees and of bees, and improved the stock of the island. He shortened the time between seed-time and harvest. He organised the fishing and navigation. He drained the bog between the observatory and the cemetery hills, dammed up the water in a lake and ran it down the ravine to turn the millwheel of his monastery. The piety of moderns has 'restored' the post-Columban cathedral, and likewise the bog. He tended the sick, comforted the afflicted, admonished and advised the erring, and was a holy and wholesome terror to evildoers. He took special pains to exclude from his island citadel all persons of bad character. But the chief purpose of the island monastery was to train the successive bands of missionary monks who sallied forth—often with Columba at their head —into the islands and mainland of Pictish Scotland, and established therein a network of monastic settlements (*i.e.* radiating foci of practical idealism) which owed allegiance to Iona and looked to it for inspiration.

VICTOR BRANFORD
St. Columba

SAINT CUTHBERT, c. 635-85

Among the spiritual descendants of Columba none is more famous than Cuthbert. As a shepherd lad, tending his flock by night on the hills of Lammermoor, he saw the vision which determined his vocation. Suddenly the dark sky shone with a broad tract of light, down which descended a host of angels, who presently mounted heavenwards, bearing with them the soul they had sought on earth. Aidan, Bishop of Lindisfarne, had died that night (651). Thirteen years later Cuthbert was drawn from Melrose, and appointed prior of the monastery of Lindisfarne, that he might reform the abuses of the house. After twelve years he withdrew to the barren island of Farne, where he built an anchorite's cell.

Legend lingers lovingly round his name. The seafowl, whom he made his companions, are called the Birds of St. Cuthbert. The little shells that are found on the coast are known as the Beads of St. Cuthbert; and by night he may still be seen, so tradition tells us, fashioning them, with a stone for his hammer, and a rock for his anvil.

> "But fain St. Hilda's nuns would learn
> If on a rock, by Lindisfarne,
> St. Cuthbert sits and toils to frame
> The seaborn beads that bear his name."

From his dear solitude he was taken, against his will, to be made Bishop of Lindisfarne (685). Two years afterwards he returned to his cell a dying man. He died March 20, 687, having received the Sacrament at the hands of Herefrith, Abbot of Lindisfarne, who tells the story of his death. Near the landing-place of the island was a rude shelter, in which some of the brethren had passed the night in prayer and chanting. When Herefrith brought the news of Cuthbert's death, the monks were singing the 60th Psalm. By an agreed signal, the light of two torches held aloft proclaimed to the watcher on the mainland that the soul of Cuthbert had departed to the Lord. Hurrying from the tower to bear the news to those who worshipped in the church, the watchman found the assembled brethren singing the same psalm.

ROWLAND E. PROTHERO
The Psalms in Human Life

KING ROBERT THE BRUCE, 1274-1329

Well indeed might Scotland, well may mankind, revere King Robert's name, for never, save Alfred the Great, did monarch so profit by adversity. Vacillating and infirm of purpose, a courtier and a timeserver at the footstool of Edward, during the days of Wallace, and betrayed into sacrilege and bloodshed on the very step of the altar at Dumfries, he redeemed all by a constancy, a patriotism, a piety, alike in his troubles and his prosperity, which rendered him the pride and example of his contemporaries, and has been the theme of history and of a grateful posterity in all succeeding ages.

The Christian, the patriot, the wisest monarch, and the most accomplished knight of his age, and more endearing than all, the owner of a heart kind and tender as a woman's, we may indeed bless his memory, and visiting his tomb, pronounce over it his epitaph in the knightly words with which Sir Hector mourned over Sir Lancelot: 'There thou liest, thou that were never matched of earthly knight's hands! And thou wert the most courteous knight that ever bare shield! And thou wert the kindest man that ever struck with sword! And thou wert the goodliest person that ever came among press of knights! And thou wert the meekest man and

182

the gentlest that ever ate in hall among ladies! And thou wert the sternest knight to thy mortal foe that ever put spear in rest!'—Such, and more than this, was Bruce.

EARL OF CRAWFORD (1812-80)
Lives of the Lindsays

THE GUDEMAN OF BALLANGEIGH

James V (1512-42) used frequently to traverse the vicinity of his several palaces, in various disguises, in search of adventures. The two comic songs, entitled *The Gaberlunzie man*, and *We'll gang na mair a roving* are said to have been founded upon the success of his amours, when travelling in the disguise of a beggar. An adventure he had at the village of Cramond, four miles from Edinburgh, is said to have nearly cost him his life.

While, one evening, visiting a pretty girl, of the lower rank, who resided in that village, to whom he had rendered his addresses acceptable, while returning home, he was beset by four or five persons. Naturally gallant, and an admirable master of his weapon, the king took post on the high and narrow bridge, over the Almond river, and defended himself bravely with his sword. A peasant who was threshing in a neighbouring barn, came out upon the noise, and whether moved by compassion, or by natural gallantry, took the weaker side, and laid about him with his flail so effectually, as to disperse the assailants, well threshed, even according to the letter. He then conducted the king into his barn, where his guest requested a basin and towel, to remove the stains of the broil. This being procured with difficulty, James employed himself in learning what was the summit of his deliverer's earthly wishes, and found that they were bounded by the desire of possessing, in property, the farm of Braehead, upon which he laboured

183

as a bondsman. The lands chanced to belong to the crown, and James directed him to come to the palace of Holyrood, and enquire for the gudeman of Ballangeigh.

The poor man came as appointed, and, as the king had given orders for his admission, he was soon brought into the royal presence. James, still dressed in his travelling attire, received him as the gudeman of Ballangeigh, conducted him from one apartment to another, by way of shewing him the palace, and then asked him if he would like to see the king. John Howison, for such was his name, said, that nothing would give him so much pleasure, if he was only brought into the king's hall, without giving offence. The gudeman of Ballangeigh, of course, undertook that the king would not be angry. "But," said John, "how am I to know his grace from the nobles who will be all about him?" "Easily," replied the king, "all the others will be bareheaded—the king alone will wear his bonnet." On John being introduced into the great hall, which was filled by the nobility and officers of the crown, he was somewhat frightened, and drew near to his attendant but was unable to distinguish the king. "I told you that you would know him by his wearing his hat," said his conductor, "Then," said John, after he had looked round the room, "it must be either you or me, for all but us are bareheaded."

The king laughed at John's fancy, and, that the good yeoman might have mirth also, he made him a present of the farm of Braehead, which he had wished so much to possess, on condition, that he and his successors should be ready to present a ewer and basin, for the king to wash his hands, when his majesty should come to Holyrood palace, or should pass the bridge of Cramond. Accordingly, in the year 1822, when Geo. IV. came to Scotland, a descendant of John Howison, who still possesses the estate which was given to his ancestor, appeared at a solemn festival, and offered his majesty water from a silver ewer, that he might perform the service by which he held his land.

Annals of Edinburgh

JOHN KNOX, c. 1515-72

It seems to me hard measure that this Scottish man, now after three hundred years, should have to plead like a culprit before the world; intrinsically for having been, in such way as it was then possible to be, the bravest of all Scotchmen! Had he been a poor Half-and-half, he could have crouched into the corner, like so many others; Scotland had not been delivered; and Knox had been without blame. He is the one Scotchman to whom, of all others, his country and the world owe a debt. He has to plead that Scotland would forgive him for having been worth to it any million "unblamable" Scotchmen that need no forgiveness! He bared his breast to the battle; had to row in French galleys, wander forlorn in exile, in clouds and storms, was censured, shot-at through his windows; had a right sore fighting life: if this world were his place of recompense, he had made but a bad venture of it. I cannot apologise for Knox. To him it is very indifferent, these two-hundred-and-fifty years or more, what men say of him. But we, having got above all these details of his battle, and living now in clearness on the fruits of his victory, we, for our own sake, ought to look through the rumours and controversies enveloping the man, into the man himself.

THOMAS CARLYLE (1795-1881)
Heroes and Hero Worship

MARY STUART, QUEEN OF SCOTS, TO THE EARL OF BOTHWELL

My Lord,

If the displeasure of your absence, of your forgetfulness, the fear of danger promised by every one to your so loved person, may give me consolation, I leave it to you to judge, seeing the mishap that my cruel lot and continual misadventure has hitherto promised me following the misfortunes and fears as well of late, as of a long time by past, the which you do know. But for all that I will nowise accuse you, neither of your little remembrance, neither of your little care, and least of all of your promise broken, or of the coldness of your writing, since I am else so far made yours that that which pleases you is acceptable to me; and my thoughts are so willingly subdued unto yours that I suppose that all that cometh of you proceeds not of any of the causes aforesaid, but rather of such as be just and reasonable, and such as I desire myself, which is the final order that you promised to take for the surety and honourable service of the only supporter of my life. For which alone I will preserve the same, and without the which I desire nought but sudden death. And to testify unto you how lowly I submit myself to your commandments I have sent you of homage by Pareis the ornament of the head which is the chief guide of the other members. Inferring thereby that by the seizing of you in the possession of the spoil of which that is the principal, the remnant cannot be but subject unto you, and with consenting of the heart.

In place whereof, since I have else left it unto you, I send unto you one sculpture of hard stone colored with black, engraved with tears and bones. The stone I compare to my heart, that as it is covered in one sure sepulture of harbor of your commandments, and, above all, of your name and memory, that are therein enclosed as is my heart in this ring, never to come forth while death grant unto you one trophy of victory to my bones, as the ring is filled, in sign you have made one full conquest of me, of my heart, and in that my bones are left unto you in remembrance of your victory and my acceptable love and willingness, for to be better bestowed than I merit. The annealing that is about is black, which signifies the steadfastness of her that sends the same. The tears are without number, so are the fears to displease you, the tears for your absence, the disdain that I cannot be in outward effect yours, as I am without faintness of heart and spirit, and of good reason, though my merits were much greater than that of the most profit that ever was, and such as I desire to be, and shall take pains in conditions to imitate, for to be bestowed worthily under your governance. My only wealth receive, therefore, in as good part the same, as I have received of your marriage in extreme joy, that which shall not part forth of my bosom till that marriage of our bodies be made in public, as a sign of all that I either hope or desire of bliss in this world.

Yet, my heart, fearing to displease you, as much in the reading hereof, as it delights me in the writing, I will make an end, after I have kissed your hand with as great affection as I pray God (oh, the only supporter of my life!) to give you long and blessed life, and to me your good favor, as the only good that I desire, and to the which I pretend. I have shown unto the bearer of this that which I have learned, knowing the credit that you give him; as she also doth, that will be forever unto you an humble and obedient lawful wife that forever dedicates unto you her heart, her body, without any change unto him I have made the possessor of my heart, of which you may hold you assured, that unto death shall no ways be changed, for evil nor good shall never make me go from it.

PRISONER IN ENGLAND

Following upon the disastrous battle of Langside, May 13th, 1568, Mary and her escort, having abandoned hope of reaching Dumbarton, galloped for the wilds of the South-West. They halted at Sanquhar, reached Dundrennan on the 15th (where she sent a letter to Elizabeth seeking protection and requesting her to do her the honour to receive her) and in company with some twenty attendants including Lords Herries, Fleming and Claud Hamilton, she crossed the Solway on Sunday afternoon, the 16th, landing at Workington at seven o'clock. Next day she was brought by Richard Lowther to Cockermouth, and on the 18th to Carlisle Castle.

On May 28th Mary received Sir Francis Knollys, the vice-chamberlain and Lord Scrope, the warden, in her apartments in Carlisle Castle and urged her right of personal access to Queen Elizabeth. On June 8th Elizabeth wrote to assure Mary that she would be as careful of Mary's "life and honour" as Mary herself could be, and that it would be one of "her highest wordly pleasures" to receive her once she was acquitted of this "crime," i.e. the murder of Darnley. It was at this time that the report from which the following is taken was sent by Knollys to Cecil, Lord Burghley:

"This ladie and prynces is a notable woman; she semethe to regard no ceremonious honor besyde the acknolegying of hyr estate regalle: she shoethe a disposition to speak motche, to be bold, to be plesant, and to be very famylyare. She shoethe a great desyer to be avenged of hyr enymyes, she shoethe a redines to expone hyr selffe to all perylls in hoope off victorie, she delytethe motche to here of hardiness and valiancye, commendyng by name all approved hardye men of hyr countrye, althoe they be hyr enemyes, and she concealithe no cowardnes even in hyr frendes. The thynge that moste she thirstethe after is victorye, and it semeth to be indifferent to hyr to have hyr enemies demynysshed eyther by the sword of hyr frendes, or by the liberall promyses and rewardes of hyr purse, or by devysyon and qwarylls raised amongst theym selffes: so that for victories sake payne and parylle semethe plesant unto hyr: and in respect off victorie, welthe and all things semethe to hyr contemptible and vyle. Nowe what is to be done with sotche a ladie and pryncesse, or whether sotche a pryncesse and ladie be to be norysshed in one's bosome? or whether it be good to halte and disembyll with sotche a ladye, I referr to your judgement."

JAMES I, 1566-1625

To his son, Prince Henry, upon his leaving Scotland to take possession of the Crown of England, 1603

(The spelling has been modernised)

My Son, that I see you not before my parting, impute it to this great occasion, wherein time was so precious; but that shall by God's grace be recompensed by your coming to me shortly, and continual residence with me ever after. Let not this news make you proud, or insolent, for a king's son and heir was ye before, and no more are ye yet. The augmentation that is hereby like to fall unto you, is but in cares and heavy burthens. Be, therefore, merry, but not insolent; keep a greatness, but *sine fastu*; be resolute, but not wilful; keep your kindness, but in honourable sort; choose none to be your playfellows but them that are well born; and above all things, never give good countenance to any but according as ye shall be informed that they are in estimation with me. Look upon all Englishmen that shall come to visit you as your loving subjects, not with that ceremony as towards strangers, and yet with such heartiness as at this time they deserve. This gentleman whom this bearer accompanies is worthy, and of good rank, and

now my familiar servitor; use him, therefore, in a more
homely sort nor other. I send you herewith my book
lately printed; study and profit in it as ye would deserve
my blessing; and as there can nothing happen unto you
whereof ye will not find the general ground therein,
if not the very particular point touched, so must ye
level every man's opinion or advices unto you as ye find
them agree or discord with the rules there set down,
allowing and following their advices that agree with
the same, mistrusting and frowning upon them that
advise you to the contrary. Be diligent and earnest in
your studies, that at your meeting with me I may praise
you for your progress in learning. Be obedient to your
master, for your own weal, and to procure my thanks;
for in reverencing him ye obey me, and honour yourself.
Farewell.

> Your loving father,
>
> JAMES R.

Historical Documents

WAT OF HARDEN, *c.* 1550-1629

We may form some idea of the style of life maintained
by the Border warriors from the anecdotes, handed down
by tradition, concerning Walter Scott of Harden, who
flourished towards the middle of the sixteenth century.
This ancient laird was a renowned freebooter, and used
to ride with a numerous band of followers. The spoil
which they carried off from England, or from their
neighbours was concealed in a deep and impervious glen,
on the brink of which the old tower of Harden is situated.
From thence the cattle were brought out, one by one,
as they were wanted, to supply the rude and plentiful
table of the laird. When the last bullock was killed and
devoured, it was the lady's custom to place on the table

a dish, which, on being uncovered, was found to contain a pair of clean spurs, a hint to the riders, that they must shift for their next meal. Upon one occasion, when the village herd was driving the cattle out to pasture, the old laird heard him call loudly *to drive out Harden's cow.* "Harden's cow!" echoed the affronted chief; "is it come to that pass? By my faith they shall soon say Harden's *kye.*" Accordingly he sounded his bugle, mounted his horse, set out with all his followers, and returned next day with "a bow of kye and a basson'd (brindled) bull." On his return with this gallant prey, he passed a very large haystack. It occurred to the provident laird, that this would be extremely convenient to fodder his new stock of cattle; but as no means of transporting it occurred, he was fain to take leave of it with this apostrophe, now proverbial: "By my soul, had ye your feet, ye should not stand lang there!" In short, as Froissart says of a similar class of feudal robbers, nothing came amiss to them, that was not *too heavy, or too hot.*

SIR WALTER SCOTT (1771-1832)
The Border Minstrelsy

SIR DAVID LINDESAY, 1490-1555

He was a man of middle age;
In aspect manly, grave, and sage,
  As on King's errand come;
But in the glances of his eye,
A penetrating, keen, and sly
  Expression found its home;
The flash of that satiric rage,
Which, bursting on the early stage,
Branded the vices of the age,
  And broke the keys of Rome.
On milk-white palfrey forth he paced;

His cap of maintenance was graced
  With the proud heron-plume.
From his steed's shoulder, loin, and breast,
  Silk housings swept the ground,
With Scotland's arms, device, and crest
  Embroider'd round and round. . . .
So bright the King's armorial coat,
That scarce the dazzled eye could note,
In living colours, blazon'd brave,
The Lion, which his title gave;
A train, which well beseem'd his state,
But all unarm'd, around him wait.
  Still is thy name in high account,
  And still thy verse has charms,
Sir David Lindesay of the Mount,
  Lord Lion King-at-arms!

SIR WALTER SCOTT (1771-1832)
Marmion

EPIGRAM ON A COUNTRY LAIRD

Not quite so wise as Solomon

Bless Jesus Christ, O Cardoness,
  With grateful, lifted eyes,
Who taught that not the soul alone,
  But *body* too shall rise;
For had He said "The soul alone
  From death I will deliver,"
Alas, alas! O Cardoness,
  Then hadst thou lain for ever.

ROBERT BURNS (1759-96)

JAMES RENWICK, 1662-88

The Reformed Presbyterians, or Cameronians, were founded by the Scottish Covenanter Richard Cameron. A schoolmaster at Falkland, he became a preacher and leader of those who disliked episcopacy. He joined the Sanquhar Declaration (June 22nd, 1680) disowning allegiance to Charles II, was outlawed and killed in a skirmish at Airds Moss, Ayrshire, on July 20th, 1680. The last of the Cameronians who suffered on the scaffold was James Renwick, though his sentence was due to his political tenets rather than to his religious opinions.

Among the crowd who had witnessed Cargill's execution in the Grassmarket of Edinburgh was a lad of nineteen, the son of a Nithsdale weaver. The lad was James Renwick. So stirred was he by the scene that he cast in his lot with the persecuted remnant of the Cameronians. Ordained to the ministry after six months' study at Groningen, he returned to Scotland, and began to preach in October 1683. On his shoulders, young though he was, rested the burden of the struggle. The spirit which he threw into his work is revealed by a passage from one of his letters from Holland. "Courage yet," he writes, "for all that is come and gone. The loss of men is not the loss of the cause. What is the matter though we all fall? the cause shall not fall." Thus inspired, Renwick speedily became the soul of the movement among the Cameronian societies, who disowned the king, and declared war against him as the subverter of the religion and liberty of the nation.

During the "Killing Times" vigorous search was made for Renwick. But he evaded capture, and it was not till January, 1688, that he was taken. On him were found the notes of his last two sermons, one of which was on Ps. 46, 10, "Be still, then, and know that I am God: I will be exalted among the heathen, and I will be exalted in the earth." He was charged with denying the authority of King James VII, teaching the unlawfulness of paying the tax called "cess," and exhorting the people to carry arms at field-meetings. The charges were admitted, and he was sentenced to death. On February 7, 1688, he was executed at the Grassmarket in Edinburgh. More than once his words were drowned by drums. But he sang a part of Ps. 103, the psalm which was always chanted by "the saints" at the celebration of the Sacrament; and as he was turned over the ladder, his last words were: "Lord, into Thy hands I commend my spirit; for Thou hast redeemed me, O Lord, Thou God of Truth"—(Ps. 31, 6).

ROWLAND E. PROTHERO
The Psalms in Human Life

BLOWS THE WIND TO-DAY

Blows the wind to-day, and the sun and the rain are
    flying,
  Blows the wind on the moors to-day and now,
Where about the graves of the martyrs the whaups are
    crying,
  My heart remembers how!

Grey recumbent tombs of the dead in desert places,
  Standing stones on the vacant wine-red moor,
Hills of sheep, and the howes of the silent vanished races,
  And winds, austere and pure:

Be it granted me to behold you again in dying,
  Hills of home! and to hear again the call;
Hear about the graves of the martyrs the peewees crying,
  And hear no more at all.

R. L. STEVENSON (1850-94)

PRINCE CHARLES EDWARD STUART
AND FLORA MACDONALD

Prince Charles Edward, after the battle of Culloden, was conveyed to what is called the Long Island, where he lay for some time concealed. But intelligence having been obtained where he was, and a number of troops having come in quest of him, it became absolutely necessary for him to quit that country without delay. Miss Flora Macdonald then a young lady, animated by what she thought the sacred principle of loyalty, offered, with the magnanimity of a Heroine, to accompany him in an open boat to Sky, though the coast they were to quit was guarded by ships. He dressed himself in women's clothes, and passed as her supposed maid, by the name of Betty Bourke, an Irish girl. They got off undiscovered, though several shots were fired to bring them to, and landed at Mugstot, the seat of Sir Alexander Macdonald. Sir Alexander was then at Fort Augustus, with the Duke of Cumberland; but his lady was at home. Prince Charles took his post upon a hill near the house. Flora Macdonald waited on Lady Margaret, and acquainted her of the enterprise in which she was engaged. Her ladyship, whose active benevolence was ever seconded by superior talents, shewed a perfect presence of mind, and readiness of invention, and at once settled that Prince Charles should be conducted to old Rasay, who was himself concealed with some select friends. The plan was instantly communicated to Kingsburgh, who was dispatched to the hill to inform the Wanderer, and carry him refreshment. When Kingsburgh approached, he started up, and advanced, holding a large knotted stick, and in appearance ready to knock him down, till he said, "I am Macdonald of Kingsburgh, come to serve your highness." The Wanderer answered, "It is well," and was satisfied with the plan.

Flora Macdonald dined with Lady Margaret, at whose table there sat an officer of the army, stationed here with a party of soldiers, to watch for Prince Charles in case of his flying to the isle of Sky. She afterwards often laughed in good humour with this gentleman, on her having so well deceived him.

After dinner, Flora Macdonald on horseback, and her supposed maid, and Kingsburgh, with a servant carrying some linen, all on foot, proceeded towards that gentleman's house. Upon the road was a small rivulet which they were obliged to cross. The Wanderer, forgetting his assumed sex, that his clothes might not be wet, held them up a great deal too high. Kingsburgh mentioned this to him, observing, it might make a discovery. He said he would be more careful for the future. He was as good as his word; for the next brook they crossed, he did not hold up his clothes at all, but let them float upon the water. He was very awkward in his female dress. His size was so large, and his strides so great, that some women whom they met reported that they had seen a very big woman, who looked like a man in women's clothes, and that perhaps it was (as they expressed themselves) the Prince, after whom so much search was making.

At Kingsburgh he met with a most cordial reception; seemed gay at supper, and after it indulged himself in a cheerful glass with his worthy host. As he had not had his clothes off for a long time, the comfort of a good bed was highly relished by him, and he slept soundly till next day at one o'clock.

The mistress of Corrichatachin told me, that in the forenoon she went into her father's room, who was also in bed, and suggested to him her apprehensions that a party of the military might come up, and that his guest and he had better not remain here too long. Her father said, "Let the poor man repose himself after his fatigues; and as for me, I care not, though they take off this old grey head ten or eleven years sooner than I should die in the course of nature." He then wrapped himself in the bed-clothes, and again fell fast asleep.

On the afternoon of that day, the Wanderer, still in the same dress, set out for Portree, with Flora Macdonald and a man servant. His shoes being very bad, Kingsburgh provided him with a new pair, and taking up the old ones, said, "I will faithfully keep them till you are safely settled at St. James's. I will then introduce myself by shaking them at you, to put you in mind of your night's entertainment and protection under my roof."—He smiled, and said, "Be as good as your word!"—Kingsburgh kept the shoes as long as he lived. After his death, a zealous Jacobite gentleman gave twenty guineas for them.

JAMES BOSWELL (1740-95)
Journal of a Tour to the Hebrides

THE ETTRICK SHEPHERD

In Scottish phrase, James Hogg (1770-1835) had ' an unco guid consate o' himsel',' as well he might, for his poetical gifts were of no common order, and raised him far above the general run of rural bards. He was born near Ettrick Kirk in 1770, and was trained to his father's calling of shepherd. Like most other men of mark, he inherited his bright intellect from his mother, Margaret Laidlaw, who used to sing to him as a child the old Border ballads. It was her unrivalled knowledge of these that brought the Hoggs a visit from Walter Scott, in his search for material for the third volume of his *Border Minstrelsy*. By that time, 1803, Hogg had published a small volume of *Pastorals*, etc., which fell quite flat. He was at some field work when they brought him word that ' the Shirra and some o' his gang' were at the cottage, and wanted to see him. Mrs. Hogg delighted

197

Scott by chanting the ballad of *Auld Maitland*. He asked, her if it had ever been in print. ' O na, na, sir,' said she, ' there never was ane o' my sangs prentit till ye prentit them yoursel', an' ye hae spoilt them a' the gither. They were made for singing, an no' for reading, an' they'll never be sung nae mair.' Scott laughed merrily, and answered the dame by a couplet from Wordsworth. ' Ye'll find,' she persisted, ' that it's a' true that I'm tellin' ye.' And so it has proved; for, as James Hogg himself said, ' from that day to this, these songs, which were the amusement of many a long winter evening, have never been sung more.'

Few people read the Ettrick Shepherd now; some love his verse—*When the Kye comes Hame*, for example— without any suspicion of the authorship; but the late Professor Ferrier's judgment holds good, pronouncing him to be, ' after Burns, *proximus sed longo intervallo*, the greatest poet that has ever sprung from the bosom of the common people.'

SIR HERBERT MAXWELL
The Story of the Tweed

BRAXFIELD, THE HANGING JUDGE

The giant of the bench was Braxfield. His very name makes people start yet. Strong built and dark, with rough eyebrows, powerful eyes, threatening lips, and a low growling voice, he was like a formidable blacksmith. His accent and his dialect were exaggerated Scotch; his language, like his thoughts, short, strong, and conclusive.

Our commercial jurisprudence was only rising when he was sinking, and, being no reader, he was too old in life and habit to master it familiarly. But within the range of the feudal and the civil branches, and in every matter depending on natural ability and practical sense, he was very great; and his powers arose more from the force of his reasoning, and his vigorous application of principle, than from either the extent or the accuracy of his learning. I have heard good observers describe with admiration how, having worked out a principle, he followed it to its application, fearlessly and triumphantly, dashing all unworthy obstructions aside, and pushed on to his result with the vigour and disdain of a consummate athlete. And he had a colloquial way of arguing, in the form of question and answer, which, done in his own clear, abrupt style, imparted a dramatic directness of vivacity to the scene.

With this intellectual force, as applied to law, his merits, I fear, cease. Illiterate and without any taste for refined enjoyment, strength of understanding which gave him power without cultivation, only encouraged him to a more contemptuous disdain of natures less coarse than his own. Thousands of his sayings have been preserved, and the staple of them is indecency. Almost the only story of him I ever heard that had some fun in it without immodesty, was when a butler gave up his place because his lordship's wife was always scolding him. "Lord!" he exclaimed, "ye've little to complain o'; ye may be thankfu' ye're no married to her."

It is impossible to condemn his conduct as a criminal judge too gravely, or too severely. It was a disgrace to the age. A dexterous and practical trier of ordinary cases, he was harsh to prisoners even in his jocularity, and to every counsel whom he chose to dislike. But all the stains on his administration of the common business of his court disappear in the indelible iniquity of the political trials of 1793 and 1794. In these he was the Jeffreys of Scotland. "Let them bring me prisoners, and I'll find them law," used to be openly stated as his suggestion, when an intended political prosecution was marred by anticipated difficulties. Mr. Horner, who was one of the jurors in Muir's case, told me that when he was passing behind the bench to get into the box, Braxfield, who knew him, whispered—"Come awa', Maister Horner, come awa', and help us to hang ane o' thae daamed scoondrels!"

HENRY, LORD COCKBURN (1779-1854)
Memorials of my own Time

THE SKYLARK

Bird of the wilderness,
Blithesome and cumberless,
Sweet be thy matin o'er moorland and lea!
Emblem of happiness,
Blest is thy dwelling-place—
Oh, to abide in the desert with thee!

Wild is thy lay and loud,
Far in the downy cloud,
Love gives it energy, love gave it birth.
Where, on thy dewy wing,
Where art thou journeying?
Thy lay is in heaven, thy love is on earth.

O'er fell and fountain sheen,
O'er moor and mountain green,
O'er the red streamer that heralds the day,
Over the cloudlet dim,
Over the rainbow's rim,
Musical cherub, soar, singing, away!

Then, when the gloaming comes,
Low in the heather blooms
Sweet will thy welcome and bed of love be!
Emblem of happiness,
Blest is thy dwelling-place—
Oh, to abide in the desert with thee!

JAMES HOGG (1770-1835)

THE PARENTS OF BURNS

William Burness and Agnes Brown were "Married together," 15th December, 1757:

> "Had a son, *Robert*, 25th Jan., 1759
> Had a son, *Gilbert*, 28th Sep., 1760
> Had a daughter, *Agnes*, 30th Sep., 1762
> Had a daughter, *Annabella*, 14th Nov., 1764
> Had a son, *William*, 30th July, 1767
> Had a son, *John*, 10th July, 1769
> Had a daughter, *Isabel*, 27th June, 1771."

Family Bible Record

According to Mrs. Begg (Isabel the seventh and last child of William and Agnes Burness) her mother was about the ordinary height;—a well-made, sonsy figure, with a beautiful red and white complexion—a skin the most transparent Mrs. Begg ever saw—red hair, dark eyes and eyebrows with a fine square forehead. With all her good qualities—and they were many—her temper, at times, was irascible. William Burness, the father of the poet, was a thin, sinewy figure, about five feet eight or nine inches in height, somewhat bent with toil; his haffet-locks thin and bare, with a dark, swarthy complexion. From this it will be seen that Burns inherited his *swarthy* complexion from his father—not from his mother, as stated by Cunningham: men who rise to celebrity in the world, are generally supposed to inherit their *genius* from the maternal side. If it shall be said that Burns inherited his love of ballad-lore from his mother, we may presume that he derived his strong manly sense from his father:—as to his *genius*—' the light that led astray was light from heaven.' It may be traced in most of his poems, and flashes out in his lyrics, like sheet-lightning in a summer's eve, when sung to the simple and pathetic melodies of his native land.

CAPTAIN CHARLES GRAY
Wood's Songs of Scotland, 1848

THE CHILDHOOD OF BURNS

At those years I was by no means a favourite with anybody. I was a good deal noted for a retentive memory, a stubborn sturdy something in my disposition, and enthusiastic idiot piety. I say *idiot* piety, because I was then but a child. Though it cost the schoolmaster some thrashings, I made an excellent English scholar; and by the time I was ten or eleven years of age, I was a critic in substantives, verbs, and particles. In my infant and boyish days, too, I owed much to an old woman who resided in the family, remarkable for her ignorance, credulity, and superstition. She had, I suppose, the largest collection in the country of tales and songs concerning devils, ghosts, fairies, brownies, witches, warlocks, spunkies, kelpies, elf-candles, dead-lights, wraiths, apparitions, cantraips, giants, enchanted towers, dragons, and other trumpery. This cultivated the latent seeds of poetry; but had so strong an effect on my imagination, that to this hour, in my nocturnal rambles, I sometimes keep a sharp look-out in suspicious places; and though nobody can be more sceptical than I am in such matters, yet it often takes an effort of philosophy to shake off these idle terrors. The earliest composition that I recollect taking pleasure in, was *The Vision of Mirza*, and a hymn of Addison's, beginning, *How are thy servants blest, O Lord!* I particularly remember one half-stanza, which was music to my boyish ear:

"For though on dreadful whirls we hung
   High on the broken wave——"

I met with these pieces in *Masson's English Collection*, one of my school-books. The two first books I ever read in private, and which gave me more pleasure than any two books I ever read since, were *The Life of Hannibal*, and

The History of Sir William Wallace. Hannibal gave my young ideas such a turn, that I used to strut in raptures up and down after the recruiting drum and bagpipe, and wish myself tall enough to be a soldier; while the story of Wallace poured a tide of Scottish prejudice into my veins, which will boil along there till the flood-gates of life shut on eternal rest.

ROBERT BURNS (1759-96)

FOR THE FUTURE BE PREPAR'D

For the future be prepar'd,
Guard wherever thou can'st guard;
But thy utmost duly done,
Welcome what thou can'st not shun.
Follies past, give thou to air,
Make their *consequence* thy care:
Keep the name of Man in mind,
And dishonour not thy kind.
Reverence with lowly heart
Him, whose wondrous work thou art;
Keep His Goodness still in view,
Thy trust, and thy example, too.

ROBERT BURNS (1759-96)
verses in *Friar's Carse Hermitage*

THE YOUTHFUL BURNS

In my seventeenth year to give my manners a brush I went to a country dancing school. My father had an unaccountable antipathy against these meetings, and my going was, what to this moment I repent, in opposition to his wishes. My father was subject to strong passions: from that instance of disobedience in me, he took a sort of dislike to me and it was, I believe, one cause of the dissipation which marked my succeeding years. I say dissipation, comparatively with the strictness and sobriety and regularity of Presbyterian country life: for though the Will o' the Wisp meteors of thoughtless whim were almost the sole lights of my path, yet early ingrained piety and virtue kept me for several years afterwards within the line of innocence.

The great misfortune of my life was to want an aim. I saw that my Father's situation entailed on me perpetual labour. The only two openings by which I could enter the temple of Fortune were the gate of niggardly economising or the path of little chicaning bargain-making. The former is so contracted an aperture I could never squeeze myself into it: the last I always hated: there was contamination in the very entrance. . . .

But far beyond all other impulses of my heart was *un pechant à l'adorable moitié du genre humain.* My heart was completely tinder and was eternally lighted up by some goddess or other, and as in every other warfare in this world my fortune was various. Sometimes I was received with favour; sometimes I was mortified with a repulse. At the plough, scythe or reap-hood I feared no competitor and thus I set absolute want at defiance, and as I never cared further for my labours than when I was in actual exercise, I spent the evenings in the way after my own heart.

A country lad seldom carries on a love adventure without an assisting confidant. I possessed a curiosity, zeal and intrepid dexterity that recommended me as a proper second on these occasions, and I dare say I felt as much pleasure in being in the secret of half the loves of the parish of Tarbolton as ever did statesman in knowing the intrigues of half the courts of Europe.

ROBERT BURNS (1759-96)

THE POET IS BORN NOT MADE

But, first an' foremost I should tell,
Amaist as soon as I could spell,
I to the crambo-jingle fell:
    Tho' rude an' rough—
Yet crooning to a body's sel'
    Does well enough.

I am nae poet, in a sense,
But just a rhymer like by chance,
An' hae to learning nae pretence;
    Yet, what the matter?
Whene'er my muse does on me glance,
    I jingle at her.

Your critic-folk may cock their nose,
And say, "How can you e'er propose,
You wha ken hardly verse frae prose
    To make a song?"
But, by your leaves, my learned foes,
    Ye're maybe wrong.

What's a' your jargon o' your schools—
Your Latin names for horns an' stools?
If honest nature made you fools,
    What sairs your grammar?
Ye'd better taen up spades and shools,
    Or knappin-hammers.

A set o' dull, conceited hashes
Confuse their brains in college-classes!
They gang in stirks, and come out asses,
    Plain truth to speak;
And syne they think to climb Parnassus
    By dint o' Greek.

> Gie me ae spark o' nature's fire,
> That's a' the learning I desire;
> Then tho' I drudge thro' dub an' mire
>   At plough or cart,
> My muse, tho' hamely in attire,
>   May touch the heart.

ROBERT BURNS (1759-96)
Epistle to Lapraik

BURNS AND JEAN ARMOUR

Burns first met Jean Armour (1767-1834) in 1784, soon after his mother, his brother Gilbert and he took tenancy of the farm of Mossgiel. The following letter refers to Jean's return to Mauchline after a three months' absence in Paisley in 1786.

Poor, ill-advised, ungrateful Armour came home on Friday last. You have heard all the particulars of that affair, and a black affair it is. What she thinks of her conduct now, I don't know; one thing I do know—she has made me completely miserable. Never man loved, or rather adored, a woman more than I did her; and, to confess a truth between you and me, I do still love her to distraction after all, though I won't tell her so if I were to see her, which I don't want to do.

May Almighty God forgive her ingratitude and perjury to me, as I from my very soul forgive her; and may His grace be with her and bless her in all her future life! I can have no nearer idea of the place of eternal punishment than what I have felt in my own breast on her account. I have tried often to forget her; I have run into all kinds of dissipation and riots, mason-meetings, drinking-matches, and other mischief, to drive her out of my head,—but all in vain. And now for a grand cure!—The ship is on her way home that is to take me out to Jamaica; and then, farewell dear old Scotland! and farewell dear, ungrateful Jean! for never, never shall I see you more.

You will have heard that I am going to commence poet in print; and to-morrow my works go to the press. I expect it will be a volume of about 200 pages: it is just the last foolish thing I intend to do; and then turn a wise man as fast as possible.

Letter to David Bryce, at Glasgow (June 12th, 1786)

A RED, RED ROSE

O, my luve's like a red, red rose,
    That's newly sprung in June:
O, my luve's like the melodie
    That's sweetly played in tune.

As fair art thou, my bonnie lass,
    So deep in luve am I;
And I will luve thee still, my dear,
    Till a' the seas gang dry.

Till a' the seas gang dry, my dear,
    And the rocks melt wi' the sun:
And I will luve thee still, my dear,
    While the sands o' life shall run.

And fare thee well, my only luve!
    And fare thee well a while!
And I will come again, my luve,
    Though it were ten thousand mile.

ROBERT BURNS (1759-96)

MEETING OF BURNS AND SCOTT

As for Burns, I may truly say, *Virgilium vidi tantum.*
I was a lad of fifteen in 1786-7, when he came first to
Edinburgh, but had sense and feeling enough to be much
interested in his poetry, and would have given the world
to know him: but I had very little acquaintance with
any literary people, and still less with the gentry of the
west country, the two sets that he most frequented.
Mr. Thomas Grierson was at that time a clerk of my
father's. He knew Burns, and promised to ask him to
his lodgings to dinner; but had no opportunity to keep
his word; otherwise I might have seen more of this
distinguished man. As it was, I saw him one day at
the late venerable Professor Ferguson's, where there were
several gentlemen of literary reputation, among whom
I remember the celebrated Mr. Dugald Stewart. Of
course, we youngsters sat silent, looked and listened.
The only thing I remember which was remarkable in
Burns's manner, was the effect produced upon him by
a print of Bunbury's, representing a soldier lying dead
on the snow, his dog sitting in misery on one side,—
on the other, his widow, with a child in her arms. These
lines were written beneath:

"Cold on Canadian hills, or Minden's plain,
  Perhaps that mother wept her soldier slain;
  Bent o'er her babe, her eye dissolved in dew,
  The big drops, mingling with the milk he drew.
  Gave the sad presage of his future years,
  The child of misery baptised in tears."

Burns seemed much affected by the print, or rather by
the ideas which it suggested to his mind. He actually
shed tears. He asked whose the lines were; and it
chanced that nobody but myself remembered that they
occur in a half-forgotten poem of Langhorne's, called

by the umpromising title of "The Justice of Peace." I whispered my information to a friend present; he mentioned it to Burns, who rewarded me with a look and a word, which, though of mere civility, I then received and still recollect with very great pleasure.

His person was strong and robust; his manners rustic, not clownish; a sort of dignified plainness and simplicity, which received part of its effect perhaps from one's knowledge of his extraordinary talents. His features are represented in Mr. Nasmyth's picture; but to me it conveys the idea that they are diminished, as if seen in perspective. I think his countenance was more massive than it looks in any of the portraits. I should have taken the poet, had I not known what he was, for a very sagacious country farmer of the old Scotch school, *i.e.* none of your modern agriculturists who keep labourers for their drudgery, but the *douce gudeman* who held his own plough. There was a strong expression of sense and shrewdness in all his lineaments; the eye alone, I think indicated the poetical character and temperament. It was large, and of a dark cast, which glowed (I say literally *glowed*) when he spoke with feeling or interest. I never saw such another eye in a human head, though I have seen the most distinguished men of my time. His conversation expressed perfect self-confidence, without the slightest presumption. Among the men who were the most learned of their time and country, he expressed himself with perfect firmness, but without the least intrusive forwardness; and when he differed in opinion, he did not hesitate to express it firmly, yet at the same time with modesty. I do not remember any part of his conversation distinctly enough to be quoted; nor did I ever see him again, except in the street, where he did not recognise me, as I could not expect he should. He was much caressed in Edinburgh: but (considering what literary emoluments have been since his day) the efforts made for his relief were extremely trifling.

I remember, on this occasion I mention, I thought Burns's acquaintance with English poetry was rather limited; and also that, having twenty times the abilities of Allan Ramsay and of Fergusson, he talked of them with too much humility as his models: there was doubtless national predilection in his estimate.

This is all I can tell you about Burns. I have only to add, that his dress corresponded with his manner. He was like a farmer dressed in his best to dine with the laird. I do not speak *in malam partem*, when I say, I never saw a man in company with his superiors in station or information more perfectly free from either the reality or the affectation of embarrassment. I was told, but did not observe it, that his address to females was extremely deferential, and always with a turn either to the pathetic or humorous, which engaged their attention particularly.

J. G. LOCKHART (1794-1854)
Life of Robert Burns

ROBERT BURNS TO WILLIAM NICOL
(*Classical Master, The High School, Edinburgh*)

CARLISLE,
June 1st, 1787

Kind, Honest-Hearted Willie,

I'm sitten down here, after seven and forty miles ridin', e'en as forjesket and forniaw'd as a forfoughten cock, to gie you some notion o' my land-lowperlike stravaguin, sin the sorrowfu' hour that I sheuk hands and parted with auld Reekie.

My auld, ga'd gleyde o' a meere has huchyall'd up hill and down brae, in Scotland and England, as teugh and birnie as a vera devil wi' me. It's true, she's as poor's a sang-maker and as hard's a kirk, and tipper-taipers when

210

she taks the gate, first like a lady's gentlewoman in a minuwae, or a hen on a het girdle; but she's a yauld, poutherie Girran for a' that, and has a stomack like Willie Stalker's meere that wad hae digeested tumbler-wheels, for she'll whip me aff her five stimparts o' the best aits at a down-sittin and ne'er fash her thumb. When ance her ringbanes and spavies, her crucks and cramps, are fairly soupl'd, she beets to, beets to, and ay the hindmost hour the tightest. I could wager her price to a thretty pennies, that for twa or three wooks ridin at fifty mile a day, the deil-sticket a five gallopers acqueesh Clyde and Whithorn could cast saut on her tail.

I hae dander'd owre a' the kintra frae Dumbar to Selcraig, and hae forgather'd wi' mony a guid fallow, and monie a weelfar'd hizzie. I met wi' twa dink quines in particlar, ane o' them a sonsie, fine, fodgel lass, baith braw and bonnie: the tither was a clean-shankit, straught, tight, weel-far'd winch, as blythe's a lint-white on a flowerie thorn, and as sweet and modest's a new blawn plumrose in a hazle shaw. They were baith bred to mainers by the beuk, and onie ane o' them had as muckle smeddum and rumblgumtion as the half o' some presbyteries that you and I baith ken. They play'd me sik a deevil o' a shavie that I daur say if my harigals were turn'd out, ye wad see twa nicks i' the heart o' me like the mark o' a kail-whittle in a castock.

I was gaun to write you a lang pystle, but, Gude forgie me, I gat myself sae noutouriously bitchify'd the day after rail-time, that I can hardly stoiter but and ben.

My best respecks to the guidwife and a' our common friens, especiall Mr. and Mrs. Cruickshank, and the honest guidman o' Jock's Lodge.

I'll be in Dumfries the morn gif the beast be to the fore, and the branks bid hale.

Gude be wi' you, Willie! Amen!

R.B.

ROBERT BURNS AND CLARINDA

From December 6th, 1787 to February 18th, 1788, a close epistolary correspondence was maintained between Burns and Mrs. M'Lehose who, after the first half-dozen letters had been interchanged, adopted the pastoral name of *Clarinda*. Burns took that of *Sylvander*, because he said he liked "the idea of Arcadian names in a commerce of this kind." Burns was confined indoors for nearly six weeks as a result of a fall from a coach in which he sustained a bruised knee, but he was able to visit *Clarinda* for the second time on January 4th, 1788, and the intercourse, epistolary and personal, continued with little interruption till nearly the end of March, when it was brought to a sudden termination.

Oh, what a fool I am in love! what an extraordinary prodigal of affection! Why are your sex called the tender sex, when I have never met with one who can repay me in passion? They are either not so rich in love as I am, or they are niggards where I am lavish.

O Thou whose I am, and whose are all my ways! Thou seest me here, the hapless wreck of tides and tempests in my own bosom: do Thou direct to Thyself that ardent love for which I have so often sought a return, in vain, from my fellow-creatures! If Thy goodness has yet such a gift in store for me, as an equal return of affection from her who, Thou knowest, is dearer to me than life, do Thou bless and hallow our bond of love and friendship; watch over us in all our outgoings and incomings, for good; and may the tie that unites our hearts be strong and indissoluble as the thread of man's immortal life!

Sylvander

AE FOND KISS

Ae fond kiss, and then we sever,—
Ae fareweel, and then—for ever
Deep in heart-wrung tears I'll pledge thee!
Warring sighs and groans I'll wage thee!

Who shall say that fortune grieves him,
While the star of hope she leaves him?
Me, nae chearfu' twinkle lights me,—
Dark despair around benights me.

I'll ne'er blame my partial fancy,
Naething could resist my Nancy;
But to see her, was to love her—
Love but her, and love for ever.

Had we never lov'd sae kindly—
Had we never lov'd sae blindly—
Never met—or never parted,
We had ne'er been broken-hearted!

Fare-thee-weel, thou first and fairest!
Fare-thee-weel, thou best and dearest!
Thine be ilka joy and treasure,
Peace, Enjoyment, Love and Pleasure!

Ae fond kiss, and then we sever!
Ae fareweel, alas! for ever!
Deep in heart-wrung tears I'll pledge thee
Warring sighs and groans I'll wage thee.

ROBERT BURNS (1759-96)

TRUE CONTENT

When winds frae off Ben Lomond blaw,
An' bar the doors wi' drivin' snaw,
  An' hing us owre the ingle,
I set me down to pass the time,
An' spin a verse or twa o' rhyme;
  In hamely, westlin' jingle!
When frosty winds blaw in the drifts,
  Ben to the chimla lug,
I grudge a wee the great-folk's gift,
  That live sae bien an' snug:
    I tent less, and want less
      Their roomy fire-side;
    But hanker, and canker,
      To see their cursed pride.

It's hardly in a body's pow'r,
To keep, at times, frae being sour,
  To see how things are shar'd;
How best o' chiels are whyles in want,
While coofs on countless thousands rant,
  And ken na how to ware't,
But Davie, lad, ne'er fash your head
  Tho' we hae little gear;
We're fit to win our daily bread,
  As lang's we're hale and fier:
    'Mair spier na', nor fear na',
      Auld age ne'er mind a feg;
    The last o't, the warst o't,
      Is only but to beg.

To lye in kilns and barns at e'en,
When banes are craz'd, and bluid is thin,
  Is, doubtless, great distress!
Yet then content could make us blest;

Ev'n then, sometimes, we'd snatch a taste
    Of truest happiness.
The honest heart that's free frae a'
    Intended fraud or guile,
However Fortune kick the ba',
    Has ay some cause to smile;
        An' mind still, you'll find still,
            A comfort this nae sma';
        Nae mair then, we'll care then,
            Nae further we can fa'.

What tho', like commoners of air,
We wander out, we know not where,
    But either house or hal',
Yet nature's charms, the hills and woods,
The sweeping vales, and foaming floods,
    Are free alike to all.
In days when daisies deck the ground,
    And blackbirds whistle clear,
With honest joy our hearts will bound,
    To see the coming year:
        On braes when we please then,
            We'll sit an' sowth a tune;
        Syne rhyme till't, we'll time till't,
            An sing't when we hae dune.

It's no in titles nor in rank;
It's no in wealth like Lon'on bank,
    To purchase peace and rest:
It's no in making muckle, mair;
It's no in books, it's no in lear,
    To make us truly blest:
If happiness hae not her seat
    And centre in the breast,
We may be wise, or rich, or great,
    But never can be blest;
        Nae treasures nor pleasures

> Could make us happy lang;
> The heart ay's the part ay
> That makes us right or wrang.

ROBERT BURNS (1759-96)
Epistle to Davie

BURNS AS CONVERSATIONALIST

Burns's gifts, expressed in conversation, are the theme of all that ever heard him. All kinds of gifts: from the gracefullest utterances of courtesy, to the highest fire of passionate speech; loud floods of mirth, soft wailings of affection, laconic emphasis, clear piercing insight; all was in him. Witty duchesses celebrate him as a man whose speech "led them off their feet." This is beautiful: but still more beautiful that which Mr. Lockhart has recorded, which I have more than once alluded to, how the waiters and ostlers at inns would get out of bed, and come crowding to hear this man speak! Waiters and ostlers:—they too were men, and here was a man! I have heard much about his speech; but one of the best things I ever heard of it was, last year, from a venerable gentleman long familiar with him. That it was speech distinguished by always *having something in it.* "He spoke rather little than much," this old man told me; "sat rather silent in those early days, as in the company of persons above him; and always when he did speak, it was to throw new light on the matter." I know not why any one should ever speak otherwise!—But if we look at his general force of soul, his healthy *robustness* everyway, the rugged downrightness, penetration, generous valour and manfulness that was in him,— where shall we readily find a better-gifted man?

THOMAS CARLYLE (1795-1881)
Heroes and Hero-Worship

BURNS IN DUMFRIES

"A gentleman of that county has often told me that he was seldom more grieved, than when riding into Dumfries one fine summer evening about this time to attend a county ball, he saw Burns walking alone, on the shady side of the principal street of the town, while the opposite side was gay with successive groups of gentlemen and ladies, all drawn together for the festivities of the night, not one of whom appeared willing to recognise him. The horseman dismounted, and joined Burns, who on his proposing to cross the street said: ' Nay, nay, my young friend, that's all over now '; and quoted, after a pause, some verses of Lady Grizzel Baillie's pathetic ballad:

> His bonnet stood ance fu' fair on his brow,
> His auld ane look'd better than mony ane's new;
> But now he lets 't wear ony way it will hing,
> And casts himself dowie upon the corn-bing.
>
> O were we young, as we ance hae been,
> We sud hae been galloping down on yon green,
> And linking it ower the lily-white lea!
> *An' werena my heart light, I wad die.*"

It was little in Burns's character to let his feelings on certain subjects escape in this fashion. He, immediately after reciting these verses, assumed the sprightliness of his most pleasing manner; and taking his young friend home with him, entertained him very agreeably till the hour of the ball arrived."

J. G. LOCKHART (1794-1854)
Life of Burns

ON THE EVE OF DEATH

Alas, my friend, I fear the voice of the bard will soon be heard among you no more. For these eight or ten months, I have been ailing, sometimes bedfast, and sometimes not; but these three months, I have been tortured by an excruciating rheumatism, which has reduced me to nearly the last stage. You actually would not know me if you saw me. Pale, emaciated, and so feeble as occasionally to need help from my chair, my spirits fled—fled!—but I can no more on this subject. The deuce of the matter is this: when an exciseman is off duty, his salary is reduced to £35, instead of £50. What way, in the name of thrift, shall I maintain myself, and keep a horse in country quarters, with a wife and five children at home, on £50?

Letter from BURNS to Alexander Cunningham
(July 7th, 1796)

Madam, I have written you so often without receiving any answer, that I would not trouble you again, but for the circumstances in which I am. An illness which has hung about me, will, in all probability, speedily send me beyond that *bourne, whence no traveller returns*! Your friendship, with which for so many years you honored me, was a friendship dearest to my soul. Your conversation, and especially your correspondence, were at once highly entertaining and instructive. With what pleasure did I use to break the seal! The remembrance yet adds one pulse more to my poor palpitating heart. Farewell!!—R.B.

Letter from BURNS to Mrs. Dunlop
(July 12th, 1796)

THE LITTLE VALCLUSA FOUNTAIN

The world is habitually unjust in its judgments of such men; unjust on many grounds, of which this one may be stated as the substance: It decides, like a court of law, by dead statutes; and not positively but negatively, less on what is done right, than on what is or is not done wrong. Granted, the ship comes into harbour with shrouds and tackle damaged; the pilot is blameworthy; he has not been all-wise and all-powerful: but to know *how* blameworthy, tell us first whether his voyage has been round the Globe, or only to Ramsgate and the Isle of Dogs.

With our readers in general, with men of right feeling anywhere, we are not required to plead for Burns. In pitying admiration he lies enshrined in all our hearts, in a far nobler mausoleum than that one of marble; neither will his Works, even as they are, pass away from the memory of men. While the Shakespeares and Miltons roll on like mighty rivers through the country of Thought, bearing fleets of traffickers and assiduous pearl-fishers on their waves; this little Valclusa Fountain will also arrest our eye; for this also is of Nature's own and most cunning workmanship, bursts from the depths of the earth, with a full gushing current, into the light of day; and often will the traveller turn aside to drink of its clear waters, and muse among its rocks and pines!

THOMAS CARLYLE (1795-1881)
Essay on Burns

ROB ROY, 1671-1734

A famous man is Robin Hood,
The English ballad-singer's joy!
And Scotland has a thief as good,
An outlaw of as daring mood;
   She has her brave Rob Roy!

Heaven gave Rob Roy a dauntless heart,
And wondrous length and strength of arm;
Nor craved he more to quell his foes,
   Or keep his friends from harm.

Yet was Rob Roy as *wise* as brave;
Forgive me if the phrase be strong;—
A poet worthy of Rob Roy
   Must scorn a timid song.

Say, then, that he was wise as brave;
As wise in thought as bold in deed:
For in the principles of things
   He sought his moral creed.

Said generous Rob, "What need of books?
Burn all the statutes and their shelves;
They stir us up against our kind:
   And worse, against ourselves.

"We have a passion, make a law,
Too false to guide us or control!
And for the law itself we fight
   In bitterness of soul.

"And puzzled, blinded thus, we lose
Distinctions that are plain and few;
These find I graven on my heart:
   That tells me what to do.

"The creatures see of flood and field,
And those that travel on the wind!
With them no strife can last; they live
※ In peace, and peace of mind.

"For why?—because the good old rule
Sufficeth them, the simple plan,
That they should take who have the power,
    And they should keep who can.

"Since, then, the rule of right is plain,
And longest life is but a day;
To have my ends, maintain my rights,
    I'll take the shortest way."

And thus among these rocks he lived,
Through summer's heat and winter's snow:
The eagle, he was lord above,
    And Rob was lord below.

WILLIAM WORDSWORTH (1770-1850)

DIALOGUE WITH CHARON

Mr. Hume's magnanimity and firmness were such that his most affectionate friends knew that they hazarded nothing in talking and writing to him as a dying man, and that so far from being hurt by this frankness he was rather pleased and flattered by it. . . . "When I lie down in the evening," he said, "I feel myself weaker than when I rose in the morning, and when I rise in the morning weaker than when I lay down in the evening. I am sensible that some of my vital parts are affected, so that I must soon die."

"Well," said I, "if must be so, you have at least the satisfaction of leaving all your friends, your brother's family in particular, in great prosperity!"

He said that he felt that satisfaction so sensibly that

221

when he was reading, a few days before, Lucian's *Dialogues of the Dead* amongst all the excuses which are alleged to Charon he could not find one that fitted him; he had no house to finish, he had no daughter to provide for: he had no enemies upon whom he wished to revenge himself. "I could not well imagine," he said, "what excuse I could make to Charon in order to obtain a little delay. I have done everything of consequence which I ever meant to do, and I could at no time expect to leave my relations and friends in a better situation than that in which I am now likely to leave them. I, therefore, have every reason to die contented."

He then diverted himself with inventing several jocular excuses which he supposed he might make to Charon and with imagining the very surly answers which it might suit the character of Charon to return to them. "Upon further consideration," said he, "I thought I might say to him, 'Good Charon, I have been correcting my works for a new edition. Allow me a little time to see how the public receives the alterations'! But Charon would answer: 'When you have seen the effect of these you will be for making other alterations. There will be no end of such excuses: so, honest friend, please step into the boat'!

"But I might still urge, 'Have a little patience, good Charon, I have been endeavouring to open the eyes of the public. If I live a few years longer, I may have the satisfaction of seeing the downfall of the prevailing system of superstition.' But Charon would then lose all temper and decency. 'You loitering rogue, that will not happen these many hundred years. Do you fancy I will grant you a leave for so long a term? Get into the boat this instant, you lazy, loitering rogue.'"

DAVID HUME (1711-76)
My Own Life

CARLYLE TO MRS. CARLYLE

Not unlike what the drop of water from Lazarus's finger might have been to Dives in the flame was my dearest Goody's letter to her husband yesterday afternoon. Blacklock had retired to the bank for fifteen minutes; the whirlwind was sleeping for that brief season, and I smoking my pipe in grim repose, when Alick came back with your messenger. No; I do not love you in the least—only a little *sympathy* and *admiration*, and a certain *esteem*. Nothing more! oh my dear best wee woman—but not a word of all this.

Such a day I never had in my life, but it is all over and well, and now "Home, brothers, home!"

Oh, Jeannie, how happy shall we be in this Craig o' Putta! Not that I look for an Arcadia or a Lubberland there; but we shall sit under our bramble and our saugh tree, and none to make us afraid; and my little wife will be there for ever beside me, and I shall be well and blest, and "the latter end of that man will be better than the beginning."

Surely I shall learn at length to prize the pearl of great price which God has given to me unworthy. Surely I already know that to me the richest treasure of this sublunary life has been awarded—the heart of my own noble Jane. Shame on me for complaining, sick and wretched though I be. Bourbon and Braganza, when I think of it, are but poor men to me. Oh Jeannie! oh my wife! we will never part, never through eternity itself; but I will love thee and keep thee in my heart of hearts! that is, unless I grow a very great fool—which, indeed, this talk doth somewhat betoken.

God bless thee! Ever thine,

THOMAS CARLYLE (1795-1881)

223

SCOTT AT SMAILHOLM TOWER

Thus while I ape the measure wild
Of tales that charm'd me yet a child,
Rude though they be, still with the chime
Return the thoughts of early time;
And feelings, roused in life's first day,
Glow in the line, and prompt the lay.
Then rise those crags, that mountain tower,
Which charm'd my fancy's wakening hour.
Though no broad river swept along,
To claim, perchance, heroic song;
Though sigh'd no groves in summer gale,
To prompt of love a softer tale;
Though scarce a puny streamlet's speed
Claim'd homage from a shepherd's reed;
Yet was poetic impulse given,
By the green hill and clear blue heaven.
It was a barren scene, and wild,
Where naked cliffs were rudely piled;
But ever and anon between
Lay velvet tufts of loveliest green;
And well the lonely infant knew
Recesses where the wall-flower grew,
And honey-suckle loved to crawl
Up the low crag and ruin'd wall.
I deem'd such nooks the sweetest shade
The sun in all its round survey'd;
And still I thought that shatter'd tower
The mightiest work of human power;
And marvell'd as the aged hind
With some strange tale bewitch'd my mind,
Of forayers, who, with headlong force,
Down from that strength had spurr'd their horse,
Their southern rapine to renew,
Far in the distant Cheviots blue,

And, home returning, fill'd the hall
With revel, wassel-rout, and brawl.
Methought that still with trump and clang,
The gateway's broken arches rang;
Methought grim features, seam'd with scars,
Glared through the window's rusty bars,
And ever, by the winter hearth,
Old tales I heard of woe or mirth,
Of lovers' slights, of ladies' charms,
Of witches' spells, of warriors' arms;
Of patriot battles, won of old
By Wallace wight and Bruce the bold;
Of later fields of feud and fight,
When, pouring from their Highland height,
The Scottish clans, in headlong sway,
Had swept the scarlet ranks away.
While stretch'd at length upon the floor,
Again I fought each combat o'er,
Pebbles and shells, in order laid,
The mimic ranks of war display'd;
And onward still the Scottish Lion bore,
And still the scatter'd Southron fled before.

SIR WALTER SCOTT (1771-1832)
Marmion

THE EYDENT HAND

It was a party of very young persons, most of them,
like Menzies and myself, destined for the Bar of Scotland,
all gay and thoughtless, enjoying the first flush of
manhood, with little remembrance of the yesterday, or
care of the morrow. When my companion's worthy
father and uncle, after seeing two or three bottles go
round, left the juveniles to themselves, the weather being
hot, we adjourned to a library which had one large

225

window looking northwards. After carousing here for an hour or more, I observed that a shade had come over the aspect of my friend, who happened to be placed immediately opposite to myself, and said something that intimated a fear of his being unwell. "No," said he, "I shall be well enough presently, if you will only let me sit where you are, and take my chair; for there is a confounded hand in sight of me here, which has often bothered me before, and now it won't let me fill my glass with a good will." I rose to change places with him accordingly, and he pointed out to me this hand which, like the writing on Belshazzar's wall, disturbed his hour of hilarity. "Since we sat down," he said, "I have been watching it—it fascinates my eye—it never stops—page after page is finished and thrown on that heap of MS., and still it goes on unwearied—and so it will be till candles are brought in, and God knows how long after that. It is the same every night—I can't stand a sight of it when I am not at my books."—"Some stupid, dogged, engrossing clerk, probably," exclaimed myself, or some other giddy youth in our society. "No, boys," said our host, "I well know what hand it is—'tis Walter Scott's." This was the hand that, in the evenings of three summer weeks, wrote the two last volumes of *Waverley*.

J. G. LOCKHART (1794-1854)
Life of Scott

PET MARJORIE

The child-friend of Sir Walter Scott

Sir Walter sat down in his large, green morocco elbow-chair, drew himself close to his table, and glowered and gloomed at his writing apparatus. He took out his paper, then starting up angrily, said, "Go spin, you jade, go spin. No, hang it, it won't do—I am off the fang! I can make nothing of *Waverley* to-day; I'll awa to Marjorie! Come wi' me, Maida, you thief!" The great dog rose slowly, and the pair were off. Scott taking a *maud* (plaid) with him. Maida gambolled and whisked among the snow, and his master strode across to the house of his dear friend, Mrs. William Keith. Sir Walter was in that house almost every day, and had a key, so in he and the hound went, shaking themselves in the lobby. "Marjorie! Marjorie!' shouted her friend, "where are ye, my bonnie wee croodlin' doo?" In a moment a bright, eager child of seven was in his arms, and he was kissing her all over. Out came Mrs. Keith, "Come yer ways in, Wattie." "No, not now, I am going to take Marjorie wi' me, and you may come to your tea in Duncan Roy's sedan, and bring the bairn home in your lap." "Tak' Marjorie, and it an *on-ding o' snow!*" "Hoot, awa! look here," and he displayed the corner of his plaid, made to hold lambs. "Tak' yer lamb," said she, laughing at the contrivance, and so the Pet was first well happet up, and then put, laughing silently into the plaid-neuk, and the shepherd strode off with his lamb—Maida gambolling through the snow, and running races in his mirth. Didn't he face "the angry airt," and make her bield his bosom, and into his own room with her, and lock the door, and out with the warm, rosy, little wifie, who took it all with great composure! There the two remained for three or more hours, making the house ring with their laughter. Having made the fire cheery, he set her down in his ample chair, and standing sheepishly before her, began to say his lesson, which happened to be—"Ziccoty, diccoty, dock, the mouse ran up the clock, the clock struck wan, down the mouse ran, ziccoty, diccoty, dock." This done repeatedly till she was pleased, she gave him his new lesson, gravely and slowly, timing it upon her little fingers—he saying it after her:

"Wonery, twoery, tickery, seven;
Alibi, crackaby, ten and eleven;
Im, pan, musky, dan;
Tweedle-um, twoddle-um
Twenty-wan; eerie, orie, ourie,
You, are, out."

Then he would read ballads to her in his own glorious way, the two getting wild with excitement over *Gil Morrice* or the *Baron of Smailholm*: and he would take her on his knee, and make her repeat Constance's speeches in *King John* till he swayed to and fro sobbing his fill. Fancy the gifted little creature, like one possessed, repeating:

"For I am sick, and capable of fears,
Oppressed with wrongs, and therefore full of fears:
A widow, husbandless, subject to fears,
A woman, naturally born to fears."

Scott used to say that he was amazed at her power over him, saying to Mrs. Keith, "She's the most extraordinary creature I ever met with, and her repeating of Shakespeare overpowers me as nothing else does."

JOHN BROWN (1810-82)
Marjorie Fleming

A DAY AT ABBOTSFORD

It was a clear, bright September morning, with a sharpness in the air that doubled the animating influence of the sunshine, and all was in readiness for a grand coursing match on Newark Hill. The only guest who had chalked out other sport for himself was that staunchest of anglers, Mr. Rose; but he, too, was there on his shelty, armed with his salmon-rod and landing-net, and attended by his humorous squire Hinves, and Charlie Purdie, a brother of Tom, in those days the most celebrated fisherman of the district. This little group of Waltonians, bound for Lord Somerville's preserve, remained lounging about to witness the start of the main cavalcade. Sir Walter, mounted on Sybil, was marshalling the order of procession with a huge hunting-whip; and, among a dozen frolicsome youths and maidens, who seemed disposed to laugh at all discipline, appeared, each on horseback, each as eager as the youngest sportsman in the troop, Sir Humphry Davy, Dr. Wollaston, and the patriarch of Scottish belles-lettres, Henry Mackenzie. The Man of Feeling, however, was persuaded with some difficulty to resign his steed for the present to his faithful negro follower, and to join Lady Scott in the sociable until we should reach the ground of our battue. Laidlaw, on a long-tailed wiry Highlander, yclept Hoddin Grey, which carried him nimbly and stoutly, although his feet almost touched the ground as he sat, was the adjutant. But the most picturesque figure was the illustrious inventor of the safety-lamp. He had come for his favourite sport of angling, and had been practising it successfully with Rose, his travelling companion, for two or three days preceding this, but he had not prepared for coursing fields, or had left Charlie Purdie's troop for Sir Walter's on a sudden thought; and his fisherman costume—a brown hat with flexible brims, surrounded with line upon line, and innumerable fly-hooks—jack-boots worthy of a Dutch smuggler, and a fustian surtout dabbled with the blood of salmon, made a fine contrast with the smart jackets, white-cord breeches, and well-polished jockey-boots of the less distinguished cavaliers about him. Dr. Wollaston was in black, and with his noble serene dignity of countenance might have passed for a sporting archbishop. Mr. Mackenzie, at this time in the 76th year of his age, with a white hat turned up with green, green spectacles, green jacket, and long brown leathern gaiters buttoned upon his nether anatomy, wore a dog-whistle round his neck, and had all over the air of as resolute a devotee as the gay captain of Huntly Burn. Tom Purdie and his subalterns had preceded us by a few hours with all the greyhounds that could be collected at Abbotsford, Darnick, and Melrose; but the giant Maida had remained as his master's orderly, and now gambolled about Sybil Grey, barking for mere joy like a spaniel puppy.

The order of march had been all settled and the sociable was just getting under weigh, when the Lady Anne broke from the line, screaming with laughter, and exclaimed— "Papa, papa, I knew you could never think of going without your pet."—Scott looked round, and I rather think there was a blush as well as a smile upon his face, when he perceived a little black pig frisking about his pony, and evidently a self-elected addition to the party of the day. He tried to look stern, and cracked his whip at the creature, but was in a moment obliged to join in the general cheers. Poor piggy soon found a strap round his neck, and was dragged into the background:—Scott, watching the retreat, repeated with mock pathos the first verse of an old pastoral song—

> "What will I do gin my hoggie die?
> My joy, my pride, my hoggie!
> My only beast, I had nae mae,
> And wow! but I was vogie!"

—the cheers were redoubled—and the squadron moved on.

J. G. LOCKHART (1794-1854)
Life of Scott

THE SUN UPON THE WEIRDLAW HILL

The sun upon the Weirdlaw Hill,
  In Ettrick's vale, is sinking sweet;
The westland wind is hush and still,
  The lake lies sleeping at my feet.
Yet not the landscape to mine eye
  Bears those bright hues that once it bore;
Though evening, with her richest dye,
  Flames o'er the hills of Ettrick's shore.

With listless look along the plain,
  I see Tweed's silver current glide,
And coldly mark the holy fane
  Of Melrose rise in ruin'd pride.
The quiet lake, the balmy air,
  The hill, the stream, the tower, the tree,—
Are they still such as once they were,
  Or is the dreary change in me?

Alas, the warp'd and broken board,
  How can it bear the painter's dye!
The harp of strain'd and tuneless chord,
  How to the minstrel's skill reply!
To aching eyes each landscape lowers,
  To feverish pulse each gale blows chill;
And Araby's or Eden's bowers
  Were barren as this moorland hill.

SIR WALTER SCOTT (1771-1832)

ON LOSING A FORTUNE

I have lost a large fortune, but I have ample compet-
ence remaining behind, and so I am just like an oak that
loses its leaves and keeps its branches. If I had ever
been a great admirer of money, I might have been at
this moment very rich, for I should have had all I have
lost, and much more. But I knew no mode of clipping
the wings of fortune, so I might also have lost what I
have set my heart upon, and I should then have been
like a man who had lost his whole clothes, whereas at
present I only feel like one who had forgot his greatcoat.
I am secure at (least?) of the perils which make bad
fortune really painful, for my family are provided for,
and so is my own and my wife's comforts for the time
we may live. Others will regret my losses more than
I do.

It would be gross affectation to say I am glad of such
a loss, but many things make it more indifferent to me
than I believe it would be to most people.

P.S.—I hope things go on well with you, as your
genius deserves. There is one comfort in the Fine Arts,
that the actual profit may be lost, but the pleasure of
pursuing them defies fortune.

SIR WALTER SCOTT (1771-1832)
Letter to B. R. Haydon, February 23rd, 1826

NEARING THE END

It was again a darkish cloudy day, with some occasional
mutterings of distant thunder, and perhaps the state of
the atmosphere told upon Sir Walter's nerves; but I had
never before seen him so sensitive as he was all the
morning after this inspection of Douglas. As we drove

over the high tableland of Lesmahago, he repeated I
know not how many verses from Winton, Barbour, and
Blind Harry, with, I believe, almost every stanza of
Dunbar's elegy on the deaths of the Makers (poets). It
was now that I saw him, such as he paints himself in
one or two passages of his Diary, but such as his companions in the meridian vigour of his life never saw
him—"the rushing of a brook, or the sighing of the
summer breeze, bringing the tears into his eyes not
unpleasantly." Bodily weakness laid the delicacy of the
organisation bare, over which he had prided himself in
wearing a sort of half-stoical mask. High and exalted
feelings, indeed, he had never been able to keep concealed, but he had shrunk from exhibiting to human
eye the softer and gentler emotions which now trembled
to the surface. He strove against it even now, and
presently came back from the Lament of the Makers to
his Douglases, and chanted, rather than repeated, in a
sort of deep and glowing, though not distinct recitative,
his first favourite among all the ballads:

"It was about the Lammas tide,
    When husbandmen do win their hay,
That the Doughty Douglas bowne him to ride
    To England to drive a prey,"—

down to the closing stanzas, which again left him in
tears:

"My wound is deep—I fain would sleep—
    Take thou the vanguard of the three,
And hide me beneath the bracken-bush,
    That grows on yonder lily lea."

J. G. LOCKHART (1794-1854)
Life of Scott

233

THE DEATH OF SIR WALTER

At a very early hour on the morning of Wednesday the 11th, we again placed him in his carriage, and he lay in the same torpid state during the first two stages on the road to Tweedside. But as we descended the vale of the Gala he began to gaze about him, and by degrees it was obvious that he was recognising the features of that familiar landscape. Presently he murmured a name or two—"Gala Water surely—Buckholm—Torwoodlee!" As we rounded the hill at Ladhope, and the outline of the Eildons burst on him, he became greatly excited, and when turning himself on the couch his eye caught at length his own towers, at the distance of a mile, he sprang up with a cry of delight. The river being in flood, we had to go round a few miles by Melrose bridge; and during the time this occupied, his woods and house being within prospect, it required occasionally both Dr. Watson's strength and mine, in addition to Nicolson's, to keep him in the carriage. After passing the bridge, the road for a couple of miles loses sight of Abbotsford, and he relapsed into his stupor; but on gaining the bank immediately above it, his excitement became again ungovernable.

Mr. Laidlaw was waiting at the porch, and assisted us in lifting him into the dining-room, where his bed had been prepared. He sat bewildered for a few moments, and then resting his eye on Laidlaw, said—"Ha! Willie Laidlaw! O man, how often have I thought of you!" By this time his dogs had assembled about his chair—they began to fawn upon him and lick his hands, and he alternately sobbed and smiled over them, until sleep oppressed him.

On Monday he remained in bed, and seemed extremely feeble; but after breakfast on Tuesday the 17th he appeared revived somewhat, and was again wheeled about on the turf. Presently he fell asleep in his chair, and after dozing for perhaps half an hour, started awake, and shaking the plaids we had put about him from off his shoulders, said—"This is sad idleness. I shall forget what I have been thinking of, if I don't set it down now. Take me into my own room, and fetch the keys of my desk." He repeated this so earnestly, that we could not refuse; his daughters went into his study, opened his writing-desk, and laid paper and pens in the usual order, and I then moved him through the hall and into the spot where he had always been accustomed to work. When the chair was placed at the desk, and he found himself in the old position, he smiled and thanked us, and said—"Now give me my pen, and leave me for a little to myself." Sophia put the pen into his hand, and he endeavoured to close his fingers upon it, but they refused their office—it dropped on the paper. He sank back among his pillows, silent tears rolling down his cheeks; but composing himself by and by, motioned to me to wheel him out of doors again. Laidlaw met us at the porch, and took his turn of the chair. Sir Walter, after a little while, again dropt into slumber. When he was awaking, Laidlaw said to me—"Sir Walter has had a little repose."—"No, Willie," said he—"no repose for Sir Walter but in the grave." The tears again rushed from his eyes. "Friends," said he, "don't let me expose myself—get me to bed—that's the only place."

As I was dressing on the morning of Monday the 17th of September, Nicolson came into my room, and told me that his master had awoke in a state of composure and consciousness, and wished to see me immediately. I found him entirely himself, though in the last extreme of feebleness. His eye was clear and calm—every trace of the wild fire of delirium extinguished. "Lockhart," he said, "I may have but a minute to speak to you. My dear, be a good man—be virtuous—be religious—be a good man. Nothing else will give you any comfort

when you come to lie here."—He paused, and I said—
"Shall I send for Sophia and Anne?"—"No," said he,
"don't disturb them. Poor souls! I know they were up
all night—God bless you all!"—With this he sunk into
a very tranquil sleep, and, indeed, he scarcely afterwards
gave any sign of consciousness, except for an instant on
the arrival of his sons.—They, on learning that the scene
was about to close, obtained a new leave of absence from
their posts, and both reached Abbotsford on the 19th.
About half-past one P.M., on the 21st of September, Sir
Walter breathed his last, in the presence of all his
children. It was a beautiful day—so warm, that every
window was wide open—and so perfectly still, that the
sound of all others most delicious to his ear, the gentle
ripple of the Tweed over its pebbles, was distinctly
audible as we knelt around the bed, and his eldest son
kissed and closed his eyes.

J. G. LOCKHART (1794-1854)
Life of Scott

CORONACH

He is gone on the mountain,
    He is lost to the forest,
Like a summer-dried fountain,
    When our need was the sorest.
The font, reappearing,
    From the rain-drops shall borrow,
But to us comes no cheering,
    To Duncan no morrow!

The hand of the reaper
    Takes the ears that are hoary,
But the voice of the weeper
    Wails manhood in glory,
The autumn winds rushing

Waft the leaves that are searest,
But our flower was in flushing,
When blighting was nearest.

Fleet foot on the correi,
Sage counsel in cumber,
Red hand in the foray,
How sound is thy slumber!
Like the dew on the mountain,
Like the foam on the river,
Like the bubble on the fountain,
Thou art gone, and for ever!

SIR WALTER SCOTT (1771-1832)
The Lady of the Lake

THE YOUTH OF LIVINGSTONE

The earliest recollection of my mother recalls a picture so often seen among the Scottish poor—that of the anxious housewife striving to make both ends meet. At the age of ten I was put into the factory as a "piecer," to aid by my earnings in lessening her anxiety. With a part of my first week's wages I purchased Ruddiman's *Rudiments of Latin*, and pursued the study of that language for many years afterwards, with unabated ardour, at an evening school, which met between the hours of eight and ten. The dictionary part of my labours was followed up till twelve o'clock, or later, if my mother did not interfere by jumping up and snatching the books out of my hands. I had to be back in the factory by six in the morning, and continue my work, with intervals for breakfast and dinner, till eight o'clock at night. I read in this way many of the classical authors, and knew Virgil and Horace better at sixteen than I do now.

237

In reading, everything that I could lay my hands on, was devoured except novels. Scientific works and books of travels were my especial delight; though my father, believing, with many of his time who ought to have known better, that the former were inimical to religion, would have preferred to have seen me poring over the *Cloud of Witnesses*, or Boston's *Fourfold State*. Our difference of opinion reached the point of open rebellion on my part, and his last application of the rod was on my refusal to peruse Wilberforce's *Practical Christianity*.

My reading while at work was carried on by placing the book on a portion of the spinning jenny, so that I could catch sentence after sentence as I passed at my work; I thus kept up a pretty constant study undisturbed by the roar of the machinery. To this part of my education I owe my present power of completely abstracting the mind from surrounding noises, so as to read and write with perfect comfort amidst the play of children or near the dancing and songs of savages. The toil of cotton-spinning, to which I was promoted in my nineteenth year, was excessively severe on a slim loose-jointed lad, but it was well paid for; and it enabled me to support myself while attending medical and Greek classes in Glasgow in winter, as also the divinity lectures of Dr. Wardlaw, by working with my hands in summer. I never received a farthing of aid from any one, and should have accomplished my project of going to China as a medical missionary in the course of time by my own efforts, had not some friends advised my joining the London Missionary Society on account of its perfectly unsectarian character. It "sends neither episcopacy, nor presbyterianism, nor independency, but the gospel of Christ to the heathen." This exactly agreed with my ideas of what a Missionary Society ought to do; but it was not without a pang that I offered myself, for it was not quite agreeable to one accustomed to work his own way to become in a measure dependent on others. And

I would not have been much put about, though my offer had been rejected.

Looking back now on that life of toil, I cannot but feel thankful that it formed such a material part of my early education; and, were it possible, I should like to begin life over again in the same lowly style, and to pass through the same hardy training.

DAVID LIVINGSTONE (1813-73)

DAVID LIVINGSTONE, 1813-73

It is not only on Livingstone's gentleness with Africans that Stanley dwells. He portrays him minutely, examines his character, retails his conversation at some length. And this was not by any means only because he was 'good copy.' It is quite evident that to Stanley, at the time and ever after, his brief companionship with Livingstone was the supreme experience of his life. He had come close to moral greatness, and he was startled, captivated, subjected by it. His description of Livingstone seems instinct with wonder and devotion—real wonder and sincere devotion. Here is the gist of it.

'I defy any one to be in his society long without thoroughly fathoming him, for in him there is no guile, and what is apparent on the surface is the thing that is in him. . . . I grant he is not an angel, but he approaches to that being as near as the nature of a living man will allow. . . . You may take any point in his character, and analyse it carefully, and I would challenge any man to find a fault in it. . . . His gentleness never forsakes him; his hopefulness never deserts him. No harassing anxieties, distraction of mind, long separation from home and kindred, can make him complain. He thinks "all will come out right at last"; he has such faith in the goodness of Providence. . . . His religion is neither demonstrative nor loud, but manifests itself in a quiet practical way and is always at work. . . . Without it Livingstone, with his ardent temperament, his enthusiasm, his high spirit and courage, must have become uncompanionable and a hard master. Religion has tamed him and made him a Christian gentleman.'

SIR REGINALD COUPLAND
Livingstone's Last Journey

BYRON AND ABERDEEN

From the early age at which Byron was taken to Scotland, as well as from the circumstance of his mother being a native of that country, he had every reason to consider himself—as, indeed, he boasts in *Don Juan*—"half a Scot by birth, and bred a whole one." He preserved through life his recollection of the mountain scenery in which he was brought up; and in a passage of *Don Juan* his allusion to the romantic bridge of Don, and to other localities of Aberdeen, shows an equal fidelity and fondness of retrospect:

As Auld Lang Syne brings Scotland, one and all,
  Scotch plaids, Scotch snoods, the blue hills and clear
    streams,
The Dee, the Don, Balgounie's brig's black wall,
  All my boy feelings, all my gentler dreams
Of what I *then dreamt*, clothed in their own pall,
  Like Banquo's offspring;—floating past me seems
My childhood in this childishness of mine;—
I care not—'tis a glimpse of "Auld Lang Syne."

He adds in a note, "The Brig of Don, near the ' auld town ' of Aberdeen, with its one arch and its black deep salmon stream, is in my memory as yesterday. I still remember the awful proverb which made me pause to cross it, and yet lean over it with a childish delight, being an only son, at least by the mother's side. The saying, as recollected by me, was this, but I have never heard or seen it since I was nine years of age:

"Brig o' Balgounie, *wight* (strong) is thy wa',
    Wi' a wife's ae son on a mare's ae foal,
    Down shalt thou fa'."

To meet with an Aberdonian was, at all times, a delight to him; and when the late Mr. Scott, who was a native of Aberdeen, paid him a visit at Venice in the year 1819, in talking of the haunts of his childhood, one of the places he particularly mentioned was Wallace-nook, a spot where there is a rude statue of the Scottish chief still standing. From first to last, indeed, these recollections of the country of his youth never forsook him. In his early voyage into Greece, not only the shapes of the mountains, but the kilts and hardy forms of the Albanese,—all, as he says, " carried him back to Morven"; and, in his last fatal expedition, the dress which he himself chiefly wore at Cephaloni was a tartan jacket.

T. MOORE (1779-1852)
Life of Byron

TWO SCOTS OLD LADIES

Except Mrs. Siddons in some of her displays of magnificent royalty, nobody could sit down like the lady of Inverleith. She would sail like a ship from Tarshish, gorgeous in velvet or rustling in silk, and done up in all the accompaniments of fan, ear-rings and finger-rings, falling sleeves, scent-bottle, embroidered bag, hoop and train—all superb, yet all in purest taste; and managing all this seemingly heavy rigging with as much ease as a full-blown swan does its plumage, she would take possession of the centre of a large sofa, and at the same moment, without the slightest visible exertion, would cover the whole of it with her bravery, the graceful folds seeming to lay themselves over it like summer waves. The descent from her carriage too, where she sat like a nautilus in its shell, was a display which no one in these days could accomplish or even fancy. The mulberry coloured coach, spacious but apparently not too large for what it carried—though she alone was in it; the handsome jolly coachman and his splendid hammer-cloth loaded with lace; the two respectful liveried foot-men, one on each side of the richly carpeted step; these were lost sight of amidst the slow majesty with which the lady came down, and touched the earth. She pre-sided, in this imperial style, over her son's excellent dinners, with great sense and spirit, to the very last day almost of a prolonged life.

Lady Dow (who lived in George Square) was still more highly bred, as was attested by her polite cheerfulness and easy elegance. The venerable faded beauty, the white well-coiled hair, the soft hand sparkling with old brilliant rings, the kind heart, the affectionate manner, the honest gentle voice, and the mild eyes, account for the love with which her old age was surrounded. She was about the last person (so far as I recollect) in Edinburgh who kept a private sedan chair. Hers stood in the lobby, and was as handsome and comfortable as silk, velvet and gilding could make it. And, when she wished to use it, two well-known respectable chairmen, enveloped in her livery cloaks, were the envy of their brethren. She and Mrs. Rockhead both sat in the Tron Church; and well do I remember how I used to form one of the cluster that always took its station to see these beautiful relics emerge from the coach and the chair.

HENRY, LORD COCKBURN (1779-1854)
Memorials of His Own Time

THE EPITAPH OF
JANE WELSH CARLYLE

In her bright existence she had more sorrows than are common: but also a soft invincibility, a clearness of discernment, and a noble loyalty of heart, which are rare. For forty years she was the true and ever-loving helpmate of her husband: and by act and word unweariedly forwarded him, as none else could, in all of worth that he did or attempted. She died at London, 21st April, 1866, suddenly snatched away from him, and the light of his life as if gone out.

THOMAS CARLYLE (1795-1881)

JOHN BROWN OF HADDINGTON

For the "heroic" old man of Haddington my father had a peculiar reverence, as indeed we all have. He was our king, the founder of our dynasty; we dated from him, and he was hedged accordingly by a certain sacredness or divinity. I possess, as an heirloom, the New Testament which my father fondly regarded as the one his grandfather, when a herd-laddie, got from the professor who heard him ask for it, and promised him it if he could read a verse; and he has, in his beautiful small hand, written in it what follows: "He (John Brown of Haddington) had now acquired so much of Greek as encouraged him to hope that he might at length be prepared to reap the richest of all rewards which classical learning could confer on him, the capacity of reading in the original tongue the blessed New Testament of our Lord and Saviour. Full of this hope, he became anxious to possess a copy of the invaluable volume. One night, having committed the charge of

243

his sheep to a companion, he set out on a midnight journey to St. Andrews, a distance of twenty-four miles. He reached his destination in the morning, and went to the bookseller's shop, asking for a copy of the Greek New Testament. The master of the shop, surprised at such a request from a shepherd boy, was disposed to make game of him. Some of the professors coming into the shop questioned the lad about his employment and studies. After hearing his tale, one of them desired the bookseller to bring the volume. He did so, and drawing it down, said: "Boy, read this and you shall have it for nothing." The boy did so, acquitted himself to the admiration of his judges, and carried off his Testament, and when the evening arrived, was studying it in the midst of his flock on the braes of Abernethy."

DR. JOHN BROWN (1810-82)
Horae Subsecivae

A FIRST DAY AT WORK

It was twenty years last February since I set out, a little before sunrise, to make my first acquaintance with a life of labour and restraint; and I have rarely had a heavier heart than on that morning. I was but a slim, loose-jointed boy at the time, fond of the pretty intangibilities of romance, and of dreaming when broad awake; and, woeful change! I was now going to work at what Burns has instanced, in his "Twa Dogs," as one of the most disagreeable of all employments—to work in a quarry. Bating the passing uneasiness occasioned by a few gloomy anticipations, the portion of my life which had already gone by had been happy beyond the common lot. I had been a wanderer among rocks and woods, a reader of curious books when I could get them, a gleaner of old traditionary stories; and now I was going to exchange all my day-dreams, and all my amusements, for the kind of life in which men toil every day that they may be enabled to eat, and eat every day that they may be enabled to toil!

The quarry in which I wrought lay on the southern shore of a noble inland bay, or frith rather, with a little clear stream on the one side, and a thick fir wood on the other. It had been opened in the Old Red Sandstone of the district, and was overtopped by a huge bank of diluvial clay, which rose over it in some places to the height of nearly thirty feet, and which at this time was rent and shivered, wherever it presented an open front to the weather, by a recent frost. A heap of loose fragments, which had fallen from above, blocked up the face of the quarry, and my first employment was to clear them away. The friction of the shovel soon blistered my hands, but the pain was by no means very severe, and I wrought hard and willingly, that I might see how the huge strata below, which presented so firm and unbroken a frontage, were to be torn up and removed. Picks, and wedges, and levers, were applied by my brother-workmen; and, simple and rude as I had been accustomed to regard these implements, I found I had much to learn in the way of using them. They all proved inefficient, however, and the workmen had to bore into one of the inferior strata, and employ gunpowder. The process was new to me, and I deemed it a highly amusing one: it had the merit, too, of being attended with some such degree of danger as a boating or rock excursion, and had thus an interest independent of its novelty. We had a few capital shots: the fragments flew in every direction; and an immense mass of the diluvium came toppling down, bearing with it two dead birds, that in a recent storm had crept into one of the deeper fissures, to die in the shelter. I felt a new interest in examining them. The one was a pretty cock goldfinch, with its hood of vermilion, and its wings inlaid with the gold to which it owes its name, as unsoiled and smooth as if it had been preserved for a museum. The other, a somewhat rarer bird, of the woodpecker tribe, was variegated with light blue and a grayish yellow. I was engaged in admiring the poor little things, more disposed to be sentimental, perhaps, than if I had been ten years older, and thinking of the contrast between the warmth and jollity of their green summer haunts, and the cold and darkness of their last retreat, when I heard our employer bidding the workmen lay by their tools. I looked up and saw the sun sinking behind the thick fir wood beside us, and the long dark shadows of the trees stretching downwards towards the shore.

HUGH MILLER (1802-56)
The Old Red Sandstone

WEEK-END WITH BARRIE

This week-end at Barrie's flat will make so strange a story that I must assure the reader that in telling it I have made no exaggeration and have carefully overhauled my memory. Maybe I suffered from delusions; I do not deny the possibility; the point is that if delusions did seize me they were so potent as to become inextricable from fact.

After Barrie had greeted me he showed me my bedroom and a shiver went down my spine when he told me, unnecessarily as I still think, that it had been "Michael's" room. (Michael Llewelyn-Davies had been drowned in 1922, almost four years to the day.) And now his manservant asked me for my keys. I had come South with only one suitcase, which contained the castoff underclothes of the tour. There were other and even more intimate things in it. I had never stayed before

246

at a house where a manservant in a brown brass-buttoned uniform asked you (in a tone of voice brooking no denial) for your keys.

This Thurston I have subsequently found out was a grand and sterling character. He spoke various languages, and would correct any loose statements about Ovid that he chanced to overhear while he was serving dinner. He had a ghostly face; he was from a Barrie play—so was Barrie, and the flat, and everything in it; the enormous cavern of a fireplace, the wooden settle and old tongs and bellows, and the sense the place gave you that the walls might be walked through if you had been given the secret. Barrie trudged the room smoking a pipe; on the desk lay another pipe already charged, ready for immediate service; he coughed as he trudged and smoked, a cruel cough that provoked a feeling of physical pain in my chest; and his splutterings and gaspings and talk struggled on one from the other. At last he came to sit facing me in front of the smouldering logs, and for a while the silence was broken by groans only to be heard in our two imaginations—the groans of men separated for ever by a chasm of shyness and uneasiness. Until midnight we lingered on. He offered me no refreshment. Thurston apparently went home to sleep each night. Or perhaps he merely dematerialised. Barrie knew I had dined on the train, but a nightcap would have been fortifying to me, I am sure; for already the spell of the flat high amongst the roofs of Adelphi was gripping me.

Next morning Thurston came into my bedroom with tea. He abruptly picked up my trousers and coat and disappeared with them. I had brought no other suit with me. For a frightful half-hour I imagined he was about to send them to the cleaners; and I could do nothing to prevent him. He brought them back neatly brushed, with my polished shoes. He showed me the bathroom, the most unkept I have ever known. The

247

towels were damp and soiled; and round about the shelves were one or two shaving brushes congealed in ancient soap. A rusty razor blade on a window ledge was historical.

Barrie had his private bathroom; the unclean towels puzzled me. Was it the custom to bring your own towels when staying with distinguished people for a week-end? I dried myself as best I could, and now Thurston directed me to the breakfast-room, where he attended to me in complete silence, only once speaking to inform me that Sir James was staying in bed for a while but would be glad if I dined with him that evening. The formality of it all was perplexing. This was not my idea of the Barrie way of life. In after years it occurred to me that probably no other guest of my humble station in life had entered the flat for years and years and years.

I spent the day at Lord's and returned to Adelphi Terrace House at seven o'clock, where to my dismay a company of people were assembling. I forget all their names and titles, but the sight of E. V. Lucas consoled me, because of his large humanity. Nobody was dressed for dinner, which was thoughtful of Thurston; clearly he had revealed to Barrie that a dinner-jacket was not part of my miscellaneous luggage. I can remember nothing of the dinner-party save the occasional low chuckle of Lucas.

Next morning—Sunday—Thurston again served tea in my bedroom and took away my coat and trousers and waited on me, and watched me carefully at breakfast. He told me that Sir James had gone away until Monday; would I be in for dinner? I replied in as easy and affable a negative as I could muster and render audible. I spent the day in the parks and dined in Soho, and just before midnight I ascended the lift to the flat and let myself in with my latchkey and turned on the light. Not a sound. A cold collation had been laid for me on the table, with a bottle of hock and a silver box of cigarettes. I explored the bookcases, almost on tiptoe; there was a row of volumes of the Scottish philosophers—Hume, Mackintosh, Hamilton. I sat at Barrie's desk but got up immediately for fear I might be caught in the act. The great chimney corner, with no fire in it, glowered at me.

Thurston went through the usual ritual when I awoke after a middling night. The bathroom remained dishevelled. Having dressed I went into the breakfast-room, where at the table sat Margaret Ogilvie, to the life. She turned out not to be a figment of my now tottering brain, but Barrie's sister Maggie. How she came to be present, wearing a dressing-gown, was not explained. She was as gracious as could be, after the manner of all Barrie's women. She had "charm." She asked if I would call on her in her boudoir after dinner to-morrow evening and take part in a little musical "conversazione"—for she loved music and would enjoy singing and playing to me. I did not dare inquire where the boudoir might chance to be situated or secreted.

After another day at Lord's I came back to the flat at dusk. Once more a cold collation and a bottle of hock waited for me. Once more the place was silent and, as far as I could tell without poking and peering and looking under tables and behind curtains, it was un-peopled. I poured me out a glass of wine, then, as I drank, I heard the rumble of the lift and presently the door opened and a young man entered, in a dinner jacket. Without a sign of curiosity at my presence or at the absence of others, he remarked to me that it had been a lovely day. He sat on a couch, smoked a cigarette, and talked for a few minutes about the cricket at Lord's; he hadn't yet been able to look in at the match himself, but he had enjoyed my account of Saturday's play in the "M.G." I was liking him very much when he arose, and with an apology left the room and the flat. To this day I do not know who he was—probably young Simon out of *Mary Rose*.

Barrie was waiting for me next evening alone; we dined together and under the glow of a perfect Burgundy we thawed somewhat. He told me of his early days as a journalist and vowed he could never have made a footing in the London journalism of the present time—which was terribly true. He said that he had never been much interested in the theatre except as one who wrote for it. But it was difficult to keep him off cricket and he pooh-poohed my fears that perhaps I was wasting myself writing about it. He excused himself from attendance at his sister's musical "conversazione" on the grounds that he was unable to distinguish one note from another. But he led me from the dining-room through another room to the boudoir. I can only suppose it had been there all the time; it was remotely Victorian in fragrance and appearance; and there was an upright piano with a fluted silk front.

Barrie handed me over to Maggie and escaped. She played a composition of her own called "1914-1918" with a battle section in the middle and a finale of bells and thanksgiving. She next sang a number of Scotch songs in an expressive if wan voice. When the music was over she asked me about my early life and of my struggles. I looked young for my years in those days and probably rather "lost." Next morning she was at breakfast waiting for me. She told me that during the night she had been in communication with my mother "on the other side" and that my mother and she had loved one another at once, and that my mother was proud of me and that they, the two of them, would watch over and take care of me. I was naturally ready to perspire with appre-hension. Was I to be mothered or Wendy'd in this flat in the tree—I mean chimney tops? The interruption here of Thurston was a relief and a blessing, much as I felt drawn to the softness and kindliness of her nature.

Thurston led me to Barrie who wanted to say good-bye before I left; he was in bed in a bandbox of a room, bare and uncomfortable—what little I could see of it through thick tobacco smoke, for his pipe was in full furnace as he lay there, frail in pyjamas, like a pigmy with one of those big pantomime heads. He hoped I had enjoyed my stay and would come again; the flat was open to me at any time: I had only to give him short notice.

Thurston carried my suitcase down the lift cage. He got me a taxi. In my highly emotional condition—feeling I had emerged from another dimension, and only just emerged—I forgot to tip him. I called on Barrie at the flat once or twice after this experience; but never stayed the night. I prefer my Barrie plays on the stage in front of me, where I can see what they are doing; I don't like them taking place behind my back in the night.

NEVILLE CARDUS
Autobiography

THE VISIONARY SCOT

That the Scot is largely endowed with the commercial imagination his foes will be ready to acknowledge. Imagination may consecrate the world to a man, or it may merely be a visualizing faculty which sees that as already perfect which is still lying in the raw material. The Scot has the lower faculty in full degree; he has the forecasting leap of the mind which sees what to make of things—more, sees them made and in vivid operation. To him there is a railway through the desert where no railway exists, and mills along the quiet stream. And his *perfervidum ingenium* is quick to attempt the realizing of his dreams. That is why he makes the best of colonists. . . . Galt is his type—Galt, dreaming

251

in boyhood of the fine water power a fellow could bring round the hill, from the stream where he went a-fishing (they have done it since), dreaming in manhood of the cities yet to rise amid Ontario's woods (they are there to witness to his foresight). Indeed, so flushed and riotous can the Scottish mind become over a commercial prospect that it sometimes sends native caution by the board, and a man's really fine idea becomes an empty balloon, to carry him off to the limbo of vanities. There is a megalomaniac in every parish of Scotland. Well, not so much as that; they're owre canny for that to be said of them. But in every district almost you may find a poor creature who for thirty years has cherished a great scheme by which he means to revolutionize the world's commerce, and amass a fortune in monstrous degree. He is generally to be seen shivering at the Cross, and (if you are a nippy man) you shout carelessly in going by, ' Good morning, Tamson; how's the scheme?' And he would be very willing to tell you, if only you would wait to listen. ' Man,' he will cry eagerly behind you, ' if I only had anither wee wheel in my invention—she would do, the besom! I'll sune have her ready noo.' Poor Tamson!

GEORGE DOUGLAS (BROWN) (1869-1902)
The House with the Green Shutters

Humour and Sentiment

SCOTTISH CHARACTER

So far as one can look into that commonplace round
of things which historians never tell us about, there
have rarely been seen in this world a set of people who
have thought more about right and wrong, and the
judgment about them of the upper powers. Long-
headed, thrifty industry—a sound hatred of waste,
imprudence, idleness, extravagance—the feet planted
firmly upon the earth—a conscientious sense that the
worldly virtues are, nevertheless, very necessary virtues,
that without these, honesty for one thing is not possible,
and that without honesty no other excellence, religious
or moral, is worth anything at all—this is the stuff of
which Scotch life was made, and very good stuff it is.
. . . Among other good qualities, the Scots have been
distinguished for humour—not for venomous wit, but
for kindly, genial humour, which half loves what it
laughs at—and this alone shows clearly enough that
those to whom it belongs have not looked too exclusively
on the gloomy side of the world. I should rather say
that the Scots had been an unusually happy people.
Intelligent industry, the honest doing of daily work,
with a sense that it must be done well, under penalties;
the necessaries of life moderately provided for; and a
sensible content with the situation of life in which men
are born—this through the week, and at the end of it
the "Cotter's Saturday Night"—the homely family,
gathered reverently and peacefully together, and irradi-
ated with a sacred presence.—Happiness! such happiness
as we human creatures are likely to know upon this
world; will be found there, if anywhere.

J. A. FROUDE (1818-94)

AN ADMONITION TO YOUNG LASSIES

A Bonnie ' No ' with smiling looks again
 I wald ye learned, sen they so comely are.
As touching ' Yes,' if ye suld speak so plain,
 I might reprove you to have said so far.
 Nocht that your grant, in ony ways, micht gar[1]
Me loathe the fruit that courage ocht to choose;
 But I wald only have you seem to skar,[2]
And let me tak it, feigning to refuse;

And warsle, as it war against your will,
 Appearing angry, though ye have no ire:
For have, ye hear, is halden half a fill.[3]
 I speak not this, as trowing for to tire:
 But as the forger when he feeds his fire
With sparks of water maks it burn more bauld;
 So, sweet denial doubles but desire,
And quickens courage fra becoming cauld.

Wald ye be made of, ye maun mak it nice;
 For dainties here are delicate and dear,
But plenty things are prized to little price;[4]
 Then though ye hearken, let no wit ye hear,
 But look away, and len them aye your ear:
For, follow love, they say, and it will flee.
 Wald ye be loved, this lesson maun ye leir:[5]
Flee whilom love, and it will follow thee.

ALEXANDER MONTGOMERIE (c. 1540-1610)

[1] make [2] discourage [3] possession, you hear, is held to halve desire
[4] things that are plentiful are little valued [5] must you learn

ANCIENT HISTORY

My brother and I derived much enjoyment, not to say instruction, from the singing of old ballads, and the telling of legendary stories, by a kind old female relative, the wife of a decayed tradesman, who dwelt in one of the ancient closes of Peebles. At her humble fireside under the canopy of a huge chimney, where her half-blind and superannuated husband sat dozing in a chair, the battle of Corunna and other prevailing news was strangely mingled with disquisitions on the Jewish wars. The source of this interesting conversation was a well-worn copy of L'Estrange's translation of *Josephus*, a small folio of date 1720. The envied possessor of the work was Tam Fleck, "a flichty chield," as he was considered, who, not particularly steady at his legitimate employment, struck out a sort of profession by going about in the evenings with his *Josephus*, which he read as the current news; the only light he had for doing so being usually that imparted by the flickering blaze of a piece of parrot coal. It was his practice not to read more than from two to three pages at a time, interlarded with sagacious remarks of his own by way of foot-notes, and in this way he sustained an extraordinary interest in the narrative. Retailing the matter with great equability in different households, Tam kept all at the same point of information, and wound them up with a corresponding anxiety as to the issue of some moving event in Hebrew annals. Although in this way he went through a course of *Josephus* yearly, the novelty somehow never seemed to wear off.

"Weel, Tam, what's the news the nicht?" would old Geordie Murray say, as Tam entered with his *Josephus* under his arm, and seated himself at the family fireside.

"Bad news, bad news," replied Tam. "Titus has begun to besiege Jerusalem—it's gaun to be a terrible business";

and then he opened his budget of intelligence, to which all paid the most reverential attention. The protracted and severe famine which was endured by the besieged Jews was a theme which kept several families in a state of agony for a week; and when Tam in his readings came to the final conflict and destruction of the city by the Roman general, there was a perfect paroxysm of horror.

W. CHAMBERS (1800-83)
Memoirs

THE FRUITS OF THE UNION

Bailie Nicol Jarvie upholds the Union of the Parliaments, 1707.

When the cloth was removed, Mr. Jarvie compounded with his own hands a very small bowl of brandy-punch, the first which I had ever the fortune to see.

"The limes," he assured us, "were from his own little farm yonder-awa" (indicating the West Indies with a knowing shrug of his shoulders), "and he had learned the art of composing the liquor from auld Captain Coffinkey, who acquired it," he added in a whisper, "as maist folk thought, among the Buccaneers. But it's excellent liquor," said he, helping us round; "and good ware has aften come frae a wicked market. And as for Captain Coffinkey, he was a decent man when I kent him, only he used to swear awfully.—But he's dead, and gaen to his account, and I trust he's accepted—I trust he's accepted."

We found the liquor exceedingly palatable, and it led to a long conversation between Owen and our host, on the opening which the Union had afforded to trade between Glasgow and the British colonies in America and the West Indies, and on the facilities which Glasgow possessed of making up *sortable* cargoes for that market.

Mr. Jarvie answered some objection which Owen made on the difficulty of sorting a cargo for America, without buying from England, with vehemence and volubility.

"Na, na, sir, we stand on our ain bottom—we pickle in our ain pock-neuk.—We hae our Stirling serges, Musselburgh stuffs, Aberdeen hose, Edinburgh shalloons, and the like, for our woollen or worsted goods—and we hae linens of a' kinds better and cheaper than you hae in Lunnon itsel'—and we can buy your north o' England wares, as Manchester wares, Sheffield wares, and Newcastle earthenware, as cheap as you can at Liverpool—and we are making a fair spell at cottons and muslins. —Na, na! let every herring hing by its ain head, and every sheep by its ain shank, and ye'll find, sir, us Glasgow folk no sae far ahint but what we may follow. —This is but poor entertainment for you, Mr. Osbaldistone" (observing that I had been for some time silent); "but ye ken cadgers maun aye be speaking about cart-saddles."

SIR WALTER SCOTT (1771-1832)
Rob Roy

LAND OF CONGYRATION

Part of a letter from Win. Jenkins to Mrs. Mary Jones

O Mary! this is the land of congyration. The bell knolled when we were there. I saw lights, and heard lamentations. The gentleman, our landlord, has got another house, which he was fain to quit, on account of a mischievous ghost, that would not suffer people to lie in their beds. The fairies dwell in a hole of Kairmann, a mounting hard by; and they steal away the good women that are in the straw, if so be as how there an't a horshoe nailed to the door. And I was shown an old vitch, called Elspath Ringavey, with a red petticoat,

bleared eyes, and a mould of grey bristles on her sin.
That she mought do me no harm, I crossed her hand with
a taster, and bid her tell my fortune; and she told me
such things—descriving Mr. Clinker to a hair—but it
shall ne'er be said that I minchioned a word of the
matter. As I was troubled with fits, she advised me to
bathe in the loff, which was holy water; and so I went
in the morning to a private place, along with the house-
maid, and we bathed in our birth-day soot, after the
fashion of the country; and behold, whilst we dabbled
in the loff, Sir George Coon started up with a gun; but
we clapt our hands to our faces, and passed by him to
the place where we had left our smocks. A civil gentleman would have turned his head another way. My
confit is, he knew not which was which; and, as the
saying is, *all cats in the dark are grey*.

TOBIAS SMOLLETT (1721-71)
Humphry Clinker

A JACOBITE TRIAL

Edward Waverley attends a Jacobite trial at Carlisle.

It was the third sitting of the court, and there were
two men at the bar. The verdict of GUILTY was already
pronounced. Edward just glanced at the bar during the
momentous pause which ensued. There was no mistak-
ing the stately form and noble features of Fergus
Mac-Ivor, although his dress was squalid and his countenance tinged with the sickly yellow hue of long and close
imprisonment. By his side was Evan Maccombich.
Edward felt sick and dizzy as he gazed on them; but he
was recalled to himself as the Clerk of the Arraigns
pronounced the solemn words: "Fergus Mac-Ivor of
Glennaquoich, otherwise called Vich Ian Vohr, and Evan
Mac-Ivor, in the Dhu of Tarrascleugh, otherwise called

Evan Dhu, otherwise called Evan Maccombich, or Evan Dhu Maccombich—you, and each of you, stand attainted of high treason. What have you to say for yourselves why the Court should not pronounce judgment against you, that you die according to law?"

Fergus, as the presiding Judge was putting on the fatal cap of judgment, placed his own bonnet upon his head, regarded him with a steadfast and stern look, and replied in a firm voice, "I cannot let this numerous audience suppose that to such an appeal I have no answer to make. But what I have to say, you would not bear to hear, for my defence would be your condemnation. Proceed, then, in the name of God, to do what is permitted to you. Yesterday, and the day before, you have condemned loyal and honourable blood to be poured forth like water. Spare not mine. Were that of all my ancestors in my veins, I would have peril'd it in this quarrel." He resumed his seat, and refused again to rise.

Evan Maccombich looked at him with great earnestness, and, rising up, seemed anxious to speak; but the confusion of the court, and the perplexity arising from thinking in a language different from that in which he was to express himself, kept him silent. There was a murmur of compassion among the spectators, from an idea that the poor fellow intended to plead the influence of his superior as an excuse for his crime. The Judge commanded silence, and encouraged Evan to proceed.

"I was only ganging to say, my lord," said Evan, in what he meant to be in an insinuating manner, "that if your excellent honour, and the honourable Court, would let Vich Ian Vohr go free just this once, and let him gae back to France, and no to trouble King George's government again, that ony six o' the very best of his clan will be willing to be justified in his stead; and if you'll just let me gae down to Glennaquoich, I'll fetch them up to ye mysel', to head or hang, and you may begin wi' me the very first man."

Notwithstanding the solemnity of the occasion, a sort of laugh was heard in the court at the extraordinary nature of the proposal. The Judge checked this indecency, and Evan, looking sternly around, when the murmur abated, "If the Saxon gentlemen are laughing," he said, "because a poor man, such as me, thinks my life, or the life of six of my degree, is worth that of Vich Ian Vohr, it's like enough there may be very right; but if they laugh because they think I would not keep my word, and come back to redeem him, I can tell them they ken neither the heart of a Hielandman nor the honour of a gentleman."

There was no further inclination or laugh among the audience, and a dead silence ensued.

The Judge then pronounced upon both prisoners the sentence of the law of high treason, with all its horrible accompaniments. The execution was appointed for the ensuing day. "For you, Fergus Mac-Ivor," continued the Judge, "I can hold out no hope of mercy. You must prepare against to-morrow for your last sufferings here, and your great audit hereafter."

"I desire nothing else, my lord," answered Fergus, in the same manly and firm tone.

The hard eyes of Evan, which had been perpetually bent on his Chief, were moistened with a tear. "For you, poor ignorant man," continued the Judge, "who, following the ideas in which you have been educated, have this day given us a striking example how the loyalty due to the king and state alone, is, from your unhappy ideas of clanship, transferred to some ambitious individual, who ends by making you the tool of his crimes—for you, I say, I feel so much compassion, that if you can make up your mind to petition for grace, I will endeavour to procure it for you. Otherwise——"

"Grace me no grace," said Evan; "since you are to shed Vich Ian Vohr's blood, the only favour I would accept from you is—to bid them loose my hands and

gie me my claymore, and bide you just a minute sitting
where you are!"

"Remove the prisoners," said the Judge; "his blood be
upon his own head!"

SIR WALTER SCOTT (1771-1832)
Waverley

THE SPAEWIFE

O, I wad like to ken—to the beggar-wife says I—
Why chops are guid to brander and nane sae guid to fry.
An' siller, that's sae braw to keep, is brawer still to gie.
—*It's gey an' easy speirin'*, says the beggar-wife to me.

O, I wad like to ken—to the beggar-wife says I—
Hoo a' things come to be whaur we find them when we
        try,
The lasses in their claes an' the fishes in the sea.
—*It's gey an' easy speirin'*, says the beggar-wife to me.

O, I wad like to ken—to the beggar-wife says I—
Why lads are a' to sell an' lasses a' to buy;
An' naebody for dacency but barely twa or three.
—*It's gey an' easy speirin'*, says the beggar-wife to me.

O, I wad like to ken—to the beggar-wife says I—
Gin death's as shure to men as killin' is to kye,
Why God has filled the yearth sae fu' o' tasty things to
        pree.
—*It's gey an' easy speirin'*, says the beggar-wife to me.

O, I wad like to ken—to the beggar-wife says I—
The reason o' the cause an' the wherefore o' the why,
Wi' mony anither riddle brings the tear into my e'e.
—*It's gey an' easy speirin'*, says the beggar-wife to me.

R. L. STEVENSON (1850-94)

THE HIGHLAND LAW

"But in the thicket of the wilderness, and in the mist of the mountain, Kenneth, son of Eracht, keep thou unsoiled the freedom which I leave thee as a birthright. Barter it not neither for the rich garment, nor for the stone roof, nor for the covered board, nor for the couch of down—on the rock or in the valley, in abundance or in famine—in the leafy summer, and in the days of the iron winter—Son of the Mist! be free as thy forefathers. Own no Lord—receive no law—take no hire—give no stipend—build no hut—enclose no pasture—sow no grain;—let the deer of the mountain be thy flocks and herds—if these fail thee, prey upon the goods of our oppressors—of the Saxons, and of such Gael as are Saxons in their souls, valuing herds and flocks more than honour and freedom. Well for us that they do so —it affords the broader scope for our revenge. Remember those who have done kindness to our race, and pay their services with thy blood, should the hour require it."

SIR WALTER SCOTT (1771-1832)
The Legend of Montrose

THE END O' AN AULD SANG

In his novel *Redgauntlet* Scott describes how Prince Charles made a descent on Cumberland. His adherents are in hot debate about their future movements.

Amid this scene of confusion, a gentleman, plainly dressed in a riding-habit, with a black cockade in his hat, but without any arms, except a *couteau-de-chasse*, walked into the apartment without ceremony. He was a tall, thin, gentlemanly man, with a look and bearing decidedly military. He had passed through their guards, if in the confusion they now maintained any, without stop or question, and now stood, almost unarmed, among armed men, who, nevertheless, gazed on him as on the angel of destruction.

"You look coldly on me, gentlemen," he said. "Sir Richard Glendale—my Lord ——, we were not always such strangers. Ha, Pate-in-Peril, how is it with you? and you too Ingoldsby—I must not call you by any other name—why do you receive an old friend so coldly? But you guess my errand."

"And are prepared for it, General," said Redgauntlet; "we are not men to be penned up like sheep for the slaughter."

"Pshaw! you take it too seriously. Let me speak but one word with you."

"No words can shake our purpose," said Redgauntlet, "were your whole command, as I suppose is the case, drawn round the house."

"I am certainly not unsupported," said the General; "but if you would hear me——"

"Hear *me*, sir," said the Wanderer, stepping forward; "I suppose I am the mark you aim at. I surrender myself willingly, to save these gentlemen's danger. Let this at least avail in their favour."

An exclamation of "Never, never!" broke from the little body of partisans, who threw themselves round the unfortunate Prince, and would have seized or struck down Campbell, had it not been that he remained with his arms folded, and a look, rather indicating impatience because they would not hear him, than the least apprehension of violence at their hand.

At length he obtained a moment's silence. "I do not," he said, "know this gentleman" (making a profound bow to the unfortunate Prince)—"I do not wish to know him; it is a knowledge which would suit neither of us."

"Our ancestors, nevertheless, have been well acquainted," said Charles, unable to suppress, even in that hour of dread and danger, the painful recollections of fallen royalty.

"In one word, General Campbell," said Redgauntlet, "is it to be peace or war? You are a man of honour, and we can trust you."

"I thank you, sir," said the General; "and I reply that the answer to your question rests with yourself. Come, do not be fools, gentlemen. There was perhaps no great harm meant or intended by your gathering together in this obscure corner for a bear-bait or a cock-fight, or whatever other amusement you may have intended; but it was a little imprudent, considering how you stand with government, and it has occasioned some anxiety. Exaggerated accounts of your purpose have been laid before government by the information of a traitor in your own counsels; and I was sent down post to take the command of a sufficient number of troops, in case these calumnies should be found to have any real foundation. I have come here, of course, sufficiently supported both with cavalry and infantry to do whatever might be necessary; but my commands are—and I am sure they agree with my inclination—to make no arrests, nay, to make no further inquiries of any kind, if this good assembly will consider their own interest so far as to give up their immediate purpose, and return quietly home to their own houses."

"What!—all?" exclaimed Sir Richard Glendale—"all, without exception?"

"ALL, without one single exception," said the General; "such are my orders. If you accept my terms, say so, and make haste; for things may happen to interfere with his Majesty's kind purposes towards you all."

"His Majesty's kind purposes!" said the Wanderer. "Do I hear you aright, sir?"

"I speak the King's very words, from his very lips," replied the General. "' I will,' said his Majesty, ' deserve the confidence of my subjects by reposing my security in the fidelity of the millions who acknowledge my title —in the good sense and prudence of the few who continue, from the errors of education, to disown it.' His Majesty will not even believe that the most zealous Jacobites who yet remain, can nourish a thought of exciting a civil war, which must be fatal to their families and themselves, besides spreading bloodshed and ruin through a peaceful land. He cannot even believe of his kinsman, that he would engage brave and generous, though mistaken men, in an attempt which must ruin all who have escaped former calamities; and he is convinced that, did curiosity or any other motive lead that person to visit this country, he would soon see it was his wisest course to return to the Continent, and his Majesty compassionates his situation too much to offer any obstacle to his doing so."

"Is this real?" said Redgauntlet. "Can you mean this? Am I—are all—are any of these gentlemen at liberty, without interruption, to embark in yonder brig, which, I see, is now again approaching the shore?"

"You, sir—all—any of the gentlemen present," said the General—"all whom the vessel can contain, are at liberty to embark, uninterrupted by me; but I advise none to go off who have not powerful reasons unconnected with the present meeting, for this will be remembered against no one."

"Then, gentlemen," said Redgauntlet, clasping his hands together as the words burst from him, "the cause is lost for ever!"

SIR WALTER SCOTT (1771-1832)
Redgauntlet

THE GIPSY'S CURSE

The gipsies having been expelled from Derncleugh, Meg Merrilies curses the Laird of Ellangowan.

She was standing upon one of those high precipitous banks, which, as we before noticed, overhung the road;

so that she was placed considerably higher than Ellangowan, even though he was on horseback; and her tall figure, relieved against the clear blue sky, seemed almost of supernatural stature. We have noticed, that there was in her general attire, or rather in her mode of adjusting it, somewhat of a foreign costume, artfully adopted perhaps for the purpose of adding to the effect of her spells and predictions, or perhaps from some traditional notions respecting the dress of her ancestors. On this occasion, she had a large piece of red cotton cloth rolled about her head in the form of a turban, from beneath which her dark eyes flashed with uncommon lustre. Her long and tangled black hair fell in elf-locks from the folds of this singular head-gear. Her attitude was that of a sibyl in frenzy, and she stretched out, in her right hand, a sapling bough which seemed just pulled.

"I'll be d——d," said the groom, "if she had not been cutting the young ashes in the Dukit park!"—The Laird made no answer, but continued to look at the figure which was thus perched above his path.

"Ride your ways," said the gipsy, "ride your ways, Laird of Ellangowan—ride your ways, Godfrey Bertram! —This day have ye quenched seven smoking hearths— see if the fire in your ain parlour burn the blyther for that. Ye have riven the thack off seven cottar houses— look if your ain roof-tree stand the faster.—Ye may stable your stirks in the shealings at Derncleugh—see that the hare does not couch on the hearthstane at Ellangowan.—Ride your ways, Godfrey Bertram—what do ye glower after our folk for?—There's thirty hearts there, that wad hae wanted bread ere ye had wanted sunkets, and spent their life-blood ere ye had scratched your finger. Yes—there's thirty yonder, from the auld wife of an hundred to the babe that was born last week, that ye have turned out o' their bits o' bields, to sleep with the tod and the black-cock in the muirs!—Ride your ways, Ellangowan.—Our bairns are hinging at our weary backs—look that your braw cradle at hame be the fairer spread up—not that I am wishing ill to little Harry, or to the babe that's yet to be born—God forbid —and make them kind to the poor, and better folk than their father!—And now, ride e'en your ways; for these are the last words ye'll ever hear Meg Merrilies speak, and this is the last reise that I'll ever cut in the bonny woods of Ellangowan."

So saying, she broke the sapling she held in her hand, and flung it into the road. Margaret of Anjou, bestowing on her triumphant foes her keen-edged malediction, could not have turned from them with a gesture more proudly contemptuous. The Laird was clearing his voice to speak, and thrusting his hand in his pocket to find a half-crown; the gipsy waited neither for his reply nor his donation, but strode down the hill to overtake the caravan.

SIR WALTER SCOTT (1771-1832)
Guy Mannering

DEAR DAYS OF OLD

Home no more home to me, whither must I wander?
   Hunger my driver, I go where I must.
Cold blows the winter wind over hill and heather;
   Thick drives the rain, and my roof is in the dust.
Loved of wise men was the shade of my roof-tree.
   The true word of welcome was spoken in the door—
Dear days of old, with the faces in the firelight,
   Kind folks of old, you come again no more.

Home was home then, my dear, full of kindly faces,
   Home was home then, my dear, happy for the child.
Fire and the windows bright glittered on the moorland;
   Song, tuneful song, built a palace in the wild.
Now, when day dawns on the brow of the moorland,

Lone stands the house, and the chimney-stone is cold.
Lone let it stand, now the friends are all departed,
   The kind hearts, the true hearts, that loved the place
   of old.

Spring shall come, come again, calling up the moor-fowl,
   Spring shall bring the sun and rain, bring the bees and
   flowers;
Red shall the heather bloom over hill and valley,
   Soft flow the stream through the even-flowing hours;
Fair the day shine as it shone on my childhood—
   Fair shine the day on the house with open door;
Birds come and cry there and twitter in the chimney—
   But I go for ever and come again no more.

R. L. STEVENSON (1850-94)

AT THE PLAY

Mansie Wauch attends the Play for the first and last time.

Just at the time that the two blind fiddlers were playing
the Downfall of Paris, a hand-bell rang, and up goes the
green curtain. So, on the music stopping, and all
becoming as still as that you might have heard a pin
fall, in comes a decent old gentleman at his leisure. I
never saw a man in such distress: he stamped about,
dadding the end of his staff on the ground, and imploring
all the powers of heaven and earth to help him to find
out his runaway daughter, that had decamped with some
ne'er-do-weel loon of a half-pay captain, that keppit her
in his arms from her bedroom-window, up two pair
of stairs.

Every father and head of a family must have felt for
a man in his situation, thus to be robbed of his dear bairn,
and an only daughter too, as he told us over and over
again, as the salt, salt tears ran gushing down his

withered face. But, ye know, the thing was absurd to suppose that we should know any inkling about the matter, having never seen him or his daughter between the een before, and not kenning them by headmark; so, though we sympathised with him, we thought it best to hold our tongues, to see what might cast up better than he expected. So out he went stumping at the other side, determined, he said, to find them out, though he should follow them to the world's end.

Hardly was his back turned, and almost before ye could cry Jack Robison, in comes the birkie and the very young lady the old gentleman described, arm-in-arm together, smoodging and laughing like daft. Dog on it! it was a shameless piece of business. As true as death, before all the crowd of folk, he put his arm round her waist, and called her his sweetheart, and love, and dearie, and darling, and everything that is fine. I thought such shame to be an eyewitness to sic on-goings, that I was obliged at last to hold up my hat before my face and look down; though, for all that, the young lad, to be such a blackguard as his conduct showed, was well enough faured, and had a good coat to his back, with double gilt buttons and fashionable lapells.

The father looked to be a rich old bool, both from his manner of speaking and the rewards he seemed to offer for the apprehension of his daughter; but to be sure, when so many of us were present that had an equal right to the spuilzie, it would not be a great deal a thousand pounds when divided, still it was worth the looking after: so we just bidit a wee.

Things were brought to a bearing, howsoever, sooner than either themselves, I daresay, or anybody else present, seemed to have the least glimpse of; for just in the middle of their fine going-ons the sound of a coming foot was heard, and the lassie, taking guilt to her, cried out, "Hide me, hide me, for the sake of goodness, for yonder comes my old father!"

No sooner said than done. In he stappit her into a closet, and, after shutting the door on her, he sat down upon a chair, pretending to be asleep in the twinkling of a walking-stick. The old father came bouncing in, and seeing the fellow as sound as a top, he ran forward and gave him such a shake as if he would have shooken him all sundry, which soon made him open his eyes as fast as he had steeked them. After blackguarding the chield at no allowance, cursing him up hill and down dale, he held his staff over his crown, and gripping him by the cuff of the neck, asked him, in a fierce tone, what he had made of his daughter. Never since I was born did I ever see such brazen-faced impudence! The rascal had the brass to say at once that he had not seen word or wittens of the lassie for a month, though more than a hundred folk sitting in his company had beheld him dauting her with his arm round her jimpy waist, not five minutes before. As a man, as a father, as an elder of our kirk, my corruption was raised, so I thought that whoever spoke first would have the best right to be entitled to the reward; whereupon, just as he was in the act of rising up, I took the word out of his mouth, saying, "Dinna believe him, auld gentleman—dinna believe him, friend; he's telling a parcel of lees. Never saw her for a month! Just open that press-door, and ye'll see whether I'm speaking truth or not!"

The old man stared, and looked dumbfoundered; and the young one, instead of running forward with his double nieves to strike me, the only thing I was feared for, began a-laughing, as if I had done him a good turn. But never since I had a being did I ever witness such an uproar and noise as immediately took place. The whole house was so glad that the scoundrel had been exposed, that they set up siccan a roar of laughter, and thumped away at siccan a rate at the boards with their feet, that at long and last, with pushing and fidgeting, clapping their hands and holding their sides, down fell the place they call the gallery, all the folk in't being hurled topsy-turvy, head foremost among the sawdust on the floor below, their guffawing soon being turned to howling, each one crying louder than another at the top of their voices, "Murder, murder! hold off me; murder! my ribs are in, murder! I'm killed—I'm speechless!" and other lamentations to that effect, so that a rush to the door took place, in the which everything was overturned, and the two blind fiddlers dung head foremost over the stage, the bass fiddle cracking like thunder at every bruise. Such tearing, and swearing, and tumbling, and squealing, was never witnessed in the memory of man; so that when we had been carried off our feet that length, my wind was fairly gone, and a sick dwalm came over me, that entirely deprived me of common sense, till, on opening my eyes in the dark, I found myself leaning with my broadside against the wall on the opposite side of the close. It was some time before I minded what had happened, so, dreading skaith, I found first the one arm, and then the other, to see if they were broken; syne my head; and finally, both of my legs; but all, as well as I could discover, was skin-whole, and scart-free. On perceiving this, my joy was without bounds, having a great notion that I had been killed on the spot! So I reached round my hand, very thankfully, to take out my pocket-napkin to give my brow a wipe, when, lo and behold! the tail of my Sunday's coat was fairly off and away, docked by the hainch buttons.

So much for plays and play-actors—the first and last, I trust in grace, that I shall ever see!

D. M. MOIR (1798-1851)
Mansie Wauch

amphitheatre now filled by this mighty congregation. All up the face of the opposite hill, which swept in a gentle curve before us,—the little brook I have mentioned flowing brightly between in the gleam of the sunset—the soft turf of those simple sepulchres rising row above row, and the little flat tombstones scattered more sparingly among them, were covered with one massy cluster of listening peasantry. Near to the tent on one side were drawn up some of the carriages of the neighbouring gentry, in which, the horses being taken away, the ancient ladies were seen sitting protected from the dews of the twilight—while the younger ones occupied places on the turf immediately below them. Close in front of the preacher, the very oldest of the people seemed to be arranged together, most of them sitting on stools brought for them by their children from the village—yet fresh and unwearied after all the fatigues of the day, and determined not to go away while any part of its services remained to be performed. The exact numbers of those assembled I cannot guess, but I am sure they must have amounted to very many thousands. Neither you or I, I am confident, ever beheld a congregation of the fourth of the extent engaged together in the worship of their Maker.

The number was enough of itself to render the scene a very interesting one; but the more nearly I examined their countenances, the more deeply was I impressed with a sense of respectful sympathy for the feelings of those who composed the multitude. A solemn devotion was imprinted on every downcast eyelid and trembling lip around me—their attitudes were as solemn as their countenances—each having his arms folded in his shepherd's cloak—or leaning in pensive repose upon one of those grassy swells, beneath which

> "Each in his narrow tomb for ever laid,
> The rude forefathers of the hamlet sleep."

Here and there I could perceive some hoary patriarch of the valley sitting in such a posture as this, with the old partner of his life beside him, and below and around him two or three generations of his descendants, all arranged according to their age and propinquity—the ancient saint contemplating the group ever and anon with a sad serenity,—thinking, I suppose, how unlikely it was he should live long enough to find himself again surrounded with them all on another recurrence of the same solemnity of Midsummer. Near them might be seen perhaps a pair of rural lovers, yet unwedded, sitting hand in hand together upon the same plaid in the shadow of some tall tombstone, their silent unbreathed vows gathering power more great than words could have given them from the eternal sanctities of the surrounding scene. The innocent feelings of filial affection and simple love cannot disturb the feelings of devotion, but mingle well in the same bosom with its higher flame, and blend all together into one softened and reposing confidence, alike favourable to the happiness of earth and heaven. There was a sober sublimity of calmness in the whole atmosphere around—the sky was pure and unclouded over head, and in the west only a few fleecy clouds floated in richest hues of gold and crimson, caught from the slow farewell radiance of the broad declining sun. The shadows of the little church and its tombstones lay far and long projected over the multitude, and taming here and there the glowing colours of their garments into a more mellow beauty. All was lonely and silent around the skirts of the assemblage —unless where some wandering heifer might be seen gazing for a moment upon the unwonted multitude, and then bounding away light and buoyant across the daisied herbage into some more sequestered browsing-place.

J. G. LOCKHART (1794-1854)
Peter's Letters to his Kinsfolk

I REFUSE TO GO AND DINE

In the course of the summer, just as the roof was closing in of the school-house, my lord came to the castle with a great company, and was not there a day till he sent for me to come over, on the next Sunday, to dine with him; but I sent him word that I could not do so, for it would be a transgression of the Sabbath, which made him send his own gentleman, to make his apology for having taken so great a liberty with me, and to beg me to come on the Monday, which I accordingly did, and nothing could be better than the discretion with which I was used.

There was a vast company of English ladies and gentlemen, and his lordship, in a most jocose manner, told them all how he had fallen on the midden, and how I had clad him in my clothes, and there was wonder of laughing and diversion; but the most particular thing in the company, was a large, round-faced man, with a wig, that was a dignitary in some great Episcopalian church in London, who was extraordinary condescending towards me, drinking wine with me at the table, and saying weighty sentences, in a fine style of language, about the becoming grace of simplicity and innocence of heart, in the clergy of all denominations of Christians, which I was pleased to hear; for really he had a proud red countenance, and I could not have thought he was so mortified to humility within, had I not heard with what sincerity he delivered himself, and seen how much reverence and attention was paid to him by all present, particularly by my lord's chaplain, who was a pious and pleasant young divine, though educated at Oxford for the Episcopalian persuasion.

JOHN GALT (1779-1839)
Annals of the Parish

JEANIE DEANS AND QUEEN CAROLINE

Jeanie Deans has travelled to London to plead for her sister, who has been condemned to death for alleged child-murder. She there addresses Queen Caroline.

"My sister, my puir sister Effie, still lives, though her days and hours are numbered!—She still lives, and a word of the King's mouth might restore her to a broken-hearted auld man, that never, in his daily and nightly exercise, forgot to pray that his Majesty might be blessed with a long and a prosperous reign, and that his throne, and the throne of his posterity, might be established in righteousness. O, madam, if ever ye kend what it was to sorrow for and with a sinning and suffering creature, whose mind is sae tossed that she can be neither ca'd fit to live or die, have some compassion on our misery!—Save an honest house from dishonour, and an unhappy girl, not eighteen years of age, from an early and dreadful death! Alas! it is not when we sleep soft and wake merrily ourselves, that we think on other people's sufferings. Our hearts are waxed light within us then, and we are for righting our ain wrangs and fighting our ain battles. But when the hour of trouble comes to the mind or to the body—and seldom may it visit your Leddyship—and when the hour of death comes, that comes to high and low—lang and late may it be yours—O! my Leddy, then it isna what we hae dune for oursells, but what we hae dune for others, that we think on maist pleasantly. And the thoughts that ye hae intervened to spare the puir thing's life will be sweeter in that hour, come when it may, than if a word of your mouth could hang the haill Porteous mob at the tail of ae tow."

SIR WALTER SCOTT (1771-1832)
Heart of Midlothian

THE CLIMAX OF GENTILITY

Mrs. Birse of Clinkstyle, having set up her carriage, determines to outface her landlord's turnout.

Mrs. Birse had made sundry tentative excursions here and there in the new "viackle," but it was only when Sir Simon Frissal had returned to the locality in the beginning of the month of April that she resolved to turn out in full style. Sir Simon, as was well known, drove along to the parish kirk at the same hour precisely, every Sabbath day that he was at home and in health; and the modest scheme devised was to time the departure of the Clinkstyle carriage, so as that it should at any rate cross Sir Simon's carriage at a favourable spot if it were not found possible even to drive half alongside the laird a little space where the two kirk routes concurred. To accomplish all this Mrs. Birse judiciously coaxed and flattered the red-haired orra man, giving him assurance how well he looked when properly "cleaned," and his coat buttoned. She would fain have had a sight of his Sunday wardrobe, but had to be content with the general statement that it was "spleet new fae the nap o' the bonnet to the point o' the taebit." Sunday came, the carriage was trundled out, and it was with a kind of dignified satisfaction that Mrs. Birse saw the red-haired orra man bustling about, minus his coat and hat, "yokin'" the carriage horse. The family had taken their seats, not without a kind of protest from Miss Birse, who, to her mother's great disappointment, had as yet failed to exhibit any symptoms of satisfaction with the carriage scheme. They were ready to start, when Mrs. Birse was horrified by seeing the red-haired orra man mount the dicky with an unmistakable sample of the broad blue bonnet on his head. It was one of those substantial bonnets that were wont to be manufactured on big knitting wires, and the "pan," or top was formed of a huge bunch of worsted, wrought up right in the centre of the bonnet. The orra man spoke truly in saying it was "spleet new," for the bonnet had evidently been purchased for that very occasion, as its extraordinary circumference and bulk testified. Mrs. Birse started indignantly, and uttered an exclamation which was a sort of half protest against the orra man, and half reproach to Peter Birse, senior, who had crammed himself into one of the back corners of the "viackle," and wore an extremely uncomfortable look. But the carriage was aleady in motion, and the driver seemed no way disposed to interrupt his progress for any mere incidental utterance. He rattled on mercilessly over the roughly-causewayed road leading out from the steading of Clinkstyle to the highway proper. Then in a trice they were into the head of the stream of kirk-going people, many of whom the red-haired orra man saluted with great familiarity, nodding his portentous bonnet, and flourishing his whip, while once and again he called out to an old cronie, "Hilloa, lad; there's the style for you!" Attempts at remonstrating and checking this reckless course were, it need not be said, utterly out of the question in the circumstances. Mrs. Birse strove hard to cover her wrath with an air of sanctimonious resignation, while Peter Birse, who timidly watched her face with a lively apprehension of the after consequences, looked increasingly ill at ease, and Miss Birse and her brother Rob, in so far as they could make themselves heard, concurred, though on different grounds, in the folly of ever setting a fellow like the red-haired orra man to drive. Rob, who kept his equanimity better than any of the others, seized the opportunity of reminding his mother that he had been perfectly willing to act as driver, adding, with a feeling of satisfaction, that he "kent a hantle better aboot ca'in' horse, nor that gype did. An' here's the laird's carriage!" added Rob, as sure enough it was. And the orra man rattled on. To cross Sir Simon's carriage in proper style had been Mrs. Birse's highest ambition. But the vision of that horrible "braid bonnet" with its big "nap" passing in view of the dignified baronet lying back on his velvet cushion was enough to make one faint away, without the addition of those deplorable vulgarities on the part of the red-haired orra man in cracking his whip, and shouting to Sir Simon's coachman to "Ca' awa', min, or gae oot o' ither fowk's road."

Mrs. Birse did not faint away; but when the "viackle" reached the church, and pulled up in the midst of many loitering, eagerly-gazing onlookers, she threw open the door, and preceded her daughter into the church with a severely devotional air.

Next day the duty devolved on Peter Birse of informing the red-haired orra man that his services were no longer required at Clinkstyle. The orra man did not much mind. He swore a little, and demanded wages for the time he had laboured, which was conceded, and Peter Birse, in filling his place, was not asked to look out for another coachman.

WILLIAM ALEXANDER (1826-94)
Johnny Gibb of Gushetneuk

A TURTLE SENT TO MR. CAYENNE

I have now to note a curious thing, not on account of its importance, but to show to what lengths a correspondence had been opened in the parish with the farthest parts of the earth. Mr. Cayenne got a turtle-fish sent to him from a Glasgow merchant, and it was living when it came to the Wheatrig House, and was one of the most remarkable beasts that had ever been seen in our country-side. It weighed as much as a well-fed calf, and had three kinds of meat in its body, fish, flesh, and fowl, and it had four water-wings, for they could not be properly called fins; but what was little short of a miracle about the creature, happened after the head was cutted off, when, if a finger was offered to it, it would open its mouth and snap at it, and all this after the carcass was divided for dressing.

Mr. Cayenne made a feast on the occasion to many of the neighbouring gentry, to the which I was invited; and we drank lime-punch as we ate the turtle, which, as I understand, is the fashion in practice among the Glasgow West Indy merchants, who are famed as great hands with turtles and lime-punch. But it is a sort of food that I should not like to fare long upon. I was not right the next day; and I have heard it said, that when eaten too often, it has a tendency to harden the heart and make it crave for greater luxuries.

JOHN GALT (1779-1839)
Annals of the Parish

JACOB AND ESAU

He now called up the Bible class, and Malcolm sat beside and listened. That morning they had read one of the chapters in the history of Jacob.

"Was Jacob a good man?" he asked as soon as the reading, each of the scholars in turn taking a verse, was over. An apparently universal expression of assent followed; halting in its wake, however, came the voice of a boy near the bottom of the class: "Wasna he some double, sir?" "You are right, Sheltie," said the master; "he *was* double. I must, I find, put the question in another shape: was Jacob a bad man?"

Again came such a burst of "yeses" that it might have been taken for a general hiss. But limping in the rear came again the half dissentient voice of Sheltie: "Pairtly,

283

sir." "You think then, Sheltie, that a man may be both bad and good?" "I dinna ken, sir; I think he may be whiles ane and whiles the other, and whiles maybe it wad be ill to say which. Our colly's whiles in twa minds whether he'll do what he's telled or no."

"That's the battle of Armageddon, Sheltie, my man. It's aye raging, as gun roared or bayonet clashed. Ye maun up and do your best in't, my man. Gien ye die fechting like a man, ye'll flee up with a quiet face and wide open een; and there's a great One that will say to ye, 'Weel done, laddie!' But gien ye gie in to the enemy, he'll turn ye into a creeping thing that eats dirt; and there'll no be a hole in a' the crystal wa' of the New Jerusalem near enough to let ye creep through."

"I reckon, sir," said Sheltie, "Jacob hadna foughten out his battle."

"That's just it, my boy. And because he would not get up and fight manfully, God had to take him in hand. Ye've heard tell of generals, when their troops were rinnin' awa', having to cut this man down, shoot that ane, and lick another, till he turned them a' right face about, and drave them on to the foe like a spate (flood). And the trouble God took wi' Jacob was not lost upon him at last."

"An' what came o' Esau, sir?" asked a pale faced maiden with blue eyes. "He wasna an ill kind o' a chield, was he, sir?"

"No, Mappy," answered the master; "he was a fine chield as you say, but he needed mair time and gentler treatment to make onything o' him. Ye see he had a guid heart, but was a duller kind o' creature a'thigether, and cared for naething he couldna see or handle. He never thought muckle about God at a'. Jacob was another sort—a poet kind o' man, but a sneck-drawing creature for a' that. It was easier, however, to get the slyness out o' Jacob than the dullness out o' Esau. Punishment telled upon Jacob like upon a thin-skinned horse, whereas Esau was mair like the minister's powny, that can hardly be made to understand that ye want him to gang on."

GEORGE MACDONALD (1824-1905)
Malcolm

LOCHABER NO MORE

David Balfour, crossing from Mull to the mainland, passes an emigrant ship for America.

The passage was a very slow affair. There was no wind, and as the boat was wretchedly equipped, we could pull but two oars on one side, and one on the other. The men gave way, however, with a good will, the passengers taking spells to help them, and the whole company giving the time in Gaelic boat-songs. And what with the songs, and the sea air, and the good-nature and spirit of all concerned, and the bright weather, the passage was a pretty thing to have seen.

But there was one melancholy part. In the mouth of Loch Aline we found a great sea-going ship at anchor; and this I supposed at first to be one of the King's cruisers which were kept along that coast, both summer and winter, to prevent communication with the French. As we got a little nearer, it became plain she was a ship of merchandise; and what still more puzzled me, not only her decks, but the sea-beach also, were quite black with people, and skiffs were continually plying to and fro between them. Yet nearer, and there began to come to our ears a great sound of mourning, the people on board and those on the shore crying and lamenting one to another so as to pierce the heart.

Then I understood this was an emigrant ship bound for the American colonies.

We put the ferry-boat alongside, and the exiles leaned

over the bulwarks, weeping and reaching out their hands to my fellow-passengers, among whom they counted some near friends. How long this might have gone on I do not know, for they seemed to have no sense of time: but at last the captain of the ship, who seemed near beside himself (and no great wonder) in the midst of this crying and confusion, came to the side and begged us to depart.

Thereupon Neil sheered off; and the chief singer in our boat struck into a melancholy air, which was presently taken up both by the emigrants and their friends upon the beach, so that it sounded from all sides like a lament for the dying. I saw the tears run down the cheeks of the men and women in the boat, even as they bent at the oars; and the circumstances and the music of the song (which is one called *Lochaber no more*) were highly affecting even to myself.

R. L. STEVENSON (1850-94)
Kidnapped

PRACTICE IN ENGLAND

It happened at a small country town that Scott suddenly required medical advice for one of his servants, and, on enquiring if there was any doctor at the place, was told that there was two—one long established, and the other a new comer. The latter gentleman, being luckily found at home, soon made his appearance;—a grave, sagacious-looking personage, attired in black, with a shovel hat, in whom, to his utter astonishment, Sir Walter recognised a Scotch blacksmith, who formerly practised, with tolerable success, as a veterinary operator in the neighbourhood of Ashestiel. "How, in all the world!" exclaimed he, "Can it be possible that this is John Lundie?" "In troth it is, your honour—just *a' that's for him*." "Well, but let us hear; you were a *horse*-doctor; how do you get on?" "Ou, just extra-ordinar weel; for your honour maun ken my practice is vera sure and orthodox. I depend entirely upon twa *simples*." "And what may their names be? Perhaps it is a secret?" "I'll tell your honour," in a low tone; "my twa simples are just laudamy and calamy!" "Simples with a vengeance!" replied Scott. "But John, do you never happen to *kill* any of your patients?" "Kill? Ou ay, may be sae! Whiles they die, and whiles no; but it's the will o' Providence. *Ony how, your honour, it wad be long before it makes up for Flodden!*"

J. G. LOCKHART (1794-1854)
Life of Sir Walter Scott

CANADIAN BOAT SONG

Listen to me, as when ye heard our father
    Sing long ago the song of other shores—
Listen to me, and then in chorus gather
    All your deep voices as ye pull your oars:
Fair these broad meads—these hoary woods are grand,
But we are exiles from our fathers' land.

From the lone shieling of the misty island
    Mountains divide us, and the waste of seas—
Yet still the blood is strong, the heart is Highland,
    And we in dreams behold the Hebrides.

We ne'er shall tread the fancy-haunted valley,
    Where 'tween the dark hills creeps the small clear
        stream,
In arms around the patriarch banner rally,
    Nor see the moon on royal tombstones gleam.

When the bold kindred, in the time long-vanish'd,
    Conquer'd the soil and fortified the keep,

No seer foretold the children would be banish'd,
  That a degenerate lord might boast his sheep.

Come foreign rage—let Discord burst in slaughter!
  O then for clansmen true, and stern claymore—
The hearts that would have given their blood like water
  Beat heavily beyond the Atlantic roar.
Fair these broad meads—these hoary woods are grand;
But we are exiles from our fathers' land.

ANONYMOUS

THE HAANTIT HOOSIE

The Haunted House

The haantit hoosie is doun at the bend o' the brae,
  Nae step on its stairs, no' e'en the paw o' a poussie.
Alike are the day, the morn, and yesterday
  To the haantit hoosie.

Ma bairn, ye maunna gan there, ma wee bit toussie,[1]
  Yon's no' a place whaur a lassock can dance and play,
E'en though the gairden is gay and the grossarts[2] are
  juicy.

No, the greediest gled[3] i' the glebe, no' the corbie[4] nor
  kae[5]
  Wull pyke at the plooms[6] on the wa', nor the nibblin'
    moosie
Wull gnaw at the girnel;[7] sae pit neither finger nor tae
  I' the haantit hoosie.

LEWIS SPENCE (1874-1955)

[1] dishevelled child   [2] gooseberries   [3] kite   [4] crow   [5] jackdaw   [6] peck at
the plums   [7] meal chest

THE WHISTLE

He cut a sappy sucker from the muckle rodden-tree,[1]
He trimmed it, an' he wet it, an' he thumped it on his
    knee;
He never heard the teuchat[2] when the harrow broke her
    eggs,
He missed the craggit[3] heron nabbin'[4] puddocks in the
    seggs,[5]
He forgot to hound the collie at the cattle when they
    strayed,
But you should hae seen the whistle that the wee[6] herd
    made!

He wheepled on't at mornin' an' he tweetled on't at
    nicht,[7]
He puffed his freckled cheeks until his nose sank oot o'
    sicht,[8]
The kye were late for milkin' when he piped them up
    the closs,[9]
The kitlins[10] got his supper syne, an' he was beddit[11]
    boss;
But he cared na doit[12] nor docken[13] what they did or
    thocht or said,
There was comfort in the whistle that the wee herd
    made.

For lyin' lang o' mornin's he had clawed[14] the caup for
    weeks,
But noo he had his bonnet on afore the lave[15] had breeks;

[1] rowan   [2] lapwing   [3] crested   [4] catching frogs   [5] marshland
[6] little [7] night [8] sight [9] lane [10] kittens [11] sent to bed hungry
[12] copper coin of small value [13] dock [14] cleaned the dish (as a
punishment the person last to get up in the morning had to clean
the common bowl) [15] the others had trousers

He was whistlin' to the porridge that were hott'rin' on
    the fire,
He was whistlin' ower the travise[1] to the baillie in the
    byre;
Nae a blackbird nor a mavis,[2] that hae pipin' for their
    trade,
Was a marrow[3] for the whistle that the wee herd made.

He played a march to battle. It cam' dirlin'[4] through
    the mist.
Till the halflin'[5] squared his shou'ders an' made up his
    mind to 'list[6];
He tried a spring for wooers, though he wistna what it
    meant,
But the kitchen-lass was lauchin' an' he thocht she
    maybe kent[7];
He got ream[8] an' buttered bannocks[9] for the lovin' lilt
    he played.
Wasna that a cheery whistle that the wee herd made?

He blew them rants sae lively, schottisches, reels, an' jigs,
The foalie flang his muckle legs an' capered ower the
    rigs,
The grey-tailed futt'rat[10] bobbit oot to hear his ain
    strathspey,
The bawd[11] cam' loupin' through the corn to "Clean
    Pease Strae,"
The feet o' ilka man an' beast gat youkie[12] when he
    played—
Hae ye ever heard o' whistle like the wee herd made?

But the snaw it stopped the herdin' an' the winter brocht
    him dool,[13]

[1] division between stalls   [2] thrush   [3] match   [4] sounding, vibrating
[5] odd boy on farm (half-grown man)   [6] enlist   [7] know   [8] cream
[9] scones   [10] weasel   [11] hare came leaping   [12] itchy   [13] woe

When in spite o' hacks and chilblains he was shod again
    for school;
He couldna souch[1] the Catechis nor pipe the rule o'
    three,
He was keepit in an' lickit[2] when the ither loons[3] got
    free;
But he aften played the truant—'twas the only thing he
    played,
For the maister brunt[4] the whistle that the wee herd
    made!

CHARLES MURRAY

[1] recite   [2] punished   [3] boys   [4] burned

THE UNDOING OF WHINNY WEBSTER

From the pulpit, which was swaddled in black, the
minister had a fine sweep of all the congregation except
those in the back pews downstairs, who were lost in the
shadow of the laft. Here sat Whinny Webster, so called
because, having an inexplicable passion against them,
he devoted his life to the extermination of whins.
Whinny for years ate peppermint lozenges with impunity
in his back seat, safe in the certainty that the minister,
however much he might try, could not possibly see him.
But his day came. One afternoon the kirk smelt of
peppermints, and Mr. Dishart could rebuke none, for the
defaulter was not in sight. Whinny's cheek was working
up and down in quiet enjoyment of its lozenge, when he
started, noticing that the preaching had stopped. Then
he heard a sepulchral voice say "Charles Webster!"
Whinny's eyes turned to the pulpit, only part of which
was visible to him, and to his horror they encountered
the minister's head coming down the stairs. This took
place after I had ceased to attend the Auld Licht kirk
regularly; but I am told that as Whinny gave one wild

scream the peppermint dropped from his mouth. The minister had got him by leaning over the pulpit door until, had he given himself only another inch, his feet would have gone into the air. As for Whinny he became a God-fearing man.

SIR J. M. BARRIE (1860-1937)
Auld Licht Idylls

THE SERMON TASTER

Tam Stoddart: It'll no' dae. It'll no' dae ava. I dinna haud wi' hintin' an' hidin'. Nae guid ever cam' o' that. Playin' a kin' o' keek-a-boo wi' folk's souls. Let a man either lash oot wi't or haud his tongue. Ye dinna win souls by tricks o' talk an' play-actin' i' the pulpit. It does an immense amount o' hairm—the folk it's meent for 'ud be the vera last i' maist cases to tak' it to themsel's, but it sets a' the silly craturs i' the congregation fair bizzin' wi' excitement an' terror. It's the humble an' contrite o' hert that are easiest made believe they're vera deevils o' ineequity, singled oot for the wrath to come. But the hard nits can sit like lumps o' asbestos through the hettest harangue. Na! Na! The man hasna bin five minutes i' the place, an' can only ha'e been talkin' at large, shootin' oot his neck at random i' the hopes o' fetchin' doon somethin'. But he's owre big for his boots—an' fer owre wee for the boots o' the auld Doctor he's tryin' to fill. Heck! It's eneuch to mak' him turn in his grave—sic a sermon as that frae his auld pulpit. We're no' leevin' in Auld Testament times noo, an' he mauna come to Blawearie thinkin' to stalk muckle big game i' the sin line. I question vera much if there's a crime i' the haill community bigger than a bit poppin' flea (an' we've a' got plenty o' them), an' yet here's him bendin' the bow o' Ulysses by his wey o't, an' knockin' oot the feck o' the congregation wi' an arrow fit to smash a rhinoceros, juist like yon fool shootin' tenant o' a Yankee at the Todheid last back-en' wha took the auld mare for a stray stag an' shot a haill hirsel o' sheep in his attempts to pot it . . .

HUGH MACDIARMID (C. M. GRIEVE, b. 1892)
The Purple Patch from *Scottish Scene*

I COME FROM SCOTLAND

Monday 16 May, 1763: Temple and his brother breakfasted with me. I went to Love's to try to recover some of the money which he owes me. But, alas, a single guinea was all I could get. He was just going to dinner, so I stayed and eat a bit, though I was angry at myself afterwards. I drank tea at Davies's in Russell Street, and about seven came in the great Mr. Samuel Johnson, whom I have so long wished to see. Mr. Davies introduced me to him. As I knew his mortal antipathy at the Scotch, I cried to Davies, "Don't tell where I come from." However, he said, "From Scotland." "Mr. Johnson," said I, "indeed I come from Scotland, but I cannot help it." "Sir," replied he, "that, I find, is what a very great many of your countrymen cannot help." Mr. Johnson is a man of a most dreadful appearance. He is a very big man, is troubled with sore eyes, the palsy, and the king's evil. He is very slovenly in his dress and speaks with a most uncouth voice. Yet his great knowledge and strength of expression command vast respect and render him very excellent company. He has great humour and is a worthy man. But his dogmatical roughness of manners is disagreeable. I shall mark what I remember of his conversation.

Boswell's London Journal, 1762-1763

293

Customs, Hospitality

SCOTTISH HOSPITALITY

It was once the universal custom to place ale, wine, or some strong liquor, in the chamber of an honoured guest, to assuage his thirst should he awaken in the night.

It is a current story in Teviotdale, that, in the house of an ancient family of distinction, much addicted to the Presbyterian cause, a Bible was always put into the sleeping apartment of the guests, along with a bottle of strong ale. On some occasion there was a meeting of clergymen in the vicinity of the castle, all of whom were invited to dinner by the worthy Baronet, and several abode all night. According to the fashion of the times, seven of the reverend guests were allotted to one large barrack-room, which was used on such occasions of extended hospitality. The butler took care that the divines were presented, according to custom, each with a Bible and a bottle of ale. But after a little consultation among themselves, they are said to have recalled the domestic as he was leaving the apartment. "My friend," said one of the venerable guests, "you must know, when we meet together as brethren, the youngest minister reads aloud a portion of Scripture to the rest; only one Bible, therefore, is necessary; take away the other six, and in their place bring six more bottles of ale."

This synod would have suited the "hermit age" of Johnson, who answered a pupil who inquired for the real road to happiness, with the celebrated line, "Come, my lad, and drink some beer!"

SIR WALTER SCOTT (1771-1832)
Note to *The Bride of Lammermoor*

RUNE OF HOSPITALITY
From the island of Eigg

I saw a stranger yestreen;
I put food in the eating place,
Drink in the drinking place,
Music in the listening place;
In the sacred name of the Triune;
He blessed myself and my house,
My cattle and my dear ones;
And the lark said in her song,
    Often, often, often
Goes the Christ in the stranger's guise,
    Often often, often
Goes the Christ in the stranger's guise.

Translation by KENNETH MACLEOD

THE VALUE OF A DRAM

"Ay, ay—it's easy for your honour, and the like o'
you gentle-folks, to say sae, that hae stouth and routh,
and fire and fending, and meat and claith, and sit dry
and canny by the fireside—but an ye wanted fire, and
meat, and dry claise, and were deeing o' cauld, and had
a sair heart, whilk is warst ava, wi' just tippence in
your pouch, wadna ye be glad to buy a dram wi't, to
be eilding and claise, and a supper an heart's ease into
the bargain, till the morn's morning?"

SIR WALTER SCOTT (1771-1832)
The Antiquary

HIGHLAND HOSPITALITY

When beginning to descend the hill towards Loch Lomond we overtook two girls, who told us we could not cross the ferry till evening, for the boat was gone with a number of people to Church. One of the girls was exceedingly beautiful; and the figures of both of them, in grey plaids falling to their feet, their faces only being uncovered, excited our attention before we spoke to them: but they answered us so sweetly that we were quite delighted. At the same time they stared at us with an innocent look of wonder. I think I never heard the English language sound more sweetly than from the mouth of the elder of these girls, while she stood at the gate answering our inquiries, her face flushed with the rain; her pronunciation was clear and distinct; without difficulty, yet slow, like that of a foreign speech. . . . We were glad to be housed, with our feet on a warm hearth-stone: and our attendants were so active and good-humoured, that it was pleasant to have to desire them to do anything. The younger was a delicate and unhealthy-looking girl: but there was an uncommon meekness in her countenance, with an air of premature intelligence, which is often seen in sickly young persons. The other moved with unusual activity, which was chastened very delicately by a certain hesitation in her looks when she spoke, being able to understand us but imperfectly. They were both exceedingly desirous to get me what I wanted to make me comfortable. I was to have a gown and petticoat of the mistress's: so they turned out her whole wardrobe upon the parlour floor, talking Erse to one another and laughing all the time. It was long before they could decide which of the gowns I was to have: they chose at last, no doubt thinking it was the best, a light-coloured sprigged cotton, with long sleeves, and they both laughed when I was putting it on, with the blue linsey petticoat; and one or the other, or both together, helped me to dress, repeating at least half a dozen times, "You never had on the like of that before." They held a consultation of several minutes over a pair of coarse woollen stockings, gabbling Erse as fast as their tongues could move, and looking as if uncertain what to do: at last, with great diffidence they offered them to me, adding, as before, that I have never worn "the like of them."

The hospitality we had met on this our first entrance into the Highlands and on this day, the innocent merriment of the girls with their kindness to us, and the beautiful figure and face of the elder, comes to my mind whenever I think of the ferry house and waterfall of Loch Lomond, and I never think of the two girls but the whole image of that romantic spot is before me, a living image, as it will be to my dying day.

DOROTHY WORDSWORTH (1771-1855)
A Tour in Scotland

A BOTTLE AND A FRIEND

Here's a bottle and an honest friend
  What wad ye wish for mair, man?
Wha kens, before his life may end,
  What his share may be o' care, man?

Then catch the moments as they fly,
  And use them as ye ought, man;
Believe me, happiness is shy,
  And comes no ay when sought, man!

ROBERT BURNS (1759-96)

297

THE HEREDITARY PIPER

Our landlord is a man of consequence in this part of the country; a cadet from the family of Argyle, and hereditary captain of one of his castles—his name, in plain English, is Dougal Campbell; but as there is a great number of the same appellation, they are distinguished (like the Welsh) by patronymics; and as I have known an ancient Briton called Madoc ap-Morgan, ap-Jenkin, ap-Jones, our Highland chief designs himself Dou'l Mac-amish, mac-'oul ich-Ian, signifying Dougal, the son of James, the son of Dougal, the son of John. He has travelled in the course of his education, and is disposed to make certain alterations in his domestic economy; but he finds it impossible to abolish the ancient customs of the family; some of which are ludicrous enough. His piper, for example, who is an hereditary officer of the household, will not part with the least particle of his privileges. He has a right to wear the kilt, or ancient Highland dress, with the purse, pistol, and dirk—a broad yellow ribbon, fixed to the chanter-pipe, is thrown over his shoulder, and trails along the ground, while he performs the functions of his minstrelsy; and this, I suppose, is analogous to the pennon or flag, which was formerly carried before every knight in battle. He plays before the laird every Sunday in this way to the kirk, which he circles three times, performing the family march, which implies defiance to all the enemies of the clan; and every morning he plays a full hour by the clock, in the great hall, marching backwards and forwards all the time, with a solemn pace, attended by the laird's kinsmen, who seem much delighted with the music. In this exercise he indulges them with a number of pibrochs or airs, suited to the different passions which he would either excite or assuage.

Mr. Campbell himself, who performs very well on the violin, has an invincible antipathy to the sound of the Highland bagpipe, which sings in the nose with a most alarming twang, and, indeed, is quite intolerable to ears of common sensibility, when aggravated by the echo of a vaulted hall. He, therefore, begged the piper would have some mercy upon him, and dispense with this part of the morning service. A consultation of the clan being held on this occasion, it was unanimously agreed, that the laird's request could not be granted, without a dangerous encroachment upon the customs of the family. The piper declared he could not give up for a moment the privilege he derived from his ancestors; nor would the laird's relations forego an entertainment which they valued above all others. There was no remedy; Mr. Campbell being obliged to acquiesce, is fain to stop his ears with cotton, to fortify his head with three or four nightcaps, and every morning retire into the penetralia of his habitation, in order to avoid this diurnal annoyance.

TOBIAS SMOLLETT (1721-71)
Humphry Clinker

EPIGRAM AT ROSLIN INN

My blessings on ye, honest wife!
 I ne'er was here before;
Ye've wealth o' gear for spoon and knife—
 Heart could not wish for more.
Heav'n keep you clear o' sturt and strife,
 Till far ayont fourscore,
And while I toddle on thro' life,
 I'll ne'er gae by your door!

ROBERT BURNS (1759-96)

299

A HUNTERS' REPAST

This morning we got up by four, to hunt the roebuck, and, in half an hour, found breakfast ready served in the hall. The hunters consisted of Sir George Colquhoun and me, as strangers (my uncle not choosing to be of the party), of the *laird in person, the laird's brother, the laird's brother's son, the laird's sister's son, the laird's father's brother's son,* and all their *foster brothers,* who are counted parcel of the family. . . . But we were attended by an infinite number of *Gaellys,* or ragged Highlanders, without shoes or stockings.

The following articles formed our morning's repast: —One kit of boiled eggs; a second, full of butter; a third, full of cream; an entire cheese made of goat's milk; a large earthen pot, full of honey; the best part of a ham; a cold venison pasty; a bushel of oatmeal, made in thin cakes and bannocks, with a small wheaten loaf in the middle for the strangers; a large stone bottle full of whisky, another of brandy, and a kilderkin of ale. There was a ladle chained to the cream-kit, with curious wooden bickers, to be filled from this reservoir. The spirits were drank out of a silver quaff, and the ale out of horns; great justice was done to the collation by the guests in general; one of them, in particular, ate above two dozen of hard eggs, with a proportionable quantity of bread, butter, and honey; nor was one drop of liquor left upon the board. Finally, a large roll of tobacco was presented by way of dessert, and every individual took a comfortable quid, to prevent the bad effects of the morning air. We had a fine chase over the mountains, after a roebuck, which we killed, and I got home time enough to drink tea with Mrs. Campbell and our squire.

TOBIAS SMOLLETT (1721-71)
Humphry Clinker

FAREWELL TO THE HIGHLANDS

Farewell to the Highlands, farewell to the north,
The birthplace of Valour, the country of Worth;
Wherever I wander, wherever I rove,
The hills of the Highlands for ever I love.

Chorus
My heart's in the Highlands, my heart is not here,
My heart's in the Highlands, a-chasing the deer;
A-chasing the wild deer, and following the roe,
My heart's in the Highlands wherever I go.

Farewell to the mountains, high-cover'd with snow,
Farewell to the straths and green valleys below;
Farewell to the forests and wild-hanging woods,
Farewell to the torrents and loud-pouring floods.

Chorus

ROBERT BURNS (1759-96)

DEOCH AN DORUIS

When the landlord of an inn presented his guests with *deoch an doruis*, that is, the drink at the door, or the stirrup-cup, the draught was not charged in the reckoning. On this point a learned bailie of the town of Forfar pronounced a very sound judgment.

A., an ale-wife in Forfar, had brewed her "peck of maut" and set the liquor out of doors to cool; the cow of B., a neighbour of A., chanced to come by, and seeing the good beverage, was allured to taste it, and finally to drink it up. When A. came to take in her liquor, she found her tub empty, and from the cow's staggering and staring, so as to betray her intemperance, she easily

301

A BOOK OF SCOTLAND

divined the mode in which her "browst" had disappeared. To take vengeance on Crummie's ribs with a stick was her first effort. The roaring of the cow brought B., her master, who remonstrated with his angry neighbour, and received in reply a demand for the value of the ale which Crummie had drunk up. B. refused payment, and was convened before C., the bailie, or sitting magistrate. He heard the case patiently; and then demanded of the plaintiff A. whether the cow had sat down to her potation or taken it standing. The plaintiff answered, she had not seen the deed committed, but she supposed the cow drank the ale while standing on her feet, adding, that had she been near she would have made her use them to some purpose. The bailie, on this admission, solemnly adjudged the cow's drink to be *deoch an doruis*, a stirrup-cup, for which no charge could be made without violating the ancient hospitality of Scotland.

SIR WALTER SCOTT (1771-1832)
Note to *Waverley*

VERSIFIED REPLY TO AN INVITATION

MAUCHLIN,
Monday night, 10 o'clock

Sir,

Yours this moment I unseal,
    And faith I'm gay and hearty!
To tell the truth and shame the deil,
    I am as fou as Bartie:
But Foorsday, sir, my promise leal,
    Expect me o' your partie,
If on a beastie I can speil,
    Or hurl in a cartie.
        Yours,

ROBERT BURNS (1759-96)

HIGHLAND WHISKY

When the Lowlanders want to drink a cheer-upping cup, they go to the public-house, called the Change House, and call for a chopin of twopenny, which is a thin yeasty beverage, made of malt, not quite so strong as the table-beer of England. This is brought in a pewter stoup, shaped like a skittle; from whence it is emptied into a quaff, that is, a curious cup made of different pieces of wood, such as box and ebony, cut into little staves, joined alternately, and secured with delicate hoops, having two ears or handles. It holds about a gill, is sometimes tipt round the mouth with silver, and has a plate of the same metal at the bottom, with the landlord's cypher engraved.

The Highlanders, on the contrary, despise this liquor, and regale themselves with whisky, a malt spirit, as strong as geneva, which they swallow in great quantities, without any signs of inebriation: they are used to it from the cradle, and find it an excellent preservative against the winter cold, which must be extreme on these mountains—I am told that it is given with great success to infants, as a cordial, in the confluent smallpox, when the eruption seems to flag, and the symptoms grow unfavourable.

TOBIAS SMOLLETT (1721-71)
Humphry Clinker

A HIGHLAND FUNERAL

Yesterday we were invited to the funeral of an old lady, the grandmother of a gentleman in this neighbour-hood, and found ourselves in the midst of fifty people, who were regaled with a sumptious feast, accompanied with the music of a dozen pipers. In short, this meeting had all the air of a grand festival; and the guests did such honour to the entertainment, that many of them could not stand when they were reminded of the business on which we had met. The company forthwith taking horse, rode in a very irregular cavalcade to the place of internment, a church, at the distance of two long miles from the castle. On our arrival, however, we found we had committed a small oversight in leaving the corpse behind; so that we were obliged to wheel about and met the old gentlewoman half-way, carried upon poles by the nearest relations of her family, and attended by the *coronach*, composed of a multitude of old hags, who tore their hair, beat their breasts, and howled most hideously.

At the grave the orator or *senachie* pronounced the panegyric of the defunct, every period being confirmed by a yell of the *coronach*. The body was committed to the earth, the pipers playing a pibroch all the time, and all the company standing uncovered. The ceremony was closed with the discharge of pistols; then we returned to the castle, resumed the bottle, and by midnight there was not a sober person in the family, the females excepted. The squire and I were, with some difficulty, permitted to retire with the landlord in the evening; but our entertainer was a little chagrined at our retreat; and afterwards seemed to think it a disparagement to his family, that not above an hundred gallons of whisky had been drunk upon such a solemn occasion.

TOBIAS SMOLLETT (1721-71)
Humphry Clinker

HAGGIS AND OATCAKES

Now we are upon the article of cookery, I must own, some of their dishes are savoury, and even delicate; but I am not yet Scotchman enough to relish their singed sheep's head and haggis, which were provided, at our request, one day at Mr. Mitchelson's, where we dined.

The first put me in mind of the history of Congo, in which I had read of negroes' heads sold publicly in the markets; the last, being a mess of minced lights, livers, suet, oatmeal, onions, and pepper, enclosed in a sheep's stomach, had a very sudden effect upon mine, and the delicate Mrs. Tabby changed colour; when the cause of our disgust was instantaneously removed at the nod of our entertainer. The Scotch in general are attached to this composition with a sort of national fondness, as well as to their oatmeal bread; which is presented at every table, in thin triangular cakes, baked upon a plate of iron, called a girdle; and these many of the natives, even in the higher ranks of life, prefer to wheaten bread, which they have here in perfection.

TOBIAS SMOLLETT (1721-71)
Humphry Clinker

HAGGIS

Fair fa' your honest, sonsie face,
Great chieftain o' the pudden race

Clean a sheep's pluck thoroughly. Make incisions in the heart and liver to allow the blood to flow out, and parboil them, letting the windpipe lie over the side of the pot to permit the phlegm and blood to disgorge from the lungs; change the water after a few minutes boiling for fresh water. Another half hour's boiling will be sufficient; but throw back the half of the liver to boil until it will grate easily. Take the heart, the half of the liver and the lungs, trimming away all skins and black-looking parts, and mince them together along with a pound of good beef suet. Grate the other half of the liver. Have eight onions peeled and scalded in two waters, which chop and mix with this mince. Toast some oatmeal before the fire till it is of a light brown colour and perfectly dry. Less than two teaspoonfuls of meal will do for this quantity of meat. Spread the mince on a board and strew the meal lightly over it, with a high seasoning of pepper, salt, a little cayenne and marjoram, well mixed. Have a sheep's stomach perfectly clean, and see that there is no thin part in it in case of its bursting. Put in the meat with a half-pint of good beef gravy, or as much strong broth and the juice of a lemon or a little good vinegar as will make a thick stew. Be careful not to fill the bag too full so as to allow the meat room to swell. Press out the air and sew up the bag; prick it with a large needle when it first swells in the pot, to prevent bursting; let it boil slowly for three hours if large.

ROBERT H. CHRISTIE
Banquets of the Nations

BANNOCKS O' BEAR MEAL

Chorus
Bannocks o' bear meal,
Bannocks o' barley,
Here's to the Highlandman's
Bannocks o' barley!

Wha, in a brulyie, will
    First cry "A parley"?
Never the lads wi' the
    Bannocks o' barley.

Chorus

Wha, in his wae days,
    Were loyal to Charlie?
Wha but the lads wi' the
    Bannocks o' barley!

Chorus

ROBERT BURNS (1759-96)

A HIGHLAND CHIEFTAIN

When Fergus and Waverley met, the latter was struck with the peculiar grace and dignity of the Chieftain's figure. Above the middle size, and finely proportioned, the Highland dress, which he wore in its simplest mode, set off his person to great advantage. He wore the trews, or close trowsers, made of tartan, chequed scarlet and white; in other particulars, his dress strictly resembled Evan's excepting that he had no weapon save a dirk, very richly mounted with silver. His page, as we have said, carried his claymore; and the fowling-piece, which he held in his hand, seemed only designed for sport. He had shot in the course of his walk some young wild-ducks, as, though *close-time* was then unknown, the broods of grouse were yet too young for the sportsman. His countenance was decidedly Scottish, with all the peculiarities of the northern physiognomy, but yet had so little of its harshness and exaggeration, that it would have been pronounced in any country extremely hand-some. The martial air of the bonnet, with a single eagle's feather as a distinction, added much to the manly appearance of his head, which was besides ornamented with a far more natural and graceful cluster of close black curls than ever were exposed to sale in Bond Street.

An air of openness and affability increased the favour-able impression derived from this handsome and dignified exterior. Yet a skilful physiognomist would have been less satisfied with the countenance on the second than on the first view. The eyebrow and upper lip bespoke something of the habit of peremptory com-mand and decisive superiority. Even his courtesy, though open, frank, and unconstrained, seemed to indicate a sense of personal importance; and, upon any check or accidental excitation, a sudden, though transient lour of the eye, shewed a hasty, haughty, and vindictive temper, not less to be dreaded because it seemed much under its owner's command. In short, the countenance of the Chieftain resembled a smiling summer's day, in which, notwithstanding, we are made sensible by certain, though slight signs, that it may thunder and lighten before the close of evening.

SIR WALTER SCOTT (1771-1832)
Waverley

ARCHER OF THE SCOTTISH GUARD

Ludovic Lesly, or, as we shall more frequently call him, Le Balafré, by which name he was generally known in France, was upwards of six feet high, robust, strongly compacted in person, and hard-favoured in countenance, which latter attribute was much increased by a large and ghastly scar, which, beginning on his forehead, and narrowly missing his right eye, had laid bare the cheekbone, and descended from thence almost to the tip of his ear, exhibiting a deep seam, which was sometimes scarlet, sometimes purple, sometimes blue, and sometimes approaching to black; but always hideous, because at variance with the complexion of the face in whatever state it chanced to be, whether agitated or still, flushed with unusual passion, or in its ordinary state of weatherbeaten and sunburnt swarthiness.

His dress and arms were splendid. He wore his national bonnet, crested with a tuft of feathers, and with a Virgin Mary of massive silver for a brooch. . . .

The Archer's gorget, arm-pieces, and gauntlets, were of the finest steel, curiously inlaid with silver, and his hauberk, or shirt of mail, was as clear and bright as the frostwork of a winter morning upon fern or brier. He wore a loose surcoat, or cassock, of rich blue velvet, open at the sides like that of a herald, with a large white St. Andrew's cross of embroidered silver bisecting it both before and behind—his knees and legs were protected by hose of mail and shoes of steel—a broad strong poniard (called the *Mercy of God*) hung by his right side—the baldric for his two-handed sword, richly embroidered, hung upon his left shoulder; but, for convenience, he at present carried in his hand that unwealdy weapon, which the rules of his service forbade him to lay aside.

Quentin Durward, though, like the Scottish youth of the period, he had been early taught to look upon arms and war, thought he had never seen a more martial-looking, or more completely equipped and accomplished man-at-arms, than now saluted him in the person of his mother's brother, called Ludovic with the Scar, or Le Balafré; yet he could not but shrink a little from the grim expression of his countenance, while, with its rough moustaches, he brushed first the one and then the other cheek of his kinsman, welcomed his nephew to France, and, in the same breath, asked what news from Scotland.

SIR WALTER SCOTT (1771-1832)
Quentin Durward

AN ABERDEEN HIGH TEA

High tea in Aberdeen is like no other meal on earth. It is the meal of the day, the meal par excellence, and the tired come home to it ravenous, driven by the granite streets, hounded in for energy to stoke against that menace. Tea is drunk with the meal, and the order of it is this: First, one eats a plateful of sausages and eggs and mashed potatoes; then a second plateful to keep down the first. Eating, one assists the second plateful to its final home by mouthfuls of oatcake spread with butter. Then you eat oatcake with cheese. Then there are scones. Then cookies. Then it is really time to begin on tea—tea and bread and butter and crumpets and toasted rolls and cakes. Then some Dundee cake. Then—about half-past seven—someone shakes you out of the coma into which you have fallen and asks you persuasively if you wouldn't like another cup of tea and just *one* more egg and sausage. . . .

And all night long, on top of this supper and one of those immense Aberdonian beds which appear to be made of knotted ship's cable, the investigator, through and transcending the howl of the November sleet-wind, will hear the lorries and the drays, in platoons, clattering up and down Market Street. They do it for no reason or purpose, except to keep you awake. And in the morning when you descend with a grey face and an aching head, they provide you with an immense Aberdeen breakfast; and if you halt and gasp somewhere through the third course they send for the manager who comes and questions you gravely as to why you don't like the food?—should he send for a doctor?

LEWIS GRASSIC GIBBON (J. LESLIE MITCHELL, 1901-35)
Scottish Scene

WHA HES GUD MALT

An example of one of the few drinking songs by the old Scots "makaris" that have been preserved. In olden time the ale was brewed by the wives who sold it.

Wha hes gud malt and makis ill drink,
    Wa mot be hir werd![1]
I pray to God scho rot and stink,
    Sevin yeir abone the erd;[2]
About hir beir na bell to clink,
    Nor clerk sing, lawid nor lerd;[3]
Bot quite to hell that scho may sink

---

[1] May woe be her destiny   [2] above ground   [3] loud nor learned

The taptre whyll scho steird:[1]
    This beis my prayer
    For that man sleyar,
Whill[2] Christ in Hevin sall heird.

Wha brewis and gevis me of the best,
    Sa it be stark and staill,[3]
White and cleir, weill to degest,
      In Hevin meit hir that aill!
Lang mot scho leif, lang mot scho lest
    In lyking ane gude saill;
In Hevin or erd[4] that wyfe be best,
    Without barrat or bail[5];
      When scho is deid,
      Withowttin pleid,
    Scho pass to Hevin all haill.[6]

ANONYMOUS

[1] while she was tapping the liquor   [2] until   [3] strong and old   [4] earth
[5] trouble or sorrow   [6] entirely, at once

ON SENSIBILITY

Rusticity's ungainly form
    May cloud the highest mind;
But when the heart is nobly warm,
    The *good* excuse will find.
Propriety's cold, cautious rules
    Warm fervour may o'erlook;
But spare poor sensibility
    Th' ungentle, harsh rebuke.

ROBERT BURNS (1759-96)

NOW FAYRE, FAYREST OFF EVERY FAYRE

Sung at the marriage banquet of James IV and Margaret Tudor in Holyrood Palace, 8th August, 1503. The music also is preserved in the MS in the British Museum.

Now fayre, fayrest off every fayre,
Princess most pleasant and preclare,[1]
The lustyest one alyve that byne,[2]
  Welcum of Scotland to be Quene!

Young tender plant of pulcritud,
Descended of Imperyal blode;
Fresh fragrant flower of fayrehede shene,[3]
  Welcum of Scotland to be Quene!

Swet lusty lusum[4] lady clere,[5]
Most myghty kynges dochter dere,
Born of a princess most serene,
  Welcum of Scotland to be Quene!

Welcum the Rose both red and whyte,
Welcum the flower of our delyte!
Our secret rejoysyng from the sone beine[6]
  Welcum of Scotland to be Quene!

WILLIAM DUNBAR (c. 1460-1520)

[1] famous [2] is [3] bright [4] lovesome [5] fair [6] to be

LAMENT FOR THE MAKARIS

I that in heill[1] was and gladness
Am trublit now with great sickness
And feblit with infirmitie:—
  Timor Mortis conturbat me.

Our plesance here is all vain glory,
This fals world is but transitory,
The flesh is bruckle,[2] the Feynd is slee[3]:—
  Timor Mortis conturbat me.

The state of man does change and vary,
Now sound, now sick, now blyth, now sary,
Now dansand[4] mirry, now like to die:—
  Timor Mortis conturbat me.

No state in Erd here standis sicker;[5]
As with the wynd wavis the wicker[6]
So wavis this world's vanitie:—
  Timor Mortis conturbat me.

Unto the deid gois all Estatis,
Princis, Prelatis, and Potestatis,
Baith rich and poor of all degree:—
  Timor Mortis conturbat me.

He takis the knichtis in to field
Enarmit under helm and scheild;
Victor he is at all mellie:[7]
  Timor Mortis conturbat me.

* The fear of death troubles me

[1] health [2] brittle, feeble [3] sly [4] dancing [5] sure [6] willow
  [7] mellay

313

That strong unmerciful tyrand
Takis, on the motheris breast sowkand,[1]
The babe full of benignitie:—
   Timor Mortis conturbat me.

He takis the campion[2] in the stour,[3]
The captain closit in the tour,
The lady in bour full of bewtie:—
   Timor Mortis conturbat me.

He spairis no lord for his piscence,[4]
Na clerk for his intelligence;
His awful straik[5] may no man flee:—
   Timor Mortis conturbat me.

Art-magicians and astrologgis,
Rethoris, logicians, and theologgis,
Them helpis no conclusionis slee:—
   Timor Mortis conturbat me.

In medecine the most practicianis,
Leechis, surrigianis, and physicianis,
Themself from Death may not supplee[6]:—
   Timor Mortis conturbat me.

I see that makaris[7] amang the lave[8]
Playis here their padyanis,[9] syne gois to grave;
Sparit is nocht their facultie:—
   Timor Mortis conturbat me.

He has done petuously devour
The noble Chaucer, of makaris flour,
The Monk of Bury, and Gower, all three:—
   Timor Mortis conturbat me.

[1] sucking   [2] champion   [3] fight   [4] puissance   [5] stroke   [6] save
        [7] poets   [8] the leave, the rest   [9] pageants

The good Sir Hew of Eglintoun,
And eik[1] Heriot, and Wyntoun,
He has tane out of this cuntrie:—
    Timor Mortis conturbat me.

That scorpion fell has done infeck
Maister John Clerk, and James Afflek,
Fra ballat-making and tragedie:—
    Timor Mortis conturbat me.

Holland and Barbour he has berevit;
Alas! that he not with us levit
Sir Mungo Lockart of the Lee:—
    Timor Mortis conturbat me.

Clerk of Tranent eke he has tane,
That made the anteris[2] of Gawaine;
Sir Gilbert Hay endit has he:—
    Timor Mortis conturbat me.

He has Blind Harry and Sandy Traill
Slaim with his schour[3] of mortal hail,
Quhilk Patrick Johnstoun might nought flee:—
    Timor Mortis conturbat me.

He has reft Merseir his endite,[4]
That did in love so lively write,
So short, so quick, of sentence hie:—
    Timor Mortis conturbat me.

He has tane Roull of Aberdene,
And gentill Roull of Corstorphine;
Two better fallowis[5] did no man see:—
    Timor Mortis conturbat me.

[1] also   [2] adventures   [3] shower   [4] inditing   [5] fellows

In Dunfermline he has done roune[1]
With Maister Robert Henrysoun;
Sir John the Ross enbrast has he:—
Timor Mortis conturbat me.

And he has now tane, last of a,
Good gentil Stobo and Quintin Shaw,
Of quhom all wichtis[2] hes pitie:—
Timor Mortis conturbat me.

Good Maister Walter Kennedy
In point of deid lies verily;
Great ruth it were that so suld be:—
Timor Mortis conturbat me.

Sen he has all my brether tane,
He will naught lat me live alane;
On force I man[3] his next prey be:—
Timor Mortis conturbat me.

Sen for the deid remeid is none,
Best is that we for deid dispone,[4]
Efter our deid that live may we:—
Timor Mortis conturbat me.

WILLIAM DUNBAR (c. 1460-1520)

[1] whispered [2] wights, persons [3] must [4] make disposition

MARIE HAMILTON

Marie Hamilton's to the kirk gane,
   Wi' ribbons in her hair;
The King thought mair o' Marie Hamilton
   Than ony that were there.

Marie Hamilton's to the kirk gane
   Wi' ribbons on her breast;
The King thought mair o' Marie Hamilton
   Than he listen'd to the priest.

Marie Hamilton's to the kirk gane,
   Wi' gloves upon her hands;
The King thought mair o' Marie Hamilton
   Than the Queen and a' her lands.

She hadna been about the King's court
   A month, but barely ane,
Till she was beloved by a' the King's court,
   And the King the only man.

She hadna been about the King's court
   A month, but barely three,
Till frae the King's court Marie Hamilton,
   Marie Hamilton durstna be.

The King is to the Abbey gane,
   To pu' the Abbey tree,
To scale[1] the babe frae Marie's heart;
   But the thing it wadna be.

O she has row'd[2] it in her apron,
   And set it on the sea—
'Gae sink ye or swim ye, bonny babe,
   Ye'se get nae mair o' me.

    [1] drive away, get rid of   [2] wrapped

Word is to the kitchen gane,
    And word is to the ha',
And word is to the noble room
    Amang the Ladies a',
That Marie Hamilton's brought to bed,
    And the bonny babe's miss'd and awa'.

Scarcely had she lain down again,
    And scarcely fa'en asleep,
When up and started our gude Queen
    Just at her bed-feet;
Saying—' Marie Hamilton, where's your babe?
    For I am sure I heard it greet.'[1]

' O no, O no, my noble Queen!
    Think no sic thing to be;
'Twas but a stitch into my side,
    And sair it troubles me! '—

' Get up, get up, Marie Hamilton:
    Get up and follow me;
For I am going to Edinburgh town,
    A rich wedding for to see.'

O slowly, slowly rase she up,
    And slowly put she on;
And slowly rade she out the way
    Wi' mony a weary groan.

The Queen was clad in scarlet,
    Her merry maids all in green;
And every town that they cam to,
    They took Marie for the Queen.

               [1] wail, cry

‘ Ride hooly,[1] hooly, gentlemen,
   Ride hooly now wi’ me!
For never, I am sure, a wearier burd
   Rade in your companie.’

But little wist Marie Hamilton,
   When she rade on the brown,
That she was gaen to Edinburgh town,
   And a’ to be put down.

‘ Why weep ye sae, ye burgess wives,
   Why look ye sae on me?
O I am going to Edinburgh town,
   A rich wedding for to see.’

When she gaed up the tolbooth stairs,
   The corks frae her heels did flee;
And lang or e’er she cam down again,
   She was condemn’d to die.

When she cam to the Netherbow port,
   She laugh’d loud laughters three;
But when she came to the gallows foot
   The tears blinded her e’e.

‘ Yestreen the Queen had four Maries,
   The night she’ll hae but three;
There was Marie Seaton, and Marie Beaton,
   And Marie Carmichael, and me.

‘ O often have I dress’d my Queen,
   And put gowd upon her hair;
But now I’ve gotten for my reward
   The gallows to be my share.

‘ Often have I dress’d my Queen
   And often made her bed;

[1] gently

319

But now I've gotten for my reward
  The gallows tree to tread.

' I charge ye all, ye mariners,
  When ye sail owre the faem,
Let neither my father nor mother get wit
  But that I'm coming hame.

' I charge ye all, ye mariners,
  That sail upon the sea,
That neither my father nor mother get wit
  The dog's death I'm to die.

' For if my father and mother got wit,
  And my bold brethren three,
O mickle wad be the gude red blude
  This day wad be spilt for me!

' O little did my mother ken,
  The day she cradled me,
The lands I was to travel in
  Or the death I was to die! '

ANONYMOUS

BONNY GEORGE CAMPBELL

Hie upon Hielands,
  And laigh[1] upon Tay,
Bonny George Campbell
  Rade out on a day:
Saddled and bridled,
  Sae gallant to see,
Hame cam' his gude horse,
  But never cam' he.

[1] low

Down ran his auld mither,
    Greetin'[1] fu' sair;
Out ran his bonny bride,
    Reaving[2] her hair;
' My meadow lies green,
    And my corn is unshorn,
My barn is to bigg,[3]
    And my babe is unborn.'

Saddled and bridled
    And booted rade he;
A plume in his helmet,
    A sword at his knee;
But toom[4] cam' his saddle
    A' bluidy to see,
O hame cam' his gude horse
    But never cam' he!

ANONYMOUS

[1] weeping full sore   [2] tearing   [3] build   [4] empty

PROUD MAISIE

Proud Maisie is in the wood,
    Walking so early;
Sweet Robin sits on the bush,
    Singing so rarely.

"Tell me, thou bonny bird,
    When shall I marry me?"
"When six braw[1] gentlemen
    Kirkward shall carry ye."

"Who makes the bridal bed,
    Birdie, say truly?"
"The grey-headed sexton
    That delves the grave duly.

[1] fine

"The glow-worm o'er grave and stone
　　Shall light thee steady.
The owl from the steeple sing,
　　' Welcome, proud lady.' "

SIR WALTER SCOTT (1771-1832)
The Heart of Midlothian

ANE PLAYNT OF LUVE

O hart, My hart! that gyves na rest,
Bot wyth luve madness dois dismaie;
For all thingis ellis, ye haif na zeste,
Nor thocht; bot luve may drive awaye.
　　　Deir hart, be still,
　　　And stay this ill,
　　Thi passioun sall me slay!

O hart, My hart! haif mercie nowe,
On me thi mastir, Sorrow's selfe:
Fra hir that will na luve allowe,
Desyre na moir the horded pelf.
　　　Deir hart, in pane
　　　Quhy wilt remane?—
　　Haif mercie on thi selfe!

O hart, My hart! tho' sche be fair,
As moon bemys quhyte, or starris that schyn—
Tho' all hir partis haif na compare,
It makis nocht, gif hir hart disdeyne.
　　　Deir harte, gyve ease,
　　　Fra luve release
　　Of ane that is nocht myne.

PITTENDRIGH MACGILLIVRAY (1856-1938)

THE LAND O' THE LEAL[1]

I'm wearin' awa', John,
Like snaw-wreaths in thaw, John;
I'm wearin' awa'
    To the land o' the leal.
There's nae sorrow there, John;
There's neither cauld nor care, John;
The day is aye fair
    In the land o' the leal.

Our bonnie bairn's there, John;
She was baith gude and fair, John;
And oh! we grudged her sair[2]
    To the land o' the leal.
But sorrow's sel'[3] wears past, John,
And joy that's a-comin' fast, John—
The joy that's aye to last
    In the land o' the leal.

Sae dear's that joy was bought, John,
Sae free the battle fought, John,
That sinfu' man e'er brought
    To the land o' the leal.
Oh, dry your glist'ning ee, John!
My saul langs to be free, John;
And angels beckon me
    To the land o' the leal.

Oh, haud[4] ye leal and true, John!
Your day it's wearin' thro', John;
And I'll welcome you
    To the land o' the leal.

[1] true or loyal   [2] sorely   [3] self   [4] keep

Now fare ye weel, my ain John,
This warld's cares are vain, John;
We'll meet, and we'll be fain[1]
In the land o' the leal.

[1] fond   Attributed to LADY NAIRNE (1766-1845)

WHEN THOU ART NEAR ME

When thou art near me,
Sorrow seems to fly,
And then I think, as well I may,
That on this earth there is no one
More blest than I.

But when thou leav'st me,
Doubts and fears arise,
And darkness reigns,
Where all before was light.

The sunshine of my soul
Is in those eyes,
And when they leave me
All the world is night.

But when thou art near me,
Sorrow seems to fly,
And then I feel, as well I may,
That on this earth there dwells not one
So blest as I.

LADY JOHN SCOTT (1811-1900)

LAST MAY A BRAW WOOER

Last May a braw wooer cam down the lang glen,
And sair wi' his love he did deave me.
I said there was naething I hated like men:
The deuce gae wi'm to believe me, believe me.—
The deuce gae wi'm to believe me!

He spak o' the darts in my bonie black een,
  And vow'd for my love he was diein.
I said, he might die when he liket for Jean:
  The Lord forgie me for liein, for liein—
  The Lord forgie me for liein!

A weel-stocket mailen, himsel for the laird,
  And marriage aff-hand were his proffers:
I never loot on that I kenn'd it, or car'd,
  But thought I might hae waur offers, waur offers—
  But thought I might hae waur offers.

But what wad ye think? In a fortnight or less
  (The Deil tak his taste to gae near her!)
He up the Gate-Slack to my black cousin, Bess!
  Guess ye how, the jad! I could bear her, could bear
    her—
  Guess ye how, the jad! I could bear her.

But a' the niest week, as I petted wi' care,
  I gaed to the tryste o' Dalgarnock,
And wha but my fine fickle lover was there?
  I glowr'd as I'd seen a warlock, a warlock—
  I glowr'd as I'd seen a warlock.

But owre my left shouther I gae him a blink,
  Lest neebours might say I was saucy.
My wooer he caper'd as he'd been in drink,
  And vow'd I was his dear lassie, dear lassie—
  And vow'd I was his dear lassie!

I spier'd for my cousin fu' couthy and sweet:
  Gin she had recover'd her hearin'?
And how her new shoon fit her auld, shachl'd feet?
  But heavens! how he fell a swearin, a swearin—
  But heavens! how he fell a swearin!

325

He begged, for Guidsake! I wad be his wife,
  Or else I would kill him wi' sorrow;
So e'en to preserve the poor body in life,
  I think I maun wed him to-morrow.

ROBERT BURNS (1759-96)

THE TWA CORBIES[1]

As I was walking all alane,
I heard twa corbies making a mane:
The tane unto the tither did say,
"Whaur sall we gang and dine the day?"

"In behint yon auld fail[2] dyke,
I wot there lies a new-slain knight;
And naebody kens that he lies there
But his hawk, his hound, and his lady fair.

"His hound is to the hunting gane,
His hawk to fetch the wild-fowl hame,
His lady's ta'en anither mate,
So we may mak' our dinner sweet.

"Ye'll sit on his white hause[3]-bane,
And I'll pike out his bonny blue e'en;
Wi' ae lock o' his gowden hair
We'll theek[4] our nest when it grows bare.

"Mony a one for him maks mane,
But nane sall ken whar he is gane;
O'er his white banes, when they are bare,
The wind sall blaw for evermair."

ANONYMOUS

[1] crows   [2] turf   [3] neck   [4] thatch

RARE WILLY DROWN'S IN YARROW

' Willy's rare, and Willy's fair,
   And Willy's wondrous bonny;
And Willy heght[1] to marry me,
   Gin e'er he marryd ony.

' Yestreen I made my bed fu' braid,
   The night I'll make it narrow,
For a' the live-long winter's night
   I lie twin'd[2] of my marrow.

' O came you by yon water-side?
   Pu'd you the rose or lily?
Or came you by yon meadow green?
   Or saw you my sweet Willy?'

She sought him east, she sought him west,
   She sought him braid and narrow;
Sine, in the clifting of a craig,
   She found him drown'd in Yarrow.

ANONYMOUS

[1] promised   [2] bereaved

A CAVALIER LYRIC

My dear and only love, I pray
   That little world of thee
Be governed by no other sway
   Than purest monarchy;
For if confusion have a part,
   Which virtuous souls abhor,
And hold a synod in thine heart,
   I'll never love thee more.

As Alexander I will reign,
    And I will reign alone;
My thoughts did ever more disdain
    A rival on my throne.
He either fears his fate too much,
    Or his deserts are small,
That dares not put it to the touch
    To gain or lose it all!

But if thou wilt prove faithful then,
    And constant of thy word,
I'll make thee glorious by my pen,
    And famous by my sword;
I'll serve thee in such noble ways
    Was never heard before;
I'll crown and deck thee all with bays,
    And love thee more and more.

MONTROSE (1612-50)

THE BONNY EARL O' MORAY

Ye Highlands and ye Lawlands,
    O where hae ye been?
They hae slain the Earl o' Moray,
    And hae laid him on the green.

Now wae be to thee, Huntley!
    And whairfore did ye sae!
I bade you bring him wi' you,
    But forbade you him to slay.

He was a braw gallant,
    And he rid at the ring;
And the bonny Earl o' Moray,
    O he might hae been a king!

He was a braw gallant,
  And he play'd at the ba';
And the bonny Earl o' Moray
  Was the flower amang them a'!

He was a braw gallant,
  And he play'd at the gluve;
And the bonny Earl o' Moray,
  O he was the Queen's luve!

O lang will his Lady
  Look owre the Castle Downe,
Eere she see the Earl o' Moray
  Come sounding through the town!

ANONYMOUS

THERE'S NAE LUCK ABOOT THE HOOSE

And are ye sure the news is true?
  And are ye sure he's weel?
Is this a time to think o' wark?
  Ye jades, fling by your wheel!
Is this a time to think o' wark
  When Colin's at the door?
Rax me my cloak—I'll to the quay,
  And see him come ashore.

    For there's nae luck aboot the hoose,
      Ther's nae luck ava',
    There's little pleasure in the hoose,
      When oor gudeman's awa'.

Rise up, and mak' a clean fireside,
  Put on the muckle pat;
Gie little Kate her cotton gown,

329

And Jock his Sunday coat.
And mak' their shoon as black as slaes,
   Their stockings white as snaw;
It's a' to please my own gudeman,
   He likes to see them braw.

There are two hens into the crib,
   Have fed this month and mair,
Mak' haste and thraw their necks aboot
   That Colin weel may fare.
And spread the table neat and clean,
   Gar ilka thing look braw;
For wha can tell how Colin fared,
   When he was far awa'?

Bring down to me my bigonet,
   My bishop-satin gown,
For I maun tell the Bailie's wife,
   That Colin's come to town.
My Turkey slippers I'll put on,
   My stockings pearly blue,
And a' to pleasure our gudeman
   For he's baith leal and true.

Sae sweet his voice, sae smooth his tongue,
   His breath's like caller air,
His very fit has music in't
   As he comes up the stair.
And will I see his face again,
   And will I hear him speak?
I'm downright dizzy wi' the thought
   In troth I'm like to greet!

W. J. MICKLE (1735-88)

RAVELSTON'S MOURNING GHOST

The murmur of the mourning ghost
    That keeps the shadowy kine.
O Keith of Ravelston,
    The sorrows of thy line!

Ravelston, Ravelston,
    The merry path that leads
Down the golden morning hill,
    And through the silver meads.

Ravelston, Ravelston,
    The stile beneath the tree,
The maid that kept her mother's kine
    The song that sang she!

She sang her song, she kept her kine,
    She sat beneath the thorn,
When Andrew Keith of Ravelston,
    Rode through, the Monday morn.

His henchmen sing, his hawk-bells ring,
    His belted jewels shine.
O Keith of Ravelston,
    The sorrows of thy line!

I lay my hand upon the stile,
    The stile is lone and cold,
The burnie that goes babbling by
    Says nought than can be told.

Yet, stranger, here from year to year,
    She keeps her shadowy kine.
O Keith of Ravelston,
    The sorrows of thy line!

Step our three steps where Andrew stood;
  Why blanch thy cheeks for fear?
The ancient stile is not alone,
  'Tis not the burn I hear!

She makes her immemorial moan,
  She keeps her shadowy kine.
O Keith of Ravelston,
  The sorrows of thy line!

SYDNEY DOBELL (1824-74)

THE BONIE WEE THING

Chorus
Bonie wee thing, cannie wee thing,
  Lovely wee thing, wert thou mine,
I wad wear thee in my bosom,
  Lest my jewel it should tine.

Wishfully I look and languish
  In that bonie face o' thine,
And my heart it stounds wi' anguish,
  Lest my wee thing be na mine.

Chorus

Wit and Grace, and Love, and Beauty,
  In ae constellation shine;
To adore thee is my duty,
  Goddess o' this soul o' mine!

Chorus

ROBERT BURNS (1759-96)

332

ANNA, THY CHARMS

Anna, thy charms my bosom fire,
    And waste my soul with care;
But ah! how bootless to admire,
    When fated to despair!

Yet in thy presence, lovely Fair,
    To hope may be forgiven;
For sure 'twere impious to despair
    So much in sight of Heaven.

ROBERT BURNS (1759-96)

LOST LOVE

Who wins his love shall lose her,
    Who loses her shall gain,
For still the spirit woos her,
    A soul without a stain;
And memory still pursues her
    With longings not in vain!

He loses her who gains her,
    Who watches day by day
The dust of time that stains her,
    The griefs that leave her grey—
The flesh that yet enchains her
    Whose grace hath passed away!

Oh, happier he who gains not
    The love some seem to gain:
The joy that custom stains not
    Shall still with him remain;
The loveliness that wanes not,
    The love that ne'er can wane.

333

In dreams she grows not older
  The lands of dream among;
Though all the world wax colder,
  Though all the songs be sung,
In dreams doth he behold her
  Still fair and kind and young.

ANDREW LANG (1844-1912)

THE LOWLANDS OF HOLLAND

"The love that I hae chosen, I'll therewith be content,
The saut sea shall be frozen, before that I repent;
Repent it shall I never, until the day I dee,
But the lowlands of Holland has twined my love and me.

"My love lies in the saut sea, and I am on the side,
Enough to break a young thing's heart, wha lately was
    a bride;
Wha lately was a bonnie bride, and pleasure in her ee;
But the lowlands of Holland has twined my love and me.

"My love hae built a bonny ship, and set her on the sea,
Wi' seven-score good mariners to bear her companie;
There's three-score is sunk, and three-score dead at sea,
And the lowlands of Holland has twined my love and me.

"My love, he built another ship, and set her on the main,
And nane but twenty mariners for to bring her hame;
But the weary wind began to rise, and the sea began to
    rout,
My love then and his bonny ship turn'd withershins
    about.

334

"There shall neither coif come on my head, nor kaim
  come in my hair,
There shall neither coal nor candle light shine in my
  bower mair;
Nor will I love another ane, until the day I dee,
For I never lov'd a love but ane, and he's drown'd in the
  sea!"

"Go haud your tongue, my daughter dear, be still, and
  be content,
There are mair lads in Galloway, ye needna sair lament."
O there is nane in Galloway, there's nane at a' for me,
For I never lov'd a love but ane, and he's drown'd in
  the sea!"

ANONYMOUS

PIBROCH OF DONUIL DHU

Pibroch of Donuil Dhu,
  Pibroch of Donuil,
Wake thy wild voice anew,
  Summon Clan Conuil.
Come away, come away,
  Hark to the summons!
Come in your war array,
  Gentles and commons.

Come from deep glen, and
  From mountain so rocky;
The war-pipe and pennon
  Are at Inverlochy.
Come every hill-plaid, and
  True heart that wears one,
Come every steel blade, and
  Strong hand that bears one.

Leave untended the herd,
    The flock without shelter;
Leave the corpse uninterr'd,
    The bride at the altar;
Leave the deer, leave the steer,
    Leave nets and barges;
Come with your fighting gear,
    Broadswords and targes.

Come as the winds come, when
    Forests are rended,
Come as the waves come, when
    Navies are stranded:
Faster come, faster come,
    Faster and faster,
Chief, vassal, page and groom,
    Tenant and master.

Fast they come, fast they come;
    See how they gather!
Wide waves the eagle plume,
    Blended with heather.
Cast your plaids, draw your blades,
    Forward each man set!
Pibroch of Donuil Dhu,
    Knell for the onset!

SIR WALTER SCOTT (1771-1832)

THE CARES O' LOVE

He

The cares o' Love are sweeter far
    Than onie other pleasure;
And if sae dear its sorrows are,
    Enjoyment, what a treasure!

She
I fear to try, I dare na try
  A passion sae ensnaring;
For light's her heart and blythe's her sang
  That for nae man is caring.

ROBERT BURNS (1759-96)

RECOLLECTION OF FIRST LOVE

When I recall your form and face
More than you I recall
To come into a meeting-place
Where no leaves fall:
The years walk round this secret garth
But cannot change its guarded earth.

I have known women fonder far
Than you; more fair, more kind:
Women whose passionate faces are
Flowers in the mind:
But as a tall tree, stem on stem,
Your presence overshadows them.

They quicken from my sentient day
And stir my body's need;
But you had fixéd roots ere they
Down-dropped in seed:
They can but copy all I found
When you alone grew in this ground.

You are reborn from changeless loam
And are a changeless shade:
Your feet had paced the paths to Rome
Ere Rome was made:
Under your eyes great towers down fell
Before that Trojan citadel.

Time, who is knocking at the gate,
Cannot make you his boast:
Our garden shall be desolate
But you—a ghost
Timeless; as beauty's timeless norm
You are in passion and in form.

WILLIAM SOUTAR (1898-1943)

HELEN OF KIRKCONNELL

I wish I were where Helen lies,
Night and day on me she cries;
O that I were where Helen lies,
    On fair Kirkconnell lea!

Curst be the heart that thought the thought,
And curst the hand that fired the shot,
When in my arms burd Helen dropt,
    And died to succour me!

O think na ye my heart was sair,
When my Love dropp'd down and spak nae mair!
There did she swoon wi' meikle care,
    On fair Kirkconnell lea.

As I went down the water side,
None but my foe to be my guide,
None but my foe to be my guide,
    On fair Kirkconnell lea;

I lighted down my sword to draw,
I hackèd him in pieces sma',
I hackèd him in pieces sma',
    For her sake that died for me.

O Helen fair, beyond compare!
I'll mak a garland o' thy hair,
Shall bind my heart for evermair
    Until the day I dee!

O that I were where Helen lies!
Night and day on me she cries;
Out of my bed she bids me rise,
    Says, "Haste, and come to me!"

O Helen fair! O Helen chaste!
If I were with thee, I'd be blest,
Where thou lies low an' taks thy rest,
    On fair Kirkconnell lea.

I wish my grave were growing green,
A winding-sheet drawn owre my een,
And I in Helen's arms lying.
    On fair Kirkconnell lea.

I wish I were where Helen lies!
Night and day on me she cries;
And I am weary of the skies,
    For her sake that died for me.

Old Ballad

POEM BEFORE BIRTH

To Catherine

She carries life in her body
as a girl in a dry country carries
a pitcher of water cupped in her hands
delighting
the thirsty eyes of the dwellers
in those parched lands.

She is as quiet and as certain
as Earth in reluctant spring
which waits for a night of warm showers
dissolving
the last delay of winter
and dazzling the dawn with flowers.

ALEXANDER SCOTT (b. 1920

CARPE DIEM

Look up Pentland's towering tap,
  Buried beneath great wreaths of snaw,
O'er ilka cleugh, ilk scaur, and slap,
  As high as ony Roman wa'.

Driving their ba's frae whins or tee,
  There's no ae gowfer to be seen,
Nor douser fouk wysing ajee
  The biassed bowls on Tamson's green.

Then fling on coals, and ripe the ribs,
  And beek the house baith but and ben;
That mutchkin-stoup it hauds but dribs,
  Then let's get in the tappit hen.

Good claret best keeps out the cauld,
  And drives away the winter soon;
It makes a man baith gash and bauld,
  And heaves his saul beyond the moon.

Leave to the gods your ilka care,
  If that they think us worth their while;
They can a rowth of blessings spare,
  Which will our fashous fears beguile.

For what they have a mind to do,
    That will they do, should we gang wud;
If they command the storms to blaw,
    Then upo' sight the hailstanes thud.

But soon as e'er they cry, "Be quiet!"
    The blattering winds dare nae mair move,
But cour into their caves, and wait
    The high command of supreme Jove.

Let neist day come as it thinks fit,
    The present minute's only ours;
On pleasure let's employ our wit,
    And laugh at fortune's feckless powers.

Be sure ye dinna quat the grip
    Of ilka joy when ye are young,
Before auld age your vitals nip,
    And lay ye twafald o'er a rung.

Sweet youth's a blithe and heartsome time;
    Then lads and lasses, while it's May,
Gae pu' the gowan in its prime,
    Before it wither and decay.

ALLAN RAMSAY (1686-1758)

THE DUSTY MILLER

Hey, the dusty Miller,
    And his dusty coat,
He will win a shilling,
    Or he spend a groat:
Dusty was the coat,
    Dusty was the colour,
Dusty was the kiss
    That I gat frae the Miller.

Hey, the dusty Miller,
   And his dusty sack:
Leeze me on the calling
   Fills the dusty peck,
Fills the dusty peck,
   Brings the dusty siller;
I wad gae my coatie
   For the dusty Miller.

ROBERT BURNS (1759-96)

THE GARMENT OF GOOD LADIES

Would my good lady love me best,
And work after my will,
I should a garment goodliest,
Gar[1] make her body till.[2]

Of high honour should be her hood,
Upon her head to weir,[3]
Garnished with governance so good,
No denying[4] should her deir.[5]

Her sark should be her body next,
Of chastity so white,
With shame and dread together mixt,
The same should be perfyt.[6]

Her kirtle should be of clean constance,
Laced with lesum[7] love,
The mailyheis[8] of continuance
For never to remove.

[1] cause   [2] to   [3] wear   [4] censuring   [5] hurt   [6] perfect   [7] lawful
[8] eyelet-holes

Her gown should be of goodliness,
Well ribboned with renown,
Purfillet[1] with pleasure in ilk place,
Furrit with fine fashion.

Her belt should be of benignity,
About her midale meet;
Her mantle of humility,
To thole both wind and weet.

Her hat should be of fair having,
And her tippet of truth,
Her patelet[2] of good pansing[3],
Her neck ribbon of ruth.

Her sleeves should be of esperance,[4]
To keep her from despair;
Her gloves of the good governance,
To hide her fingers fair.

Her shoes should be of sickerness,[5]
In sign that she nought flyd,[6]
Her hose of honesty, I guess,
I should for her provide.

Would she put on this garment gay,
I durst swear by my feill,[7]
That she wore never green nor gray
That set her half so weil.

ROBERT HENRYSON (*c.* 1430-1506)

[1] embroidered   [2] ruff   [3] thought   [4] hope   [5] security   [6] fears
[7] knowledge

HAD I TWA HERTS

Had I twa herts an you but ane
   Whan we were twin'd, still for your sake
That I micht loe yet be alane
   Ae hert wud thrive, the ither break.

Had I twa tongues to speak o thee
   I culdna let a morrow come
An hearna o your cheritie
   From ane—the ither wud be dumb.

Had I fower een an twa to close
   Wi greetin o a hert forlorn,
The ither twa wud see a rose
   Ahint the gairden o your scorn.

But I am ane an sae maun find
   An answer til the mysterie;
Dee an forget, or livan mind
   Aa times ma troublit historie.

R. CROMBIE SAUNDERS (b. 1914)

LOCK THE DOOR, LARISTON

"Lock the door, Lariston, lion of Liddesdale;
Lock the door, Lariston, Lowther comes on;
   The Armstrongs are flying,
   The widows are crying,
The Castletown's burning, and Oliver's gone!

"Lock the door, Lariston,—high on the weather-gleam
See how the Saxon plumes bob on the sky—
   Yeoman and carbineer,
   Billman and halberdier,
Fierce is the foray, and far is the cry!

344

"Bewcastle brandishes high his broad scimitar;
Ridley is riding his fleet-footed gray;
    Hidley and Howard there,
    Wandale and Windermere;
Lock the door, Lariston, hold them at bay.

"Why dost thou smile, noble Elliot of Lariston?
Why does the joy-candle gleam in thine eye?
    Thou bold Border ranger,
    Beware of thy danger;
Thy foes are relentless, determined, and nigh."

Jack Elliot raised up his steel bonnet and lookit,
His hand grasped the sword with a nervous embrace;
    "Ah, welcome, brave foemen,
    On earth there are no men
More gallant to meet in the foray or chase!

"Little know you of the hearts I have hidden here;
Little know you of our moss-troopers' might—
    Linhope and Sorbie true,
    Sundhope and Milburn too,
Gentle in manner, but lions in fight!

"I have Mangerton, Ogilvie, Raeburn, and Netherbie,
Old Sim of Whitram, and all his array;
    Come all Northumberland,
    Teesdale and Cumberland,
Here at the Breaken tower end shall the fray!"

Scowled the broad sun o'er the links of green Liddesdale,
Red as the beacon-light tipped he the wold;
    Many a bold martial eye
    Mirror'd that morning sky,
Never more oped on his orbit of gold.

Shrill was the bugle's note, dreadful the warrior's shout,
Lances and halberds in splinters were borne;
     Helmet and hauberk then,
     Braved the claymore in vain,
Buckler and armlet in shivers were shorn.

See how they wane—the proud files of the Windermere!
Howard! ah, woe to thy hopes of the day!
     Hear the wide welkin rend,
     While the Scots' shouts ascend—
"Elliot of Lariston, Elliot for aye !"

JAMES HOGG (1770-1835)

BEAUTY

The source of Beauty lies beyond
The things of sense, the power of mind;
Strange and immaculate her birth;
Ageless, unheard, untimed.

Ten thousand thousand eyes have seen
The flood-lit splendours of the dawn;
Ten thousand thousand ears have heard
Man's raucous antiphon.

Across the desert of the night
The ancient constellations stride;
And rare spirits keep their tryst
At Beauty's Eastertide.

None but the lonely heart can know
The quickening impulse of her power;
Only by rood and sacrifice
Doth Beauty come to flower.

G. F. MAINE (1893-1956)

AULD LANG SYNE

Should auld acquaintance be forgot,
  And never brought to mind?
Should auld acquaintance be forgot,
  And auld lang syne?

    Chorus
For auld lang syne, my dear,
  For auld lang syne,
We'll tak a cup o' kindness yet
  For auld lang syne!

And surely you'll be[1] your pint-stoup,
  And surely I'll be mine;
And we'll tak a cup o' kindness yet
  For auld lang syne!

We twa hae run about the braes,
  And pu'd the gowans[2] fine;
But we've wander'd mony a weary fit[3]
  Sin auld lang syne.

We twa hae paidl'd in the burn,
  Frae morning sun till dine;[4]
But seas between us braid hae roar'd
  Sin auld lang syne!

And there's a hand, my trusty fiere,[5]
  And gie's a hand o' thine;
And we'll tak a right gude-willie waught,[6]
  For auld lang syne.

ROBERT BURNS (1759-96)

[1] pay for   [2] daisies   [3] foot   [4] noon   [5] comrade   [6] draught

Religious and Mystical

PSALM 23
Metrical Version

The Lord's my shepherd, I'll not want.
    He makes me down to lie
In pastures green: he leadeth me
    the quiet waters by.

My soul he doth restore again;
    and me to walk doth make
Within the paths of righteousness,
    ev'n for his own name's sake.

Yea, though I walk in death's dark vale,
    yet will I fear none ill:
For thou art with me; and thy rod
    and staff me comfort still.

My table thou hast furnished
    in presence of my foes;
My head thou dost with oil anoint,
    and my cup overflows.

Goodness and mercy all my life
    shall surely follow me:
And in God's house for evermore
    my dwelling-place shall be.

Psalter (1650)

PSALM 100
Metrical Version

All people that on earth do dwell,
Sing to the Lord with cheerful voice.
Him serve with mirth, his praise forth tell,
Come ye before him and rejoice.

Know that the Lord is God indeed;
Without our aid he did us make:
We are his flock, he doth us feed,
And for his sheep he doth us take.

O enter then his gates with praise,
Aproach with joy his courts unto:
Praise, laud, and bless his name always,
For it is seemly so to do.

For why? the Lord our God is good,
His mercy is for ever sure;
His truth at all times firmly stood,
And shall from age to age endure.

WILLIAM KETHE (1559)
Psalter (1650)

PSALM 121
Metrical Version

I to the hills will lift mine eyes,
  from whence doth come mine aid.
My safety cometh from the Lord,
  who heav'n and earth hath made.

Thy foot he'll not let slide, nor will
  he slumber that thee keeps.
Behold, he that keeps Israel,
  he slumbers not, nor sleeps.

The Lord thee keeps, the Lord thy shade
  on thy right hand doth stay:
The moon by night thee shall not smite,
  nor yet the sun by day.

The Lord shall keep thy soul; he shall
  preserve thee from all ill.
Henceforth thy going out and in
  God keep for ever will.

Psalter (1650)

PSALM 124
Metrical Version

Now Israel may say, and that truly,
If that the Lord had not our cause maintain'd;
If that the Lord had not our right sustain'd,
When cruel men against us furiously
Rose up in wrath, to make of us their prey;

Then certainly they had devour'd us all,
And swallow'd quick, for ought that we could deem;
Such was their rage, as we might well esteem.
And as fierce floods before them all things drown,
So had they brought our soul to death quite down.

The raging streams with their proud swelling waves,
Had then our soul o'erwhelmed in the deep.
But bless'd be God, who doth us safely keep,
And hath not giv'n us for a living prey
Unto their teeth, and bloody cruelty.

Ev'n as a bird out of the fowler's snare
Escapes away, so is our soul set free:
Broke are their nets, and thus escaped we.
Therefore our help is in the Lord's great name,
Who heav'n and earth by His great pow'r did frame.

W. WHITTINGHAM
Revised Version, Psalter (1650

PARAPHRASE 2

Founded on a hymn by Dr. Philip Dodderidge entitled *Jacob's Vow*, written in 1736. The paraphrase now in use is an altered version of a hymn by John Logan which dates from 1781.

O God of Bethel! by whose hand
    thy people still are fed;
Who through this weary pilgrimage
    hast all our fathers led:

Our vows, our pray'rs, we now present
    before thy throne of grace:
God of our fathers! be the God
    of their succeeding race.

Through each perplexing path of life
    our wand'ring footsteps guide;
Give us each day our daily bread,
    and raiment fit provide.

O spread thy cov'ring wings around,
    till all our wand'rings cease,
And at our Father's lov'd abode
    our souls arrive in peace.

Such blessings from thy gracious hand
    our humble pray'rs implore;
And thou shalt be our chosen God,
    and portion evermore.

351

PARAPHRASE 30

Come, let us to the Lord our God
    with contrite hearts return;
Our God is gracious, nor will leave
    the desolate to mourn.

His voice commands the tempest forth,
    and stills the stormy wave;
And though His arm be strong to smite,
    'tis also strong to save.

Long hath the night of sorrow reign'd,
    the dawn shall bring us light:
God shall appear, and we shall rise
    with gladness in His sight.

Our hearts, if God we seek to know,
    shall know Him, and rejoice;
His coming like the morn shall be,
    like morning songs His voice.

As dew upon the tender herb,
    diffusing fragrance round;
As show'rs that usher in the spring,
    and cheer the thirsty ground:

So shall His presence bless our souls,
    and shed a joyful light;
That Hallow'd morn shall chase away
    the sorrows of the night.

JOHN MORISON

PARAPHRASE 60

A composite hymn of which verse 1 is by Dr. Philip Dodderidge, verses 2 and 3 are based on Dodderidge and verse 4 is by William Cameron.

Father of peace, and God of love!
    we own thy pow'r to save,
That pow'r by which our Shepherd rose
    victorious o'er the grave.

Him from the dead thou brought'st again,
    when, by his sacred blood,
Confirm'd and seal'd for evermore,
    th' eternal cov'nant stood.

O may thy Spirit seal our souls,
    and mould them to thy will,
That our weak hearts no more may stray,
    but keep thy precepts still;

That to perfection's sacred height
    we nearer still may rise,
And all we think, and all we do,
    be pleasing in thine eyes.

OF CHRISTIANITY

There are versions of Christianity, it is true, which no self-respecting mind can do other than disown—versions so hard, so narrow, so unreal, so super-theological, that practical men can find in them neither outlet for their lives nor resting-place for their thoughts. With these we have nothing to do. With these Christ had nothing to do—except to oppose them with every word and act of His life. It too seldom occurs to those who repudiate

Christianity because of its narrowness or its unpractical-ness, its sanctimoniousness or its dullness, that these were the very things which Christ strove against and unweariedly condemned. It was the one risk of His religion being given to the common people—an inevitable risk which He took without reserve—that its infinite lustre should be tarnished in the fingering of the crowd or have its great truths narrowed into mean and unworthy moulds as they passed from lip to lip. But though the crowd is the object of Christianity, it is not its custodian. Deal with the Founder of this great Commonwealth Himself. Any man of honest purpose who will take the trouble to inquire at first hand what Christianity really is, will find it a thing he cannot get away from. Without either argument or pressure by the mere practicalness of its aims and the pathos of its compassions, it forces its august claim upon every serious life.

He who joins this Society finds himself in a large place. The Kingdom of God is a Society of the best men, working for the best ends, according to the best methods. Its membership is a multitude whom no man can number; its methods are as various as human nature; its field is the world. It is a Commonwealth, yet it honours a King; it is a Social Brotherhood, but it acknowledges the Fatherhood of God. Though not a Philosophy the world turns to it for light; though not Political it is the incubator of all great laws. It is more human than State, for it deals with deeper needs; more Catholic than the Church, for it includes whom the Church rejects. It is a Propaganda, yet it works not by agitation but by ideals. It is a Religion, yet it holds the worship of God to be mainly the service of man. Though not a Scientific Society its watchword is Evolution; though not an Ethic it possesses the Sermon on the Mount. This mysterious Society owns no wealth but distributes fortunes. It has no minutes for history keeps them; no member's roll for no one could make it. Its

entry-money is nothing; its subscription, all you have.
The Society never meets and it never adjourns. Its law
is one word—loyalty; its gospel one message—love.
Verily "Whosoever will lose his life for My sake shall
find it."

HENRY DRUMMOND (1851-97)
The Programme of Christianity

COVENANTER'S SCAFFOLD SONG

Sing with me! sing with me!
Weeping brethren, sing with me!
For now an open heaven I see,
And a crown of glory laid for me.
How my soul this earth despises!
How my heart and spirit rises!
Bounding from the flesh I sever:
World of sin, adieu for ever!

Sing with me! sing with me!
Friends in Jesus, sing with me!
All my sufferings, all my woe
All my griefs I here forego.
Farewell terror, sighing, grieving,
Praying, hearing, and believing,
Earthly trust and all its wrongings,
Earthly love and all its longings.

Sing with me! sing with me!
Blessèd spirits, sing with me!
To the Lamb our song shall be
Through a glad eternity.
Farewell earthly morn and even,
Sun and moon and stars of heaven;
Heavenly portals ope before me,
Welcome, Christ, in all Thy glory.

JAMES HOGG (1770-1835)

GO, HEART, UNTO THE LAMP OF LICHT

Go, heart, unto the lamp of licht,
    Go, heart, do service and honour,
Go, heart, and serve him day and nicht,
    Go, heart, unto thy Saviour.

Go, heart, to thy only remeid[1]
Descending from the heavenly tour:
Thee to deliver from pyne and deide,[2]
    Go, heart, unto thy Saviour.

Go, heart, but[3] dissimulatioun,
    To Christ, that took our vile nature,
For thee to suffer passioun,
    Go, heart, unto thy Saviour.

Go, heart, richt humill and meek,
    Go, heart, as leal and true servitour,
To him that heill[4] is for all seek,[5]
    Go, heart, unto thy Saviour.

Go heart, with true and haill intent,
    To Christ thy help and haill succour,
Thee to redeem he was all rent,
    Go, heart, unto thy Saviour.

To Christ, that raise from death to live,[6]
    Go, heart, unto thy latter hour,
Whais great mercy can nane discrive,[7]
    Go, heart, unto thy Saviour.

ANONYMOUS
From *The Gude and Godlie Ballatis* (1567)

[1] remedy   [2] pain and death   [3] without   [4] health
[5] sick   [6] life   [7] describe

BURNBRAE'S PRAYER

Almichty Father, we are a' thy puir an' sinfu' bairns, wha wearied o' hame and gaed awa' intae the far country. Forgive us, for we didna ken whait we were leavin', or the sair heart we gied oor Father. It was weary wark tae live wi' oor sins, but we wad never hev come back, had it no been for oor Elder Brither. He cam' a long road tae find us, and a sore travail he had afore he set us free. He's been a gude Brither tae us, and we've been a heavy chairge tae him. May he keep a firm hand o' us, and guide us in the richt road, and bring us back gin we wander, and tell us a' we need tae know till the gloamin' come. Gether us in then, we pray thee, and a' we luve, no a bairn missin', and may we sit doon forever in oor ain Father's house. Amen.

IAN MACLAREN (JOHN WATSON, D.D., 1850-1907)
Beside the Bonnie Brier Bush

LUTHER'S HYMN

A safe stronghold our God is still,
  A trusty shield and weapon;
He'll help us clear from all the ill
  That hath us now o'ertaken.
    The ancient prince of hell
    Hath risen with purpose fell;
    Strong mail of craft and power
    He weareth in this hour ;
  On earth is not his fellow.

With force of arms we nothing can,
  Full soon were we down-ridden;
But for us fights the proper Man,
  Whom God Himself hath bidden.

Ask ye who is this same?
Christ Jesus is His Name,
The Lord Sabaoth's Son;
He, and no other one,
Shall conquer in the battle.

And were this world all devils o'er,
And watching to devour us,
We lay it not to heart so sore;
Not they can overpower us.
And let the prince of ill
Look grim as e'er he will,
He harms us not a whit;
For why his doom is writ;
A word shall quickly slay him.

God's word, for all their craft and force,
One moment will not linger,
But, spite of hell, shall have its course;
'Tis written by His finger.
And, though they take our life,
Goods, honour, children, wife,
Yet is their profit small;
These things shall vanish all:
The city of God remaineth.

MARTIN LUTHER (1483-1546)
translated by THOMAS CARLYLE

from A CHRISTMAS SERMON

To be honest, to be kind—to earn a little and to spend a little less, to make upon the whole a family happier for his presence, to renounce when that shall be necessary and not be embittered, to keep a few friends but these without capitulation—above all, on the same grim condition, to keep friends with himself—here is a task for ell that a man has of fortitude and delicacy. He has an ambitious soul who would ask more; he has a hopeful spirit who should look in such an enterprise to be successful. There is indeed one element in human destiny that not blindness itself can controvert: whatever else we are intended to do, we are not intended to succeed; failure is the fate allotted. It is so in every art and study; it is so above all in the continent art of living well. Here is a pleasant thought for the year's end or for the end of life: only self-deception will be satisfied, and there need be no despair for the despairer.

R. L. STEVENSON (1850-94)
Later Essays

CHRISTMAS MEDITATION

He who by a mother's love
  Made the wandering world his own,
Every year comes from above,
  Comes the parted to atone,
  Binding Earth to the Father's throne.

Nay, thou comest every day!
  No, thou never didst depart!
Never hour has been away!
  Always with us, Lord, thou art,
  Binding, binding, heart to heart!

GEORGE MACDONALD (1824-1905)

THE BEING AND THE ATTRIBUTES

Things on the earth, *if* made, and regulated, by a Contriving Mind, must have been made according to a plan, or after a pattern: there must, therefore, be, in the higher sphere of causes, the models, of which the earthly

objects and effects are the resemblances; and according
to the laws of these causes, the earthly operations are
conducted and go on. The earthly images may be
affirmed, or may be denied, to be the representatives of
the most real and ever-enduring *archetypal ideas:* but
certain it is, that, whatever be the names by which these
likenesses are designated, the causes of them must have
pre-existed in, or been present to, in some special manner,
the Divine Mind, which was the depository of the model-
thoughts, until they were actualized in this lower
theatre.

*   *   *   *   *

For, Love is, without doubt, a tree of Life: in a
certain good sense, it is the tree of Life. It is, in fact,
the true mundane Yggdrasil. To vary our view, and
enlarge, to the utmost, the illustrating medium: Love
is the central attractive power of the universe. It is the
centre, whence all influential radiations must depart,
and to which they must return as their proper home.
There is, of necessity, an inmost Spiritual Sun to the
Universe; a central influence appertaining to the sum
total of all the forces of every world, and every system
of worlds. There must be supposed a centre; in other
words, a Sun of all Suns, material and spiritual: otherwise, related things would be out of proportion to each
other, and apparent effects would be unlawfully divorced
from their only possible causes.

God *is Love*; and, when we say so, we evoke the
omnipotent word, representative of the all-radiant idea,
which throws warmth upon the field of our world.
Possessed of this secret, we feel we are in possession of
the talisman yielding the primal causation. When we
have reached as high as Love, we have reached (to use the
humanly most significant expression) *the very heart of
God.*

WILLIAM HONYMAN GILLESPIE (1808-75)
The Argument a priori

BOSWELL AND VOLTAIRE

At last we came upon Religion. Then did he rage.
The company went to supper. M. de Voltaire and I
remained in the drawing-room with a great Bible before
us; and if ever two mortal men disputed with vehemence
we did. Yes, upon that occasion He was one Individual
and I another. For a certain portion of time there was
a fair opposition between Voltaire and Boswell. The
daring bursts of his Ridicule confounded my understanding. He stood like an Orator of ancient Rome.
Tully was never more agitated than he was. He went
too far. His aged frame trembled beneath him. He cried,
"O, I am very sick; my head turns round," and he let
himself gently fall upon an easy-chair. He recovered.

I resumed our Conversation, but changed the tone. I
talked to him serious and earnest. I demanded of him
an honest confession of his real sentiments. He gave it
me with candour and with a mild eloquence which
touched my heart. I did not believe him capable of
thinking in the manner that he declared to me was
"from the bottom of his heart." He exprest his veneration—his love—of the Supreme Being, and his entire
resignation to the will of Him who is Allwise. He
exprest his desire to resemble the Author of Goodness,
by being good himself. His sentiments go no farther.
He does not inflame his mind with grand hopes of the
immortality of the Soul. He says it may be; but he
knows nothing of it. And his mind is in perfect
tranquillity.

I was moved; I was sorry. I doubted his Sincerity.
I called to him with emotion, "Are you sincere? are
you really sincere?" He answered, "Before God, I am."

JAMES BOSWELL (1740-1795)
Letter to W. J. Temple

ENDURE, MY HEART

Endure, my heart: not long shalt thou endure
    The shame, the smart;
The good and ill are done; the end is sure;
    Endure, my heart!
There stand two vessels by the golden throne
    Of Zeus on high;
From these he scatters mirth and scatters moan,
    To men that die.
And thou of many joys hast had thy share,
    Thy perfect part;
Battle and love, and evil things and fair;
    Endure, my heart!

Fight one last greatest battle under shield,
    Wage that war well:
Then seek thy fellows in the shadowy field
    Of asphodel;
There is the knightly Hector; there the men
    Who fought for Troy;
Shall we not fight our battles o'er again?
    Were that not joy?
Though no sun shines beyond the dusky west,
    Thy perfect part
There shalt thou have of the unbroken rest;
    Endure, my heart!

ANDREW LANG (1844-1912)

YOUNG CRUSADE

O strange, unseemly woes that wait
Upon the rising of our morn:
Our plundered Spring, dream-desolate,
Scarce-budded, knows its rose unborn

Cheated of June, of joy frustrate,
Bankrupt of beauty, peace-forlorn!

Yet written timeless as the stars
Our steadfast destiny shall be;
Our barren youth that flowers in wars
Shall live in lands its faith made free:
Truth triumphs in our battle-scars;
Christ conquers in our Calvary!

MARGARET WINEFRIDE SIMPSON

THE SECRET COMMONWEALTH

The Rev. Robert Kirke (1641-92), seventh son of the minister of Aberfoyle (in which is the Bailie Nicol Jarvie inn associated with *Rob Roy*) issued about 1691 a remarkable book called *The Secret Commonwealth of Elves, Faunes and Fairies*. His contemporaries believed that he did not die a natural death but, when walking upon a small hillock to the west of the manse, sank to the ground and was carried into fairyland, where, according to local tradition, he still abides.

Mr. Kirke was a near relation of Graham of Duchray, the ancestor of the present General Graham Stirling. Shortly after his funeral, he appeared, in the dress in which he had sunk down, to a medical relation of his own and of Duchray. "Go," said he to him, "to my cousin Duchray and tell him that I am not dead. I fell down in a swoon, and was carried into fairyland, where I now am. Tell him that when he and my friends are assembled at the baptism of my child (for he had left his wife pregnant), I will appear in the room, and that if he throws the knife which he holds in his hand over my head, I will be released, and restored to human society."

The man, it seems, neglected, for some time, to deliver the message. Mr. Kirke appeared to him a second time, threatening to haunt him night and day till he executed

363

his commission, which at length he did. The time of the baptism arrived. They were seated at table; the figure of Mr. Kirke entered, but the Laird of Duchray, by some unaccountable fatality, neglected to perform the prescribed ceremony. Mr. Kirke retired by another door, and was seen no more.

PATRICK GRAHAME
Sketches of Perthshire

THE FAIRY BOY OF LEITH

This legend is found in *Pandæmonium, or the Devil's Cloyster* by Richard Bovet, 1684. The story is entitled, "A remarkable passage of one named the Fairy Boy of Leith, in Scotland, given me by my worthy friend Captain George Burton, and attested under his hand."

About fifteen years since, having business that detained me for some time in Leith, I often met some of my acquaintance at a certain house there, where we used to drink a glass of wine for our refection. The woman which kept the house was of honest reputation amongst the neighbours, which made me give the more attention to what she told me one day about a Fairy Boy (as they called him) who lived about that town. She had given me so strange an account of him, that I desired her I might see him the first opportunity, which she promised; and not long after, passing that way, she told me there was the Fairy Boy but a little before I came by; and casting her eye into the street, said, "Look you, sir, yonder he is at play with those other boys," and designing him to me, I went, and by smooth words, and a piece of money, got him to come into the house with me; where, in the presence of divers people, I demanded of him several astrological questions, which he answered with great subtility, and through all his discourse carried it with a cunning much beyond his years, which seemed not to exceed ten or eleven. He seemed to make a motion like drumming upon the table with his fingers, upon which I asked him whether he could beat a drum, to which he replied, "Yes, sir, as well as any man in Scotland; for every Thursday night I beat all points to a sort of people that used to meet under yonder hill" (pointing to the great hill between Edenborough and Leith). "How, boy," quoth I; "what company have you there?"—"There are, sir," said he, "a great company both of men and women, and they are entertained with many sorts of music besides my drum; they have, besides, plenty variety of meats and wine; and many times we are carried into France or Holland in a night, and return again; and whilst we are there, we enjoy all the pleasures the country doth afford." I demanded of him how they got under that hill? To which he replied, "That there were a great pair of gates that opened to them, though they were invisible to others, and that within there were brave larger rooms, as well accommodated as most in Scotland."

The woman of the house told me that all the people in Scotland could not keep him from the rendezvous on Thursday night; upon which, by promising him some more money, I got a promise of him to meet me at the same place, in the afternoon of the Thursday following, and so dismissed him at that time. The boy came again, at the place and time appointed, and I had prevailed with some friends to continue with me, if possible, to prevent his moving that night; he was placed between us, and answered many questions, without offering to go from us, until about eleven of the clock, he was got away unperceived of the company; but I suddenly missing him, hasted to the door, and took hold of him, and so returned him into the same room: we all watched him, and on a sudden he was again got out of the doors. I followed him close, and he made a noise in the street as if he had been set upon; but from that time I could never see him.

THE BUGLES OF DREAMLAND

Swiftly the dews of the gloaming are falling:
Faintly the bugles of Dreamland are calling.
    O hearken, my darling, the elf-flutes are blowing
    The shining-eyed folk from the hillside are flowing,
I' the moonshine the wild-apple blossoms are snowing,
And louder and louder where the white dews are falling
The far-away bugles of Dreamland are calling.

O what are the bugles of Dreamland calling
There where the dews of the gloaming are falling?
    Come away from the weary old world of tears,
    Come away, come away to where one never hears
    The slow weary drip of the slow weary years,
    But peace and deep rest till the white dews are falling
    And the blithe bugle-laughters through Dreamland
        are calling.

Then bugle for us, where the cool dews are falling,
O bugle for us, wild elf-flutes now calling—
    For Isla and I are too weary to wait
    For the dim drowsy whisper that cometh too late,
    The dim muffled whisper of blind empty fate—
    O the world's well lost now the dream-dews are
        falling,
    And the bugles of Dreamland about us are calling.

FIONA MACLEOD (WILLIAM SHARP, 1855-1905)
from *The Hills of Dream*

THE CALL OF THE ISLAND

MARY ROSE: (*gloriously*). Simon, isn't life lovely! I am so happy, happy, happy. Aren't you?

SIMON: Rather.

MARY ROSE: But you can tie up marmalade. Why don't you scream with happiness? One of us has got to scream.

SIMON: Then I know which one it will be. Scream away, it will give Cameron the jumps.

(CAMERON *draws in*)

There you are, Cameron. We are still safe, you see. You can count us—two.

CAMERON: I am ferry glad.

SIMON: Here you are (*handing him the luncheon basket*). You needn't tie the boat up. Stay there and I'll stamp out the fire myself.

CAMERON: As Mr. Blake pleases.

SIMON: Ready, Mary Rose?

MARY ROSE: I must say good-bye to my island first. Good-bye, old mossy seat, nice rowan. Good-bye, little island that likes too much to be visited. Perhaps I shall come back when I am an old lady with wrinkles, and you won't know your Mary Rose.

SIMON: I say, dear, do dry up. I can't help listening to you when I ought to be getting this fire out.

MARY ROSE: I won't say another word.

SIMON: Just as it seems to be out, sparks come again. Do you think if I were to get some stones—?

(*He looks up and she signs that she has promised not to talk. They laugh to each other. He is then occupied for a little time in dumping wet stones from the loch upon the fire.* CAMERON *is in the boat with his Euripides.* MARY ROSE *is sitting demure but gay, holding her tongue with her fingers like a child.*

Something else is happening; the call has come to MARY ROSE. *It is at first as soft and furtive as whisperings from holes in the ground, Mary Rose, Mary Rose. Then in a fury as of storm and whistling winds that might be an unholy organ it rushes upon the island, raking every bush for her. These sounds increase rapidly in volume till the mere loudness of them is horrible. They are not without an opponent. Struggling through them, and also calling her name, is to be heard music of an unearthly sweetness that is seeking perhaps to beat them back and put a girdle of safety round her. Once* MARY ROSE'S *arms go out to her husband for help, but thereafter she is oblivious of his existence. Her face is rapt, but there is neither fear nor joy in it. Thus she passes from view. The island immediately resumes its stillness. The sun has gone down.* SIMON *by the fire and* CAMERON *in the boat have heard nothing.)*

SIMON (*on his knees*): I think the fire is done for at last, and that we can go now. How cold and grey it has become. (*Smiling, but without looking up.*) You needn't grip your tongue any longer, you know. (*He rises.*) Mary Rose, where have you got to? Please don't hide. Dearest, don't. Cameron, where is my wife?

(CAMERON *rises in the boat, and he is afraid to land. His face alarms* SIMON, *who runs this way and that and is lost to sight calling her by name again and again. He returns livid.*)

Cameron, I can't find her. Mary Rose! Mary Rose! Mary Rose!

SIR J. M. BARRIE (1860-1937)
Mary Rose

THE FAIRY CHORUS

How beautiful they are,
The lordly ones
Who dwell in the hills,
In the hollow hills.

They have faces like flowers,
And their breath is a wind
That blows over summer meadows,
Filled with dewy clover.

Their limbs are more white
Than shafts of moonshine:
They are more fleet
Than the March wind.

They laugh and are glad,
And are terrible:
When their lances shake and glitter
Every green reed quivers.

How beautiful they are,
How beautiful
The lordly ones
In the hollow hills.

FIONA MACLEOD (WILLIAM SHARP, 1855-1905)
The Immortal Hour

DAFT SANG

Whan doors are steek't,[1] and a' are hame,
It's then I pu' my bauchles[2] on:
Whan folk are beddit wi' their dream
The hale world is my causey-croun.[3]

The hale world is my causey-croun;
The hackit hench my steppie-stair:
I whistle and the wind comes doun;
And on the wind I gang oniewhaur.

[1] shut fast [2] comfortable old shoes
[3] literally, the centre of the street

369

And on the wind I gang oniewhaur,
But nane will ken what I hae seen:
For the world ends—and it isna far;
But nane will ken whaur I hae been.

But nane will ken whaur I hae been
Atween the glimmer and the grey;
Nor hear the clapper o' the mune
Ding up the nicht, ding doun the day.

WILLIAM SOUTAR (1898-1943)

TIR-NAN-OG

Sir James Barrie has borrowed more than once his glamorous conception of Eternal Youth from the Gaelic belief in *Tir-nan-Og*, that Land of Heart's Desire where the blessed keep the secret of remaining ever-young and never grow up. As the early Christians spoke of a Land of Promise, so the ancient Celts spoke of a Land of Light, a Land of Ever-living, a Land of Eternal Youth. Sometimes they conceived it as below the depths of the sea; then they called it a Land under the Waves. Sometimes they thought it was a beautiful Isle of Joy; then they placed it far out in the magic West on the boundless ocean. Sometimes they associated it with one of those green knolls known to Celtic superstition as *Shians*; then they called it a place of Fairy Mansions. These abodes of the blessed in *Tir-nan Og* were peopled by fairy folk; but a few favoured human beings occasionally reached them, being drawn there during their lifetime; only— they had to have the inner vision which could see the messenger, and the mystic ear which could hear the call. The Celt has always been sensitive to haunting music, and reference is often made to the ravishing music which was heard in these fairy abodes of the blessed. It lulled to forgetfulness the favoured humans who were invited there. So, this belief in the Land of the Ever-Young has filled the Hebrides with certain fairy mounds and fairy islands from which messengers are sent occasionally to call those who visit them to this land of music and beauty and Eternal Youth.

T. RATCLIFFE BARNETT (1868-1946)
The Road to Rannoch and the Summer Isles

THE IMMORTALS

I saw the Weaver of Dream, an immortal shape of star-eyed Silence; and the Weaver of Death, a lovely Dusk with a heart of hidden flame: and each wove with the shuttles of Beauty and Wonder and Mystery.

I knew not which was the more fair: for Death seemed to me as Love, and in the eyes of Dream I saw Joy. Oh, come, come to me, Weaver of Dream! Come, come unto me, O Lovely Dusk, thou that hast the heart of hidden flame!

THE REED PLAYER

I saw one put a hollow reed to his lips. It was a forlorn, sweet air that he played, an ancient forgotten strain learned of a shepherding woman upon the hills. The Song of Songs it was that he played: and the beating of hearts was heard, and I heard sighs, and a voice like a distant bird-song rose and fell.

"Play me a song of Death," I said. Then he who had the hollow reed at his lips smiled, and he played again the Song of Songs.

FIONA MACLEOD (WILLIAM SHARP, 1855-1905)
The Silence of Amor

371

ANIMA MUNDI

Union exists beyond all thought and speech
Between the Absolute and the world of things.
From age to age the Eternal Mind doth reach
Out, out into the Universe on wings
Of self-creative thought.   The insentient dust
Is bound by birth and lineage to obey
That self-same law the mean amoeba must ;
The unselfconscious tiger stalks his prey.
But lo ! the divine, the unparalleled mutation,
Man, self-aware, the similitude of God.
By slow, infinitesimal gradation
The Spirit triumphs over brute and clod.
And when the mind takes counsel of the heart,
These twain are each of each the counterpart.

G. F. MAINE (1893-1956)

BE MIRRY, MAN

Be mirry, man! and tak nocht far in mynd
The wavering of this wrechit warld of sorrow;
To God be humill, and to thy freynd by kynd,
And with thy nychtbouris[1] glaidly len and borrow;
His chance to nycht it may be thyne tomorrow.
Be blyth in hairt for ony aventure,
For oft with wysmen it hes bene said a forrow,
Without glaidnes availis no tresour.

Mak the guid cheir of it that God the sendis,
For warldis wrak[2] but[3] weilfar nocht availis;
Na gude is thyne saif only at thow spendis,

[1] neighbours   [2] goods   [3] without

372

Remenant all thow brukis,[1] bot with bailis[2] ;
Seik to solace quhen sadness the assailis,
In dolour[3] lang thy lyfe ma nocht indure;
Quhairfoir of confort set up all thy sailis;
Without glaidnes availis no tresour.

Follow on peis, fle truble and debait;
With famous flokis hald thy cumpany;
Be charitabill and humyll in thyne estait,
For warldly honour lestis bot a cry;
For truble in erd[4] tak no mallancoly;
Be riche in patience, gif thow in gudis be pure;[5]
Quho levis mirry, he levis michtely.
Without glaidnes availis no tresour.

WILLIAM DUNBAR (1480-1520)
From *No Tressour Availis Without Glaidnes*

[1] enjoy [2] calamities [3] sorrow [4] earth [5] poor

BEYOND

When youthful faith hath fled
    Of loving take thy leave;
Be constant to the dead—
    The dead cannot deceive.

Sweet modest flowers of Spring,
    How fleet your balmy day!
And man's brief year can bring
    No secondary May,

No earthly burst again
    Of gladness out of gloom,
Fond hope and vision vain,
    Ungrateful to the tomb.

But 'tis an old belief
    That on some solemn shore,
Beyond the sphere of grief,
    Dear friends shall meet once more.

373

Beyond the sphere of time,
    And Sin and Fate's control,
Serene in endless prime
    Of body and of soul.

That creed I fain would keep,
    That hope I'll not forgo,
Eternal be the sleep
    Unless to waken so.

J. G. LOCKHART (1794-1854)

A PLEDGE

He wha tills the fairies' green
    Nae luck again shall hae.
An' he wha spills the fairies' ring
    Betide him want an' wae.

But wha gaes by the fairy ring
    Nae dule nor pine shall see;
An' he wha cleans the fairy ring
    An easy daith shall dee.

TRADITIONAL

EPILOGUE

Harp of the North, farewell! The hills grow dark,
  On purple peaks a deeper shade descending;
In twilight copse the glow-worm lights her spark,
  The deer, half seen, are to the covert wending.
Resume thy wizard elm! the fountain lending,
  And the wild breeze, thy wilder minstrelsy;
Thy numbers sweet with nature's vespers blending,
  With distant echo from the fold and lea,
And herd-boy's evening pipe and hum of housing bee.

Yet, once again farewell, thou Minstrel harp!
  Yet once again, forgive my feeble sway,
And little reck I of the censure sharp
  May idly cavil at an idle lay.
Much have I owed thy strains on life's long way,
  Through secret woes the world has never known,
When on the weary night dawn'd wearier day,
  And bitterer was the grief devour'd alone.
That I o'erlive such woes, Enchantress! is thine own.

Hark! as my lingering footsteps slow retire,
  Some Spirit of the Air has waked thy string!
'Tis now a seraph bold, with touch of fire,
  'Tis now the brush of Fairy's frolic wing.
Receding now, the dying numbers ring
  Fainter and fainter down the rugged dell,
And now the mountain breezes scarcely bring
  A wandering witch-note of the distant spell—
And now, 'tis silent all !—Enchantress, fare thee well !

SIR WALTER SCOTT (1771-1832)
The Lady of the Lake

LEADING EVENTS AND DATES
IN SCOTTISH HISTORY
A. D. 80 - 1707

80	Agricola's invasion.
84	Battle at Ardoch; Forts built between Forth and Clyde.
140	Wall of Antonine built.
208	Invasion by the Emperor Severus.
500	Coming of the Scots.
563	Columba comes to Iona.
730	War of Picts and Scots.
844	Kenneth M'Alpin king (fourteen kings in succession, 860-1034).
1005	Malcolm II.
1034	Duncan I.
1040	Macbeth.
1057	Malcolm Canmore.
1072	William the Conqueror's invasion; Malcolm does homage.
1093	Donald Bane king.
1097	Edgar.
1107	Alexander I.
1124	David I.
1153	Malcolm the Maiden.
1165	William the Lion.
1174	William captured at Alnwick; becomes vassal of Henry II.
1190	Freedom of Scotland purchased.
1214	Alexander II.
1249	Alexander III.
1263	Battle of Largs.
1286	Death of Alexander III.
1290	Maid of Norway died.
1292	John Baliol king.
1296	Baliol deposed.
1297	Wallace's revolt; Battle of Stirling Bridge.
1298	Battle of Falkirk.
1305	Execution of Wallace.
1306	Bruce crowned.
1307	Battle of Methven.
1307	Battle of Loudon Hill.
1313	Siege of Stirling Castle.
1314	Bannockburn.
1319	Siege of Berwick.
1328	Treaty of Northampton; Scotland's independence acknowledged.
1329	Death of Bruce; David II.
1332	Edward Baliol crowned.
1332	France helps the Scots.
1333	Battle of Halidon Hill.
1341	David II returns to Scotland.

376

1346   Battle of Neville's Cross.
1370   Robert II (Stewart line).
1388   Battle of Otterburn.
1390   Robert III.
1406   James I; Albany regent.
1411   Battle of Harlaw.
1412   St. Andrews University founded.
1424   James I set free.
1437   Murder of James I; James II.
1440   Douglas's black dinner.
1454   Earl of Douglas slain.
1460   James III.
1482   Lauder Bridge.
1488   Battle of Sauchieburn; James III killed; James IV.
1494   James IV invades England with Warbeck.
1502   Marriage of "the Thistle and the Rose."
1509   Printing introduced by Chapman.
1513   Battle of Flodden; James IV slain; James V.
1528   Patrick Hamilton burned at St. Andrews.
1532   Court of Session established.
1542   Rout of Solway Moss.
1542   Mary Queen of Scots.
1545   Hertford's invasion.
1546   George Wishart burned.
1547   Battle of Pinkie.
1547   Knox a prisoner.
1559   Knox in Scotland; riot at Perth.
1560   First General Assembly at Glasgow.
1561   Queen Mary returns to Scotland.
1566   Murder of Rizzio.
1567   Murder of Darnley; Carberry Hill.
1567   Abdication of Mary; James VI crowned.
1568   Mary's escape from Lochleven; Langside; Mary's flight into
       England.
1570   Regent Murray assassinated.
1578   King James begins to rule.
1582   Raid of Ruthven.
1587   Mary executed at Fotheringay.
1589   Marriage of James with Anne of Denmark.
1603   James becomes King of Great Britain.
1617   James visits Scotland.
1625   Death of James VI.
1633   Charles visits Scotland.
1637   Riot in St. Giles's.
1638   National Covenant; General Assembly, Glasgow.
1639   Duns Law; Pacification of Berwick.
1644   Montrose's rising.
1645   Philiphaugh.
1649   Charles II proclaimed king.
1650   Battle of Dunbar.

1651   Charles II crowned at Scone.
1661   Execution of Argyle.
1662   Episcopacy established.
1666   Battle of Rullion Green.
1678   Archbishop Sharp murdered.
1679   Battles of Drumclog and Bothwell Bridge.
1685   James VII; Argyle's invasion.
1689   Battle of Killiecrankie.
1692   Massacre of Glencoe.
1698   Darien Expedition sails.
1702   Accession of Queen Anne.
1704   Act of Security.
1706   Last meeting of Scottish Parliament.
1707   Union of Parliaments.

FIRST LINES OF POEMS

LIST OF AUTHORS